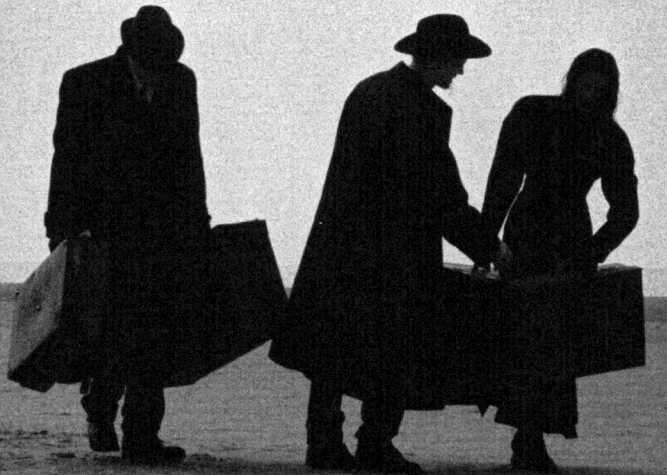

Azzedine Peter
Alaïa Lindbergh

TASCHEN

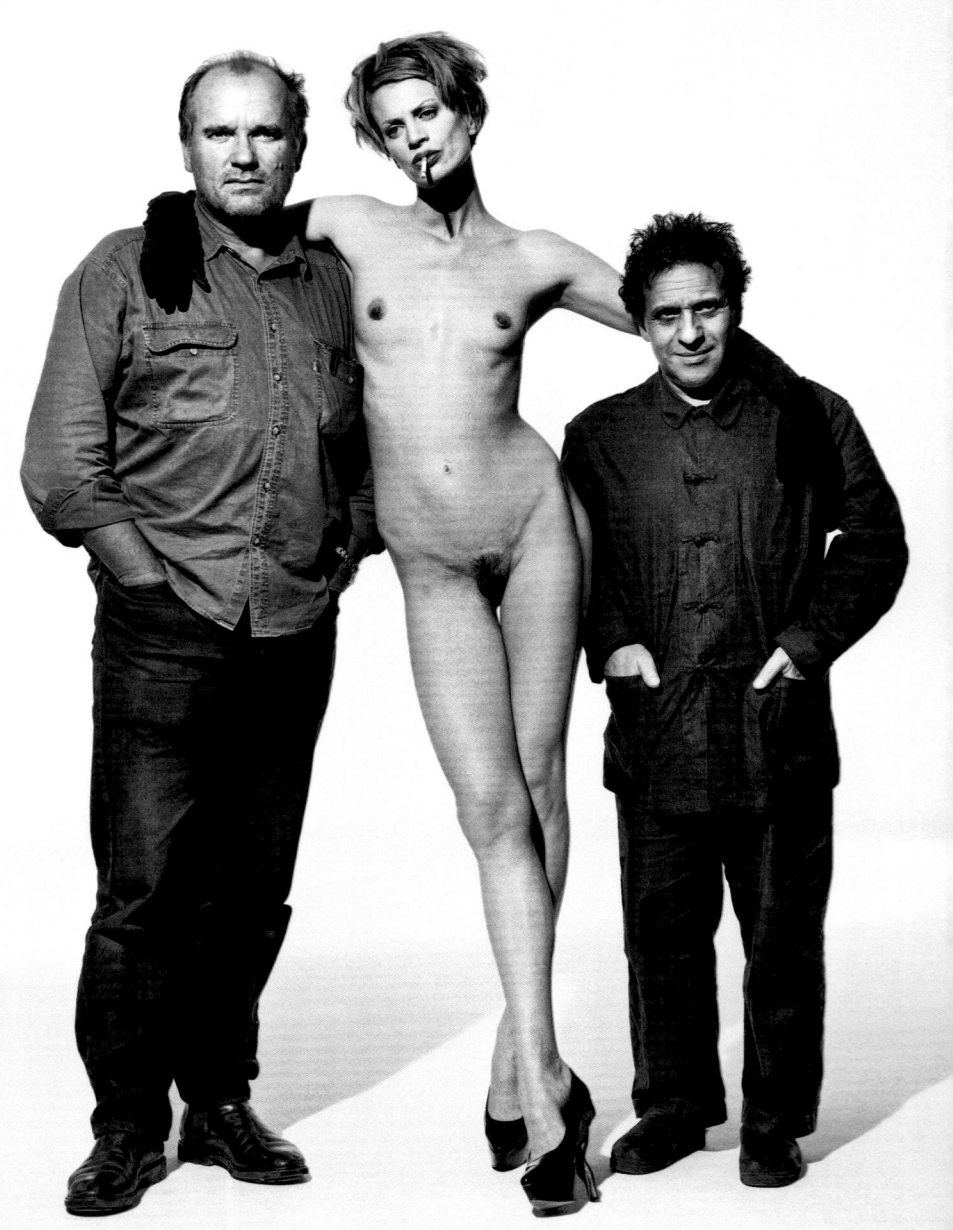

Fondation Azzedine Alaïa
Peter Lindbergh *Foundation*

Edited by
Carla Sozzani

Dedicated to
Franca Sozzani

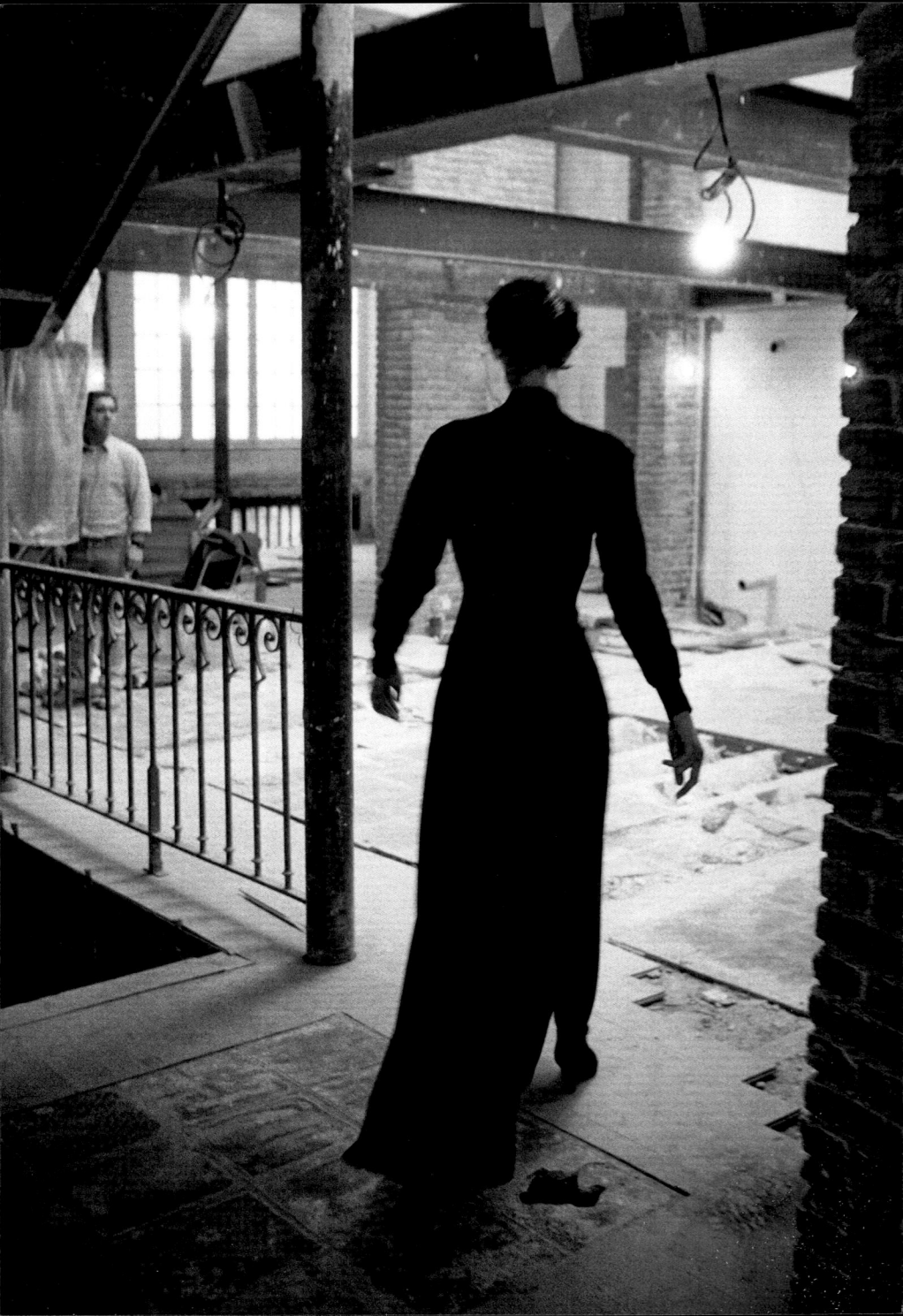

Mirror View

Olivier Saillard

Peter Lindbergh and Azzedine Alaïa celebrated photography and fashion with the kind of kindred spirit and communion that is the foundation of great artistic collaborations. Like Richard Avedon and Christian Dior in another period or, more recently, Helmut Newton and Yves Saint Laurent, they found a shared territory where each man's expression was a reflection of the other's.

Without words, the photographer and the couturier came together in an affection for iconographic themes and forms that they approached as a kind of philosophy. The dark, black tones that they both cultivated, whether in gelatin silver prints or in monochrome clothing, set their style apart; they constitute a manifesto. Lindbergh summoned them constantly to signify his quest for authenticity in the faces he brought to the light, seeking to make those who came before his lens timeless. Alaïa turned inky monochrome into clothes that defy the times, veritable sculptures for the body. Both attained this impression of a poetic realism that magnifies personalities while satisfying their creative ambition.

Although from opposing geographies and differing origins and cultures, Lindbergh and Alaïa cultivated close horizons. Born in Duisburg, a German town close to the Dutch border, Peter Lindbergh trained at the School of Applied Arts in Krefeld. Azzedine Alaïa studied sculpture at the École des Beaux-Arts in Tunis, where he grew up. The deep shadows of passers-by on that city's whitewashed walls were part of his visual world. The photographer's environment was formed by the buildings of the industrial and trading city of Duisburg and by the Dutch beaches where he used to go. Both had a taste for wide horizons, whether on the Mediterranean or in the north, where the use of blacks and swaths of muted colors sometimes dialog.

While Lindbergh made a name for himself in Germany, especially via the magazine *Stern*, then set up his studio in Paris in the late 1970s, Alaïa was an eminently discreet couturier whose technical sophistication was a secret shared by the serious clients of haute couture. Soon, the German boy with a love of noble

Vanessa Duve, *Paris*, 1989. Dress, *Winter* 1988

photography, who invoked Brassaï, Kertész, and Winogrand as his models, and this young man from Tunisia with the deftest scissors, this heir of the masters of haute couture that were Balenciaga and Vionnet, would be writing some of the most illustrious chapters in Parisian and French fashion.

Almost simultaneously, Alaïa became an architect of bodies, the man who gave the 1980s that extra touch of class. He brought out women's figures, forming a silhouette that he draped, moulded or revealed with a cutting technique that he alone mastered. Lindbergh ennobled his subjects by lighting up their souls and personalities with the precision of the contours that he cut like a tailor. Step by step they became dominant figures in their respective disciplines, joining and weaving them together. Both rejected the artifices that distanced the true subject, and their powerful collaborations came naturally to them.

And so it goes with the greats. They seem not to be struggling. Simplicity is their playground. A beach at Le Touquet, the streets of Old Paris; these indicate the shared inspirations, from black-and-white movies and broad panoramas. The models, Marie-Sophie Wilson, Linda Spierings, Linda Evangelista, and Naomi Campbell joined the great actresses and entered the mythology that inspired the couturier, in which women are always the sisters of Arletty, Greta Garbo or Josephine Baker.

The metal lofts of a machine room, repeatedly convulsive iron mechanisms, the base of the Eiffel Tower; these illustrate memories of German industrial landscapes for one, and recall the other's great love of functional design and architecture. Naked bodies and directed gazes take hold of the composition, offering contrast and cold sensuality.

In these faces that they magnify, Lindbergh and Alaïa create their great work in this strange relation between disciplines that try to be invisible, the better to reveal the other. As the couturier himself wanted, Alaïa's clothes were to be the pedestals for the smiles and gazes of the icons and models who wore them, and whom he actively helped make famous. For Lindbergh, who built his name on the image of those great models, the authenticity of the features was all that mattered. To the colors of those photographs that turn perfect beauty into an ordinary commodity, he preferred the infinite shades of blacks, of gray and white hues. Both, in unison, were the great, passionate artisans of those unadorned faces that marked the 1990s and consecrated the age of the supermodels.

"Few words are needed for one who can understand," seems to be the message of the couturier and the photographer in the snapshots that bring them together. Here, Peter Lindbergh and Azzedine Alaïa converse with the silence of knowing gestures that turns a friendly understanding into works that possess a destiny.

Azzedine Alaïa and Vanessa Duve, *Paris*, 1989. Dress, *Winter 1988*

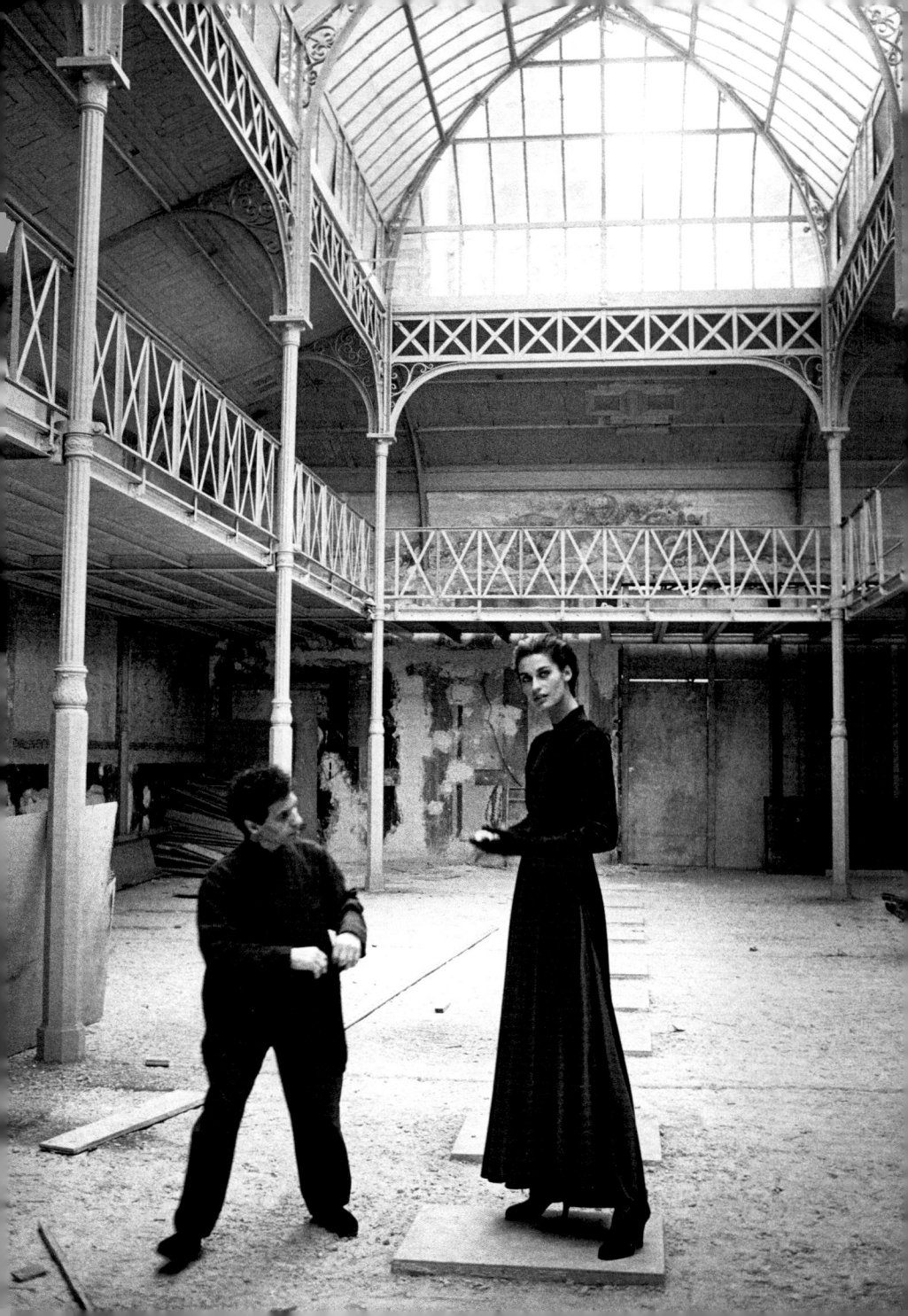

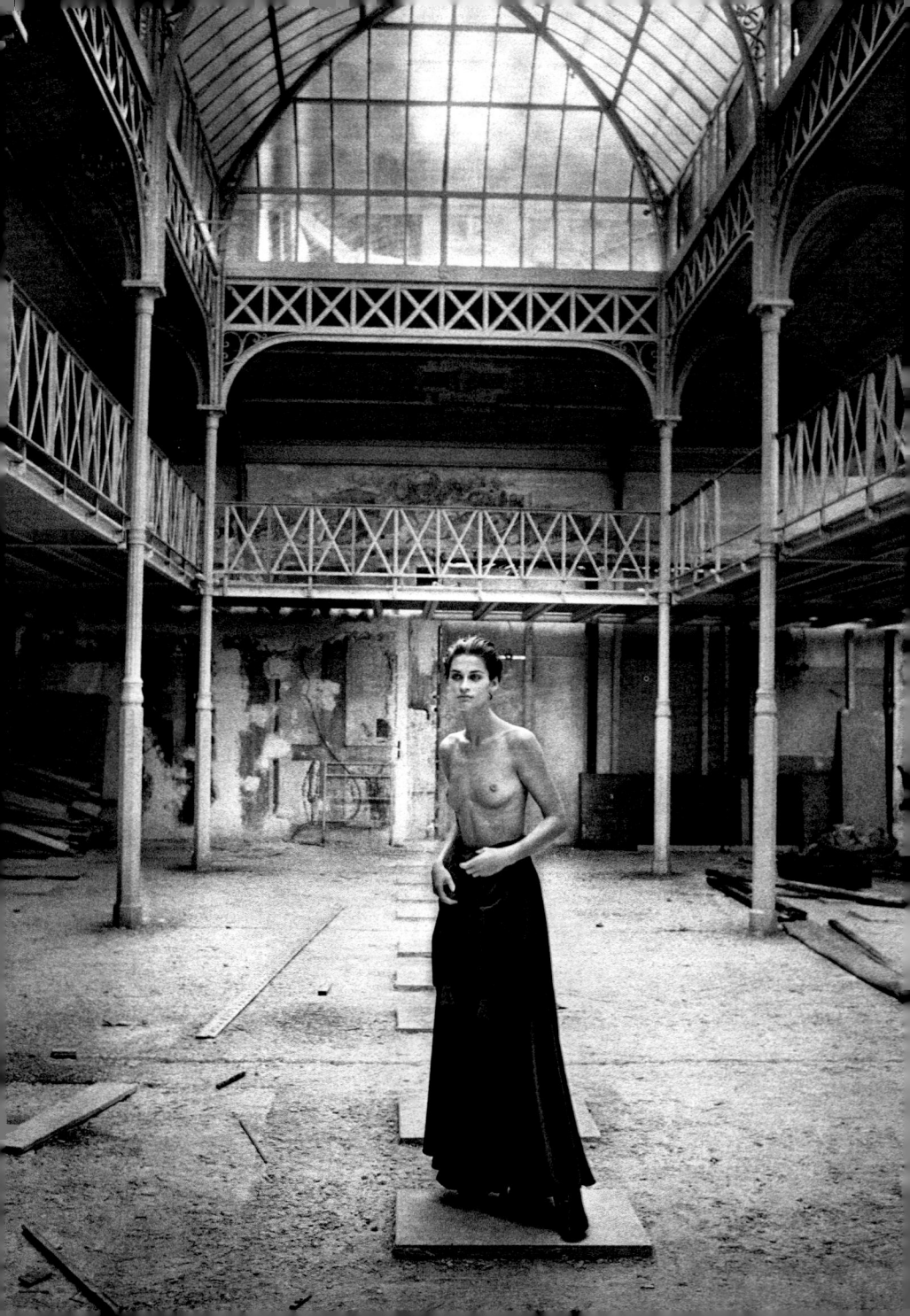

" Peter and I have known each
other since I started out.
We know each other very well.
We don't even need to talk.
Everything flows. "
Azzedine Alaïa

Vanessa Duve, *Paris*, 1989. Dress, *Winter* 1988

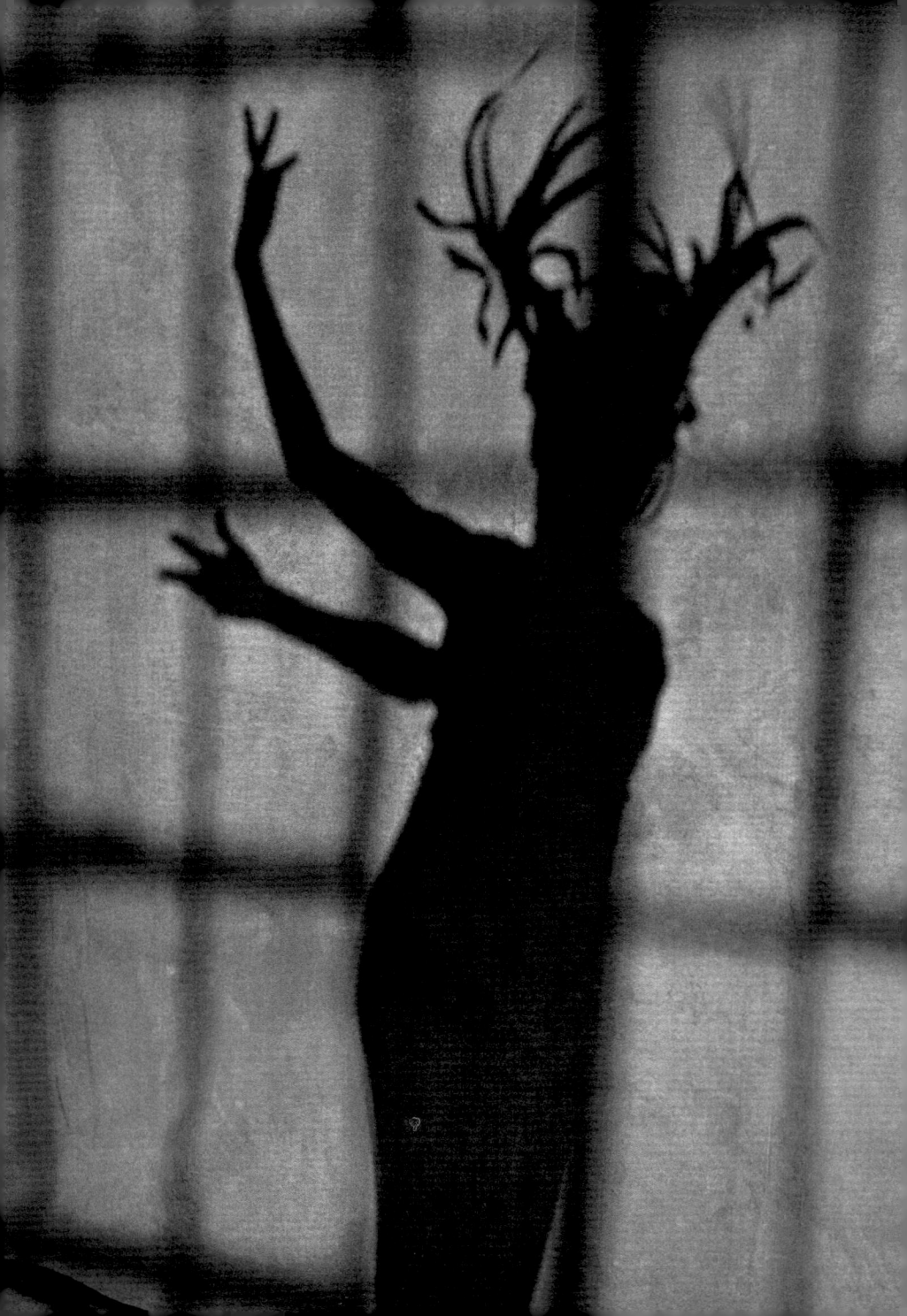

Azzedine, Peter

Paolo Roversi

There are many things that Peter, Azzedine and I have in common, but perhaps the one that most closely connects and defines us is our love for our adoptive city.

Paris has its own gravitational force, so different from New York or Berlin, and obviously profoundly different from places like Leszno, Tunis (or Ravenna, for that matter); an energy that pervades and bewitches those who choose to live here, and that inevitably becomes an integral part of the aesthetic sense of those who work here. It is not a city: it is an ideal of elegance, life, and poetry.

Even though they are not French, both Azzedine and Peter succeed in creating a new ideal of the Parisian woman: the former finding inspiration in a melancholic sophistication that reveals with unequaled elegance his profound knowledge of every single drapery fold by Madame Grès, every cut by Balenciaga, the immortal allure of Louise de Vilmorin, and every gesture and every cigarette of Arletty; the latter by carrying this ideal within himself through the streets of Paris like a dream suddenly turned into reality, with high cloud-filled skies and marvelous lights. Peter knows every corner, every bridge, every lamppost in Paris, and in his photographs the *ville lumière* is an intangible but constant reflection.

I often think about the two of them on the opposite banks of the Seine, busy drawing or conjuring up their future creations as the city sleeps; indefatigable, impassioned, obsessed up to the last, infinitesimal detail, as day after day, night after night, they outline the history of fashion, and photography, igniting the passion for one's art in the heart of the other. They both leave an indelible mark, a veritable aesthetic revolution that surpassed itself after each new collaboration, taking their art forms to a new, unrivaled peak, enthralling us all, taking our breath away.

Think only of Yasmin Le Bon crossing the street with two baguettes under her arm and a cigarette hanging from her lips, wrapped in white from head to toe: She was a harbinger of change, a different kind of Parisian woman, powerful and delicate, feminine and seductive, who led us into a new era with bold strides. Or think of the

Kristen McMenamy, *New York*, 1992

overcoats billowing in the wind of a sandstorm at Le Touquet, or Marie-Sophie's silhouette in front of the Hôtel du Nord. These are images that, as Jean-Louis Froment rightly observed, examine the present time as well as their own timelessness.

Peter and Azzedine are two unique artists, who, among so many other virtues, possess one that is particularly dear to to me, one that is rarer than you would think: they are exactly consubstantial with their work. Naturally, every artist transposes a part of himself in his work. But art and the artist are not always one and the same: quite the contrary.

Peter and Azzedine, however, are exactly like the work they created: passionate, generous, incisive, and never conventional. Their lives are a celebration and an emblem of what they convey through their art, from the grandest, most ambitious creation, to a convivial evening among friends.

This brings to mind a quotation from Charles Simic: "The best talk is around that table. Poetry and wisdom are its company. [...] One could compose an autobiography mentioning every memorable meal in one's life and it would probably make better reading than what one ordinarily gets." And maybe recounting those legendary dinner parties would be the right way to tell the story of these two memorable friends: the long tables where everyone was welcome; the endless toasts; Azzedine's hottest chili peppers, or Petra's homemade delicacies; Grigolo singing happy birthday to Franca Sozzani; Didine, the great Saint Bernard wagging his tail around the guests; the intense conversations about art, fashion and photography; the laughter, and the stories that ignited our imagination. I remember one evening a guest saying to Azzedine: Here I really understand the meaning of these three words: *liberté, égalité, fraternité.* These words have become trite and reduced to a slogan, but they are not empty cyphers. Free, generous, welcoming: Azzedine and Peter are like that. As is their art.

Lily's hands, *Los Angeles*, 1996

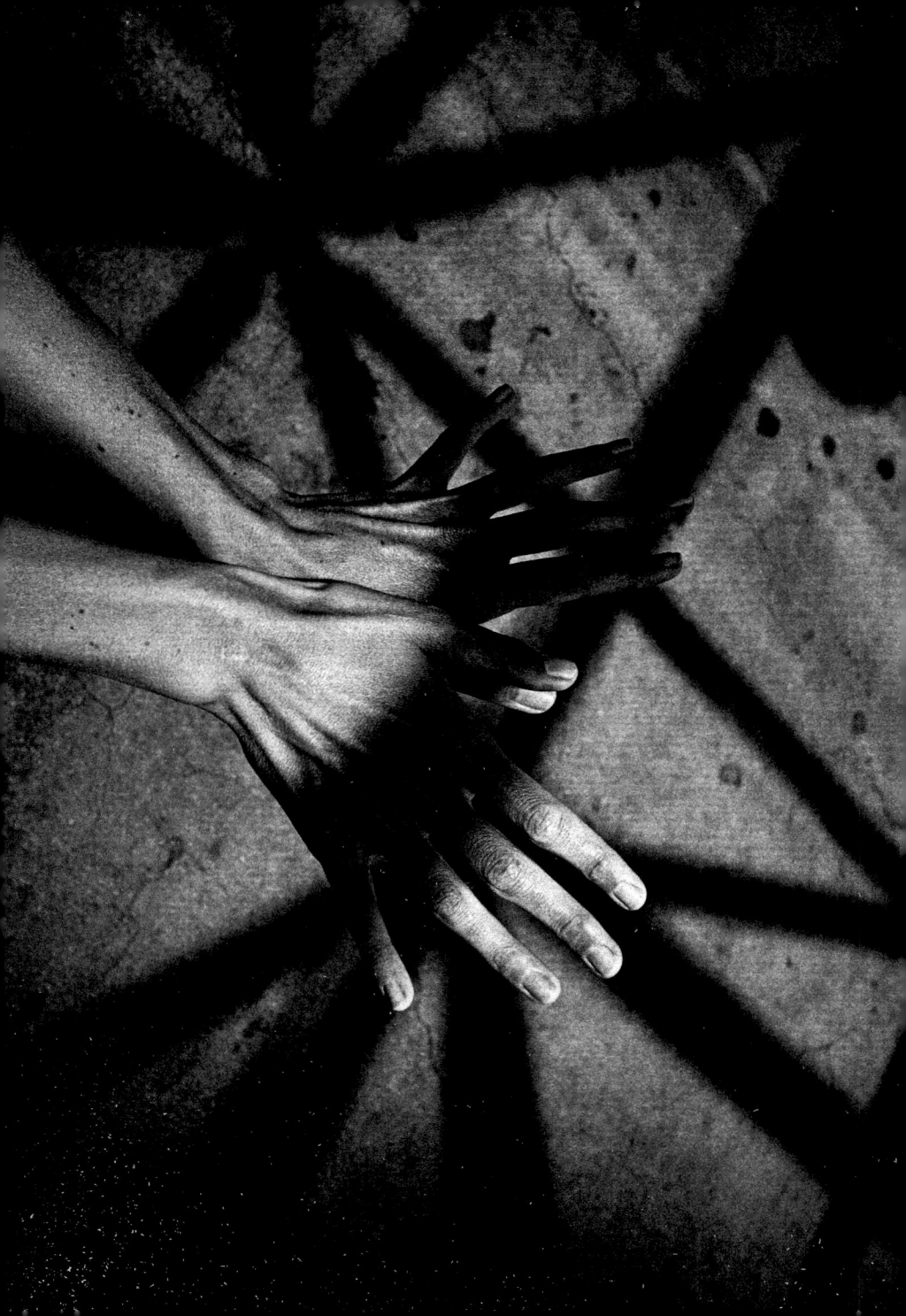

Azzedine Alaïa
and Peter Lindbergh

Fabrice Hergott

Peter Lindbergh's photography is so deeply a part of fashion photography that it is hard to know where to place him in the recent history of the medium. Just like Azzedine Alaïa, his works were often commissions, but they go well beyond their remit. Neither man saw any difference between a commissioned work and another kind. They met at the start of their careers and became friends. They were two strangers in Paris, two seemingly opposed worlds, but with the same gaze.

Lindbergh came to photography by chance, when he helped a friend who needed an assistant. He knew nothing about it at the time, but that innocence allowed him to realize that photography was his vocation, an energy that swept him vigorously ahead as often happens with converts. Success was not long in coming. With his outmoded, Old Deutschland courtesy and his warm, cheerful character, he inspired trust in his models. His activity soon became prolific. Dancing like a bee, he waited until his sitters forgot they were posing. Then the photo would be right, with everything fitting monumentally and spontaneously together. The figure, the open expression, the frame, the lighting.

It was chance, too, that brought Azzedine Alaïa, who wanted to be a sculptor, to fashion. He moved around his models in order to adjust the cut, find the hang, the fold or curve that was right for a given morphology, presence or character. He did it as if in a state of weightlessness, outside the world, absorbed in his concentration, the attention of the artist remaking the world.

Today, the qualities of Azzedine Alaïa and Peter Lindbergh seem self-evident, but this was not the case forty years ago. In those days supermodels were just models, and a model, if not already an actor or celebrity, was at best one of those slightly awkward forms that we see in De Chirico paintings. Lindbergh gave them a life. Not a fake, scripted and impersonal life, but their own life, revealing what they are

Nadja Auermann, *Tokyo*, 1996. Dress, *Haute Couture Hiver 1986*

and what they do not necessarily take the time to express, that way of appearing totally available while being perfectly inaccessible. That is exactly what Azzedine Alaïa gradually came to achieve after his arrival in Paris: the revelation, by means of a given garment, of the profound, human and extra-human nature of women, capable of giving an appearance and being themselves, while at the same time existing outside the temporality of men. This will of course be attacked as an exaggeration typical of the 1980s, perhaps the most extravagant and the most significant period of all, but one that was in fact a moment of grace, a golden age that Lindbergh and Alaïa pursued in their work. Without them, the 1980s would not have been the years of emancipation that they were, and it is no exaggeration to say that together Lindbergh and Alaïa invented the star supermodel.

Toward the end of the 1970s their gazes ushered in a veritable revolution in the world of fashion. This was when Kraftwerk wrote *Das Model*, a song that conveys the hope of models that are more human, whose beauty is more accessible. More than elsewhere, German youth thirsted for life. It wanted to see faces, to recover a lost humanity. Germany had to wait for the fall of the Berlin Wall to get over a history that had shattered everything. For years, there had been only two solutions: obliterate the past or turn toward a more distant past, the past that the Nazis hated and destroyed—the short-lived German modern art period that, in the aftermath of World War I, tried to put a face on beings, on despair and the insatiable appetite for life.

For Lindbergh, who originally wanted to be a painter, there was a need to revive what had been ransacked, to mend the broken threads. He could not fail to be interested in artists such as Otto Dix and George Grosz for their uncompromising portraits, or Max Beckmann for his play of shadows and his circuses. In the generous movement that was *Neue Sachlichkeit*, above all, there could be no missing his professional comrades, the photographers: August Sander, first of all, with his grand repertoire of trades, Erich Salomon with his human beings caught up in time, and Helmar Lerski and his light-bathed faces. Is not the very name Lindbergh, his pseudonym, an homage to the world of the 1920s, to its passionate embrace of life, to self-transcendence, to despair and the will to build new bridges over oceans and abysses?

His systematic approach and sense of observation also made August Sander the key reference for Bernd and Hilla Becher who, forty years later, photographed an entire repertoire of old buildings, of mine shafts, hangars and water towers. After the discovery of the minimal art of Joseph Kosuth, Douglas Huebler, and Lawrence Weiner, it was the conceptual photographs by Bernd and Hilla Becher that interested

Lindbergh the most. They were the founders of the Düsseldorf school of photography, the biggest in Europe after the war, to which Lindbergh probably belonged without ever asserting the link. In leaving Germany for the world of fashion in Paris and New York, he was protecting himself from the world of contemporary art, which would have limited his freedom. This position, at once real and marginal, enabled him to do what he wanted, to follow his interests, sometimes humorously. The portrait of Tina Turner wearing an Alaïa dress in the precarious position of Marc Riboud's *Painter of the Eiffel Tower* is much more than a wink. It is the manifesto of a photographer finding a balance between fashion and art, an homage to fashion and to art, but above all Lindbergh's homage to Azzedine Alaïa who dreamed of art and of Paris and whose work was both a school and an ethos for the photographer.

Alaïa, too, had known this thirst for culture. Growing up in Tunisia he had dreamed of Paris as the home of an ideal. His sensibility and his intuition told him to reconnect with the refinement, the rigor, and the culture of the court of Versailles, as most fully expressed by Madame de Pompadour and her intense activity in favor of the arts. It was during his studies at the École des Beaux-Arts, where he dreamed of Coysevox and Rodin, that he began sewing in order to make a living. He had learned how to sew with his sister. His talent and virtuosity meant he could meet the demands of a prestigious clientele that included Louise de Vilmorin and Arletty, two free women unbound by the times, with whom he became close friends. In this way he was living something of his dream of French culture while extending it in his work as a couturier, which he tirelessly perfected through his compulsive collecting of fashion. Fashion could exist only within meticulous attention to women's faces and bodies. For him the poise of a head or a way of walking were a dance that he wanted to perpetuate forever, acting as a modeler, sculptor, and painter with the ambition of the photographer who wants beauty never to die. Everything is of a piece, balanced, simple, and the eye never grows bored. His mastery of light, of texture, of black, means that both the ensemble and each centimeter are as stunning as the model's natural, spontaneous way of being. Every major work is constructed like a wall: first of all, we see nothing, then we note that everything is right and in its place, and soon we can see nothing else. And this can be transposed word for word to Peter Lindbergh's photographs.

In the work he did for the magazine *Stern* in the 1970s, Lindbergh reintroduced the relation of trust with the model as the basis of the photographer's craft. This relation was founded on lighting that respected the body and the face, a passion for the differences and varieties of bodies, and especially of faces. Having understood

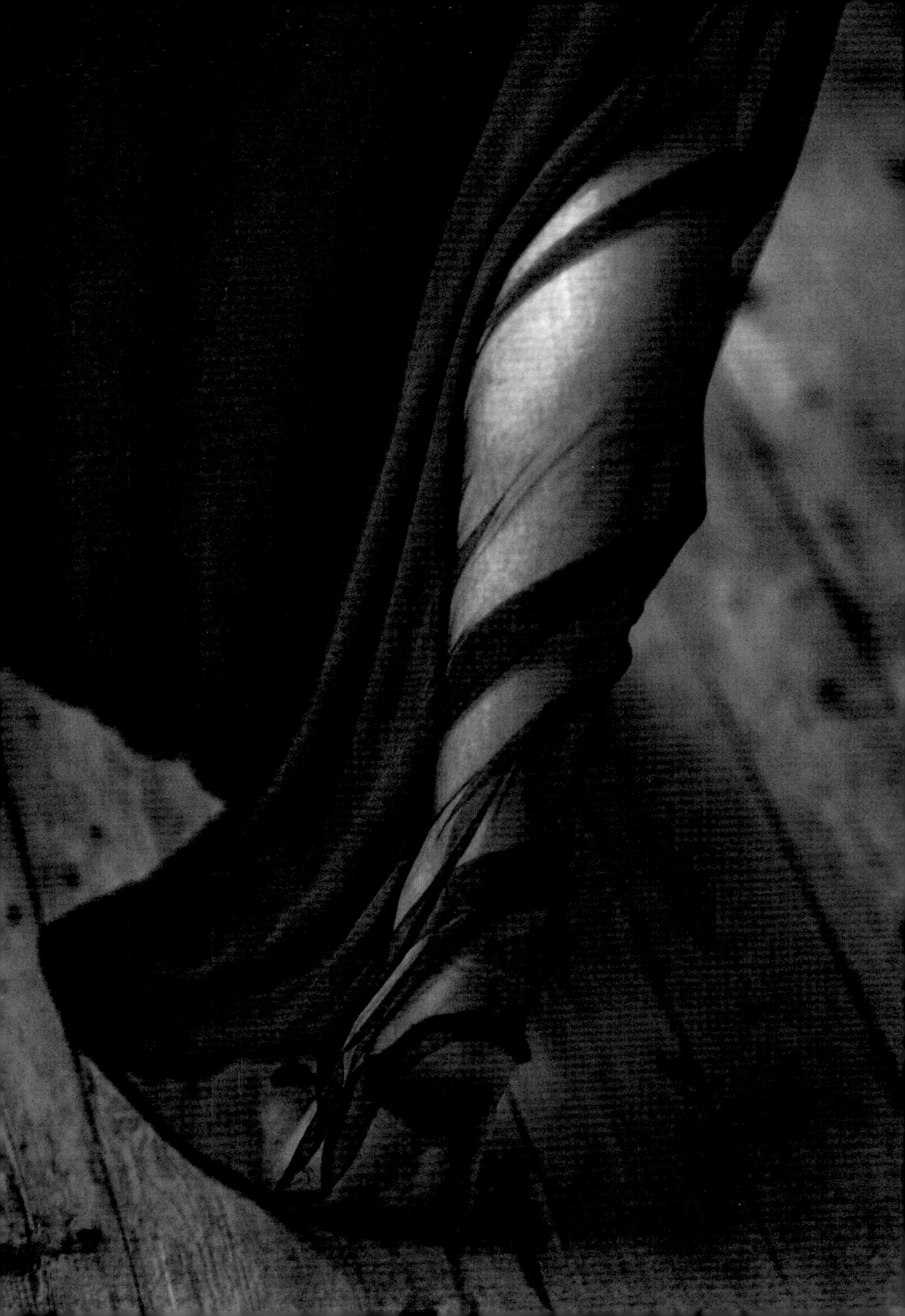

that he was interested only in black and white, in 1987 he even started asking his models to wear white shirts, the better to emphasise, even more, the uniqueness and holiness of each face. This was the culmination of a revolution that had been started ten years earlier. With his white shirts around beautiful, happy faces, the world had changed. Fashion had at last begun to serve humanity, and as a result it was lastingly transformed.

Azzedine Alaïa and Peter Lindbergh shared the same vision. They had the same kind of career path and each possessed a kind of technique, in photography or couture, that had in large part been lost. They put it in the service of their need for timelessness. Founded on mutual admiration, their friendship grew stronger with the years and with each new project. Together, they invented a large part of what made the 1980s, understanding that these new times were the age of a deep and definitive emancipation of women and that they would become an essential moment in the history of the aesthetics of the last forty years. They are both, still, our greatest contemporaries.

Alba Rohrwacher, *Paris*, 2008

"As paradoxical as it may sound,
I find black and white often
more authentic than color.
Portraits in particular appear
stronger by the reduction.**"**
Peter Lindbergh

Ariane Koizumi, *Duisburg*, 1985. Jacket, *Winter* 1984
(Following spread) Ariane Koizumi, *Duisburg*, 1985. Dress, *Summer* 1986

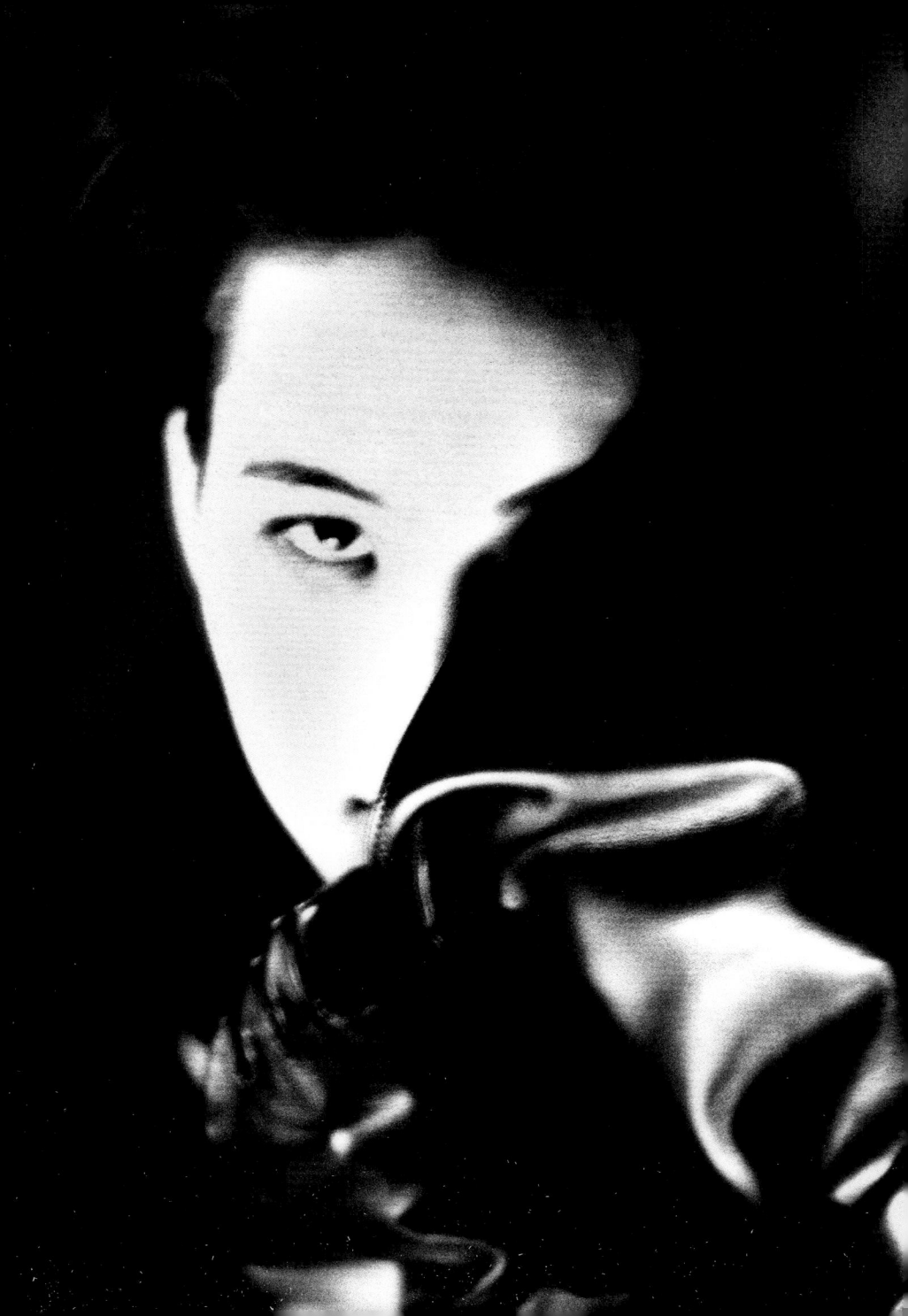

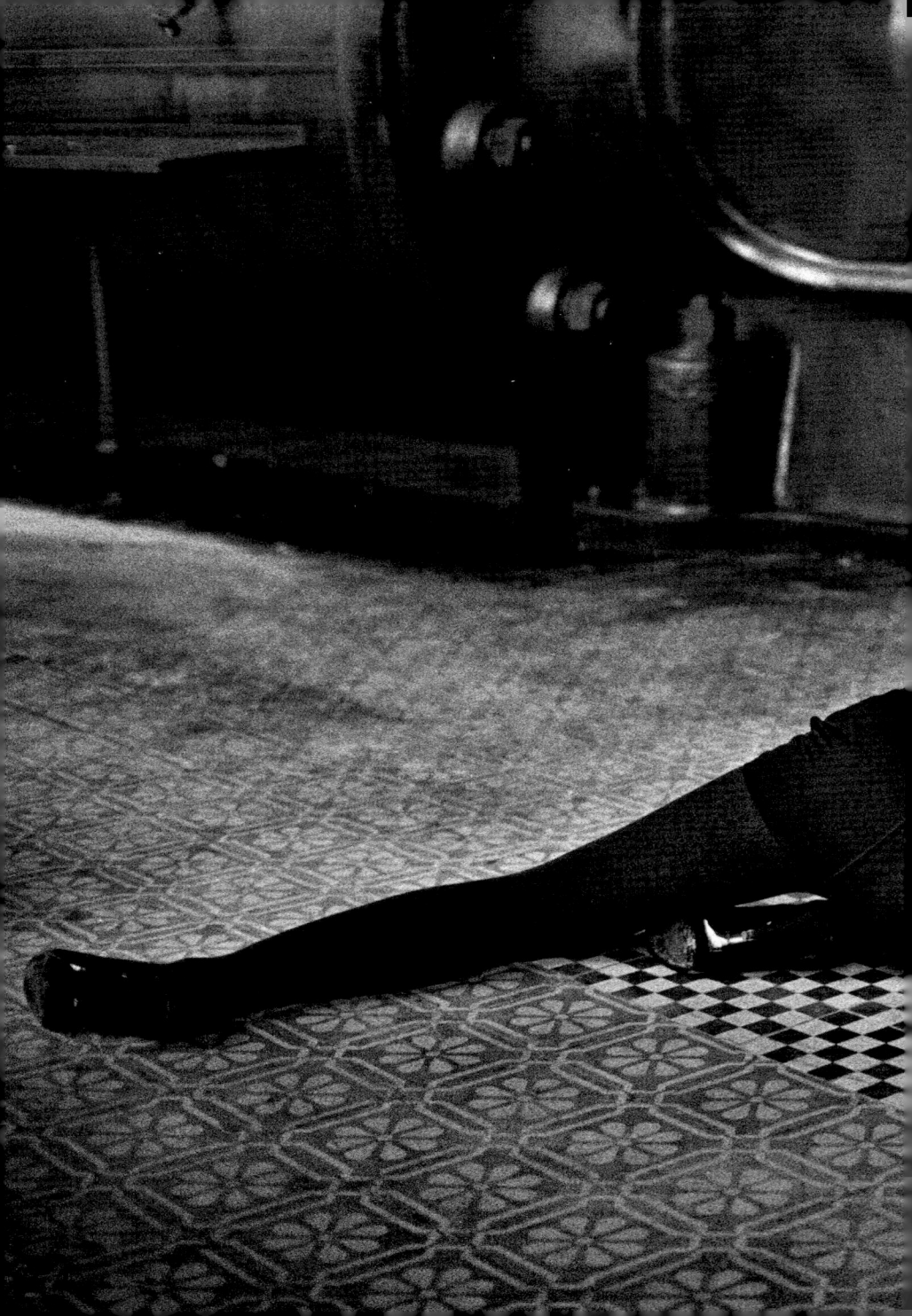

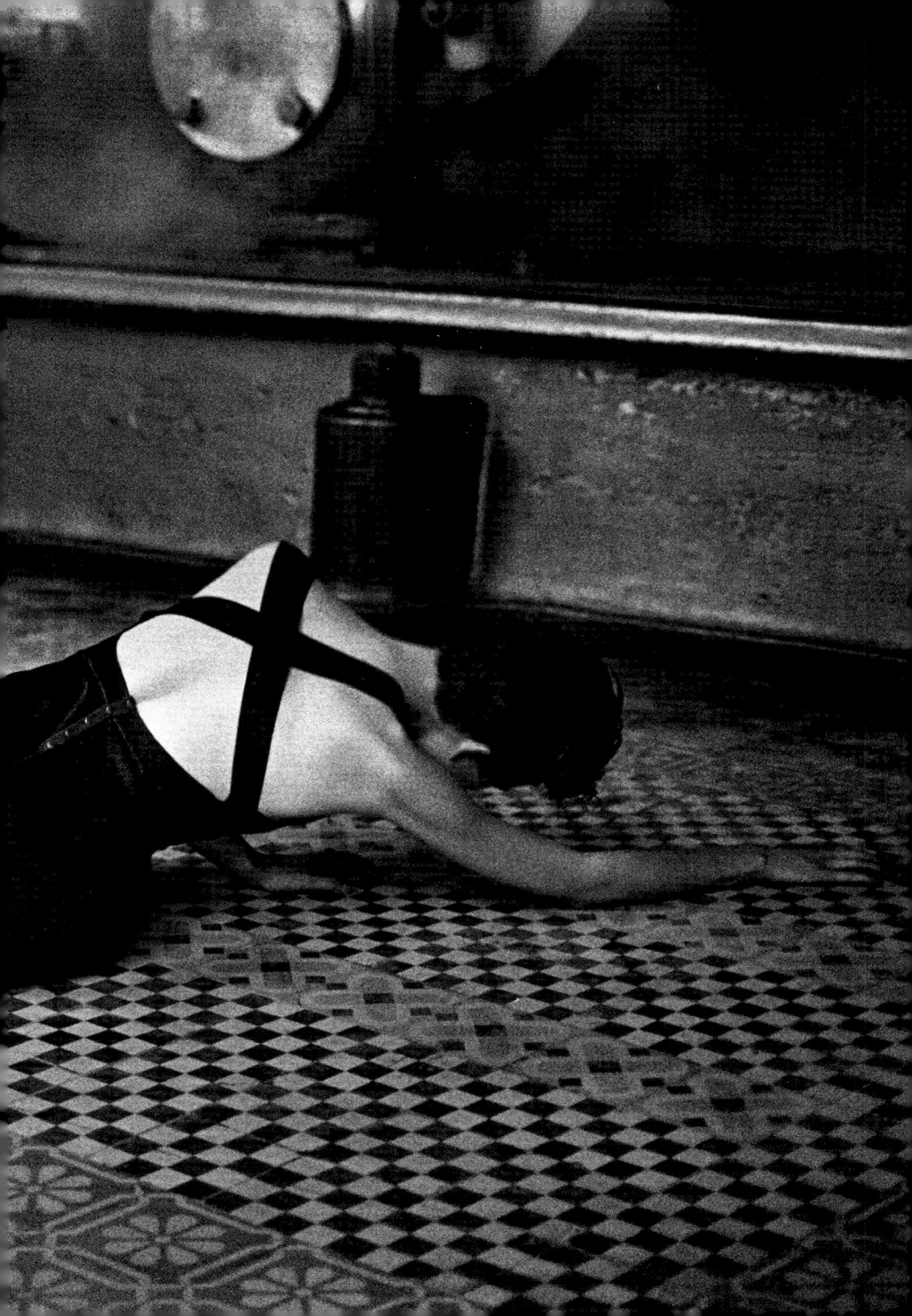

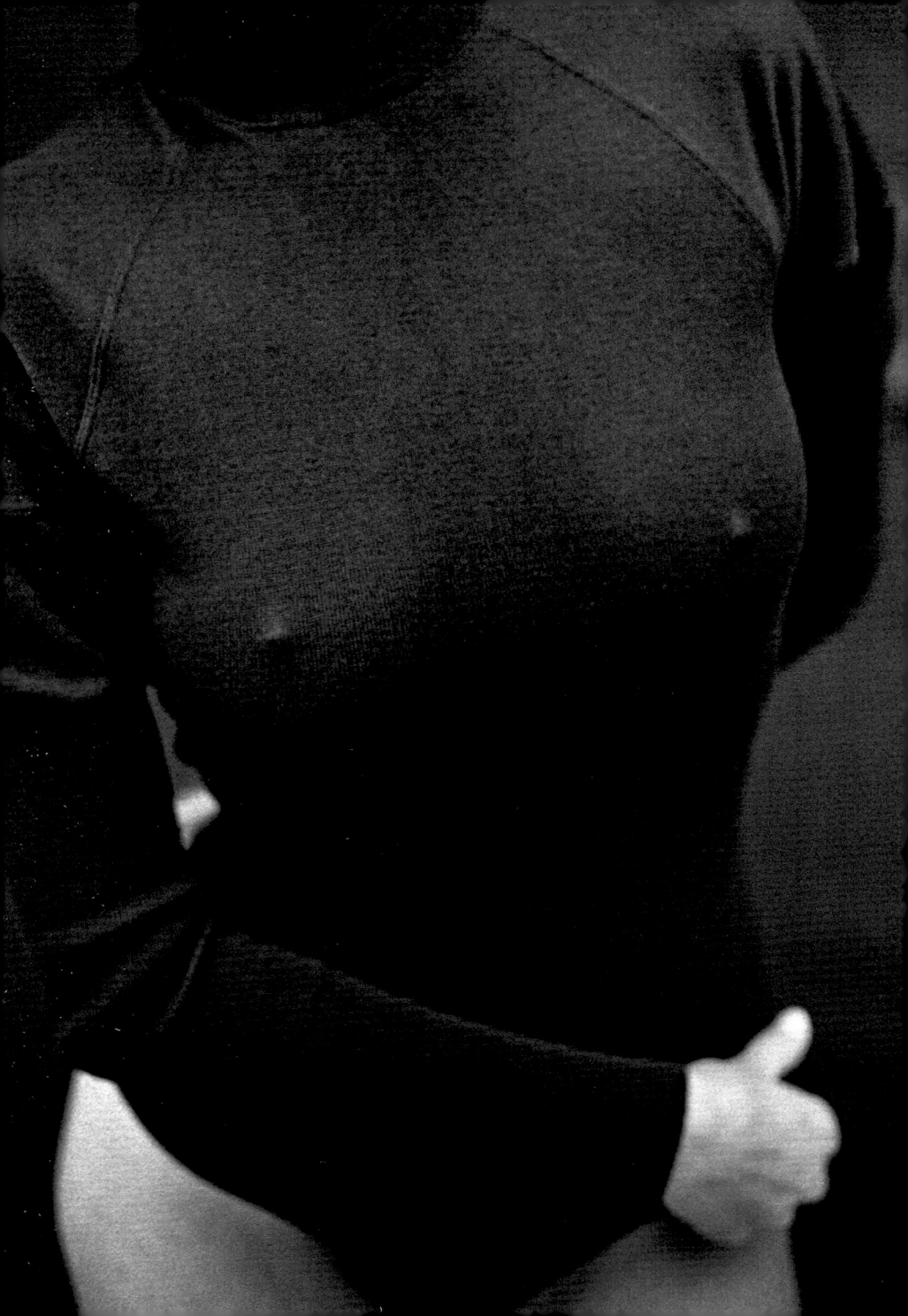

"I like black, because for me it is a very happy color."
Azzedine Alaïa

Tatjana Patitz, *Cannes*, 1989. Body, *Winter* 1989
(Following spread) Marie-Sophie Wilson, *Paris*, 1986. Dress, *Summer* 1987

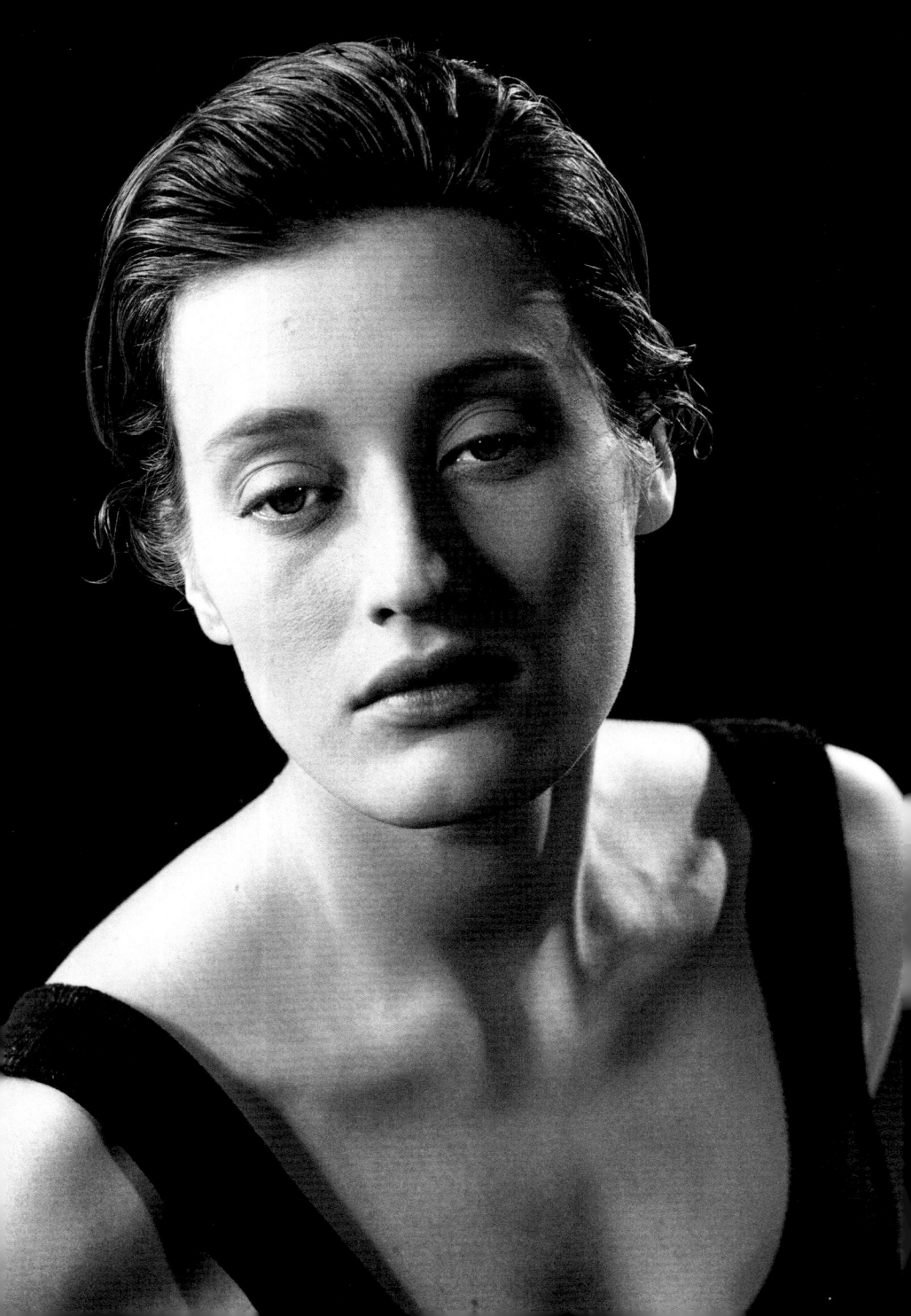

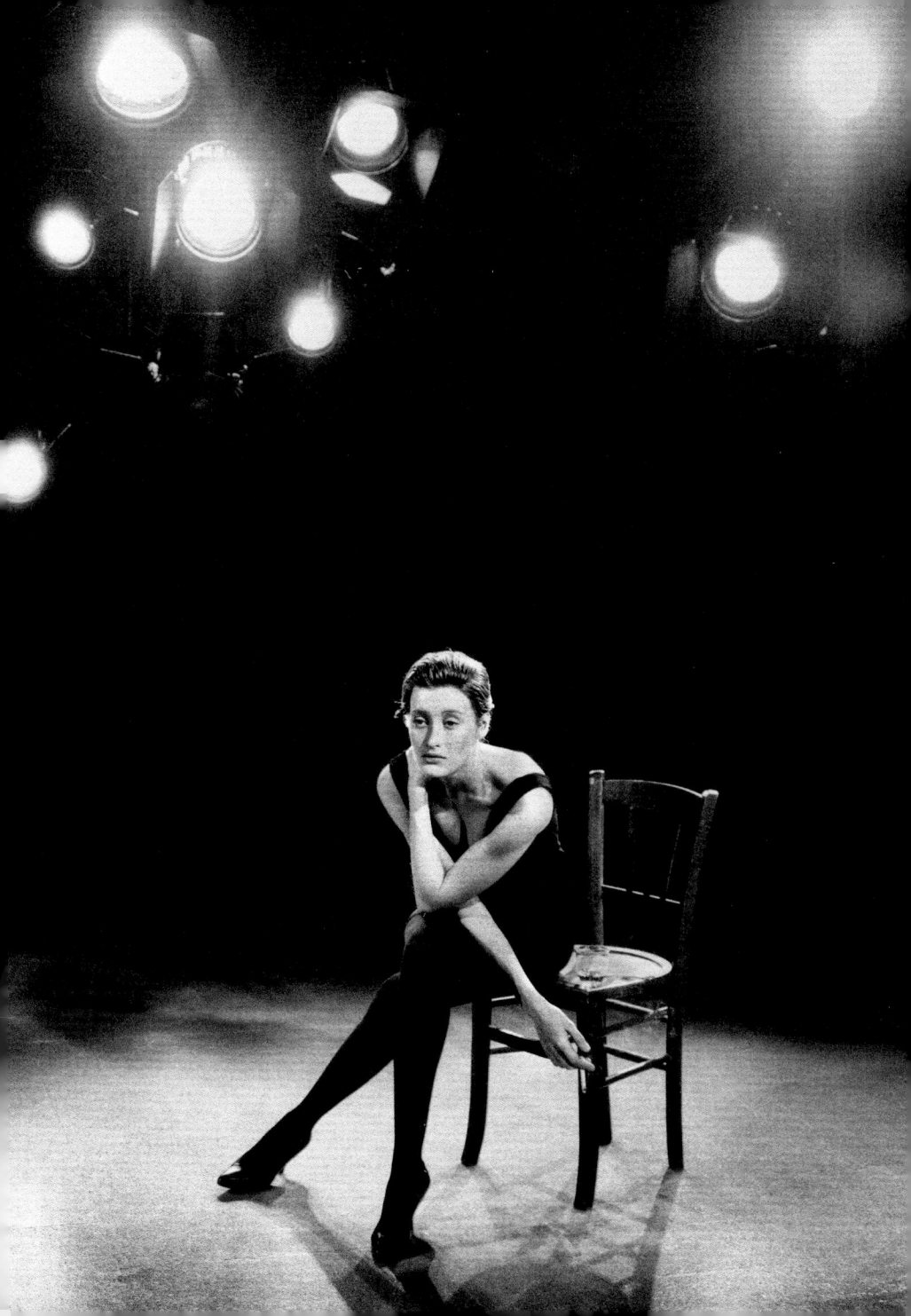

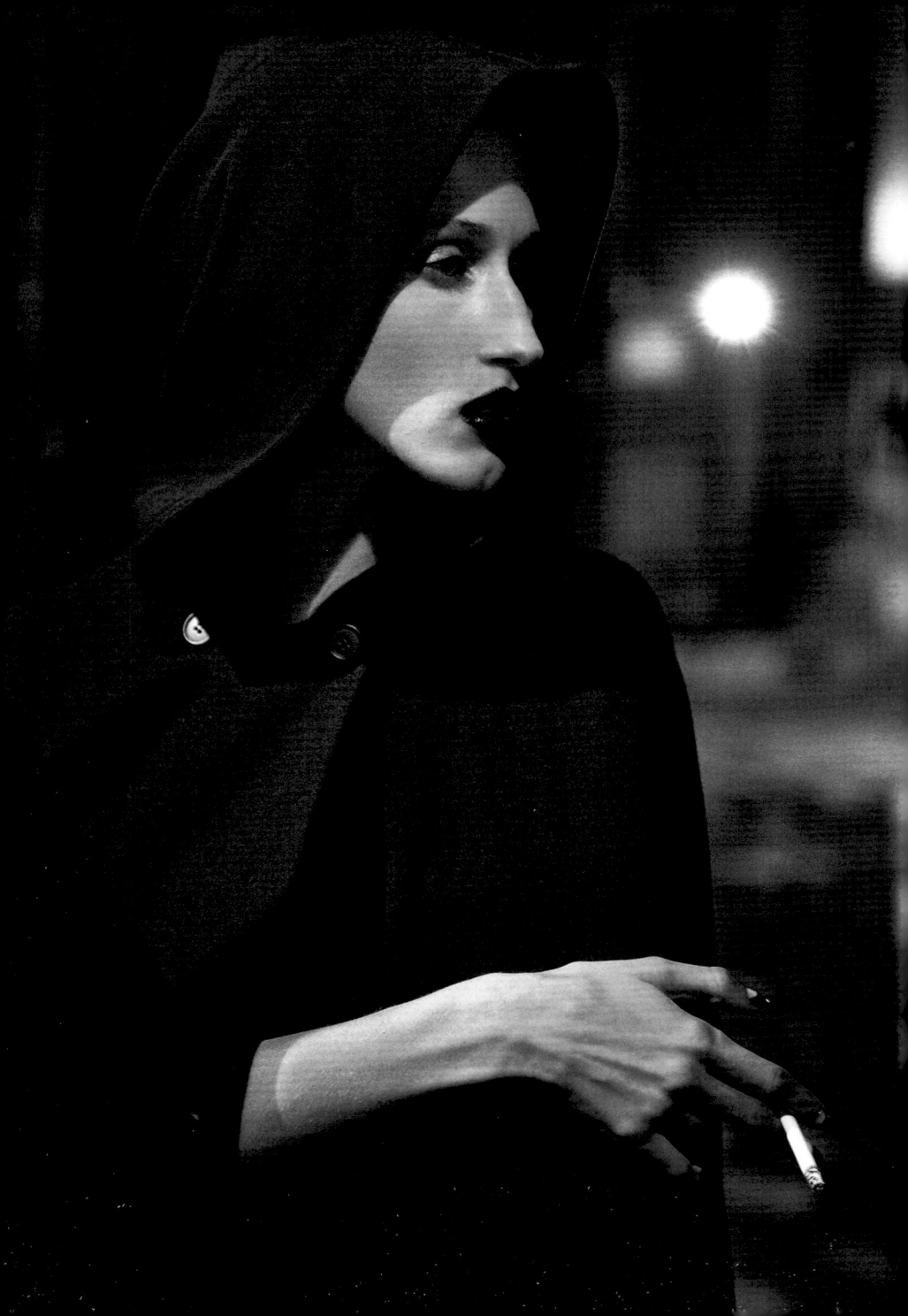

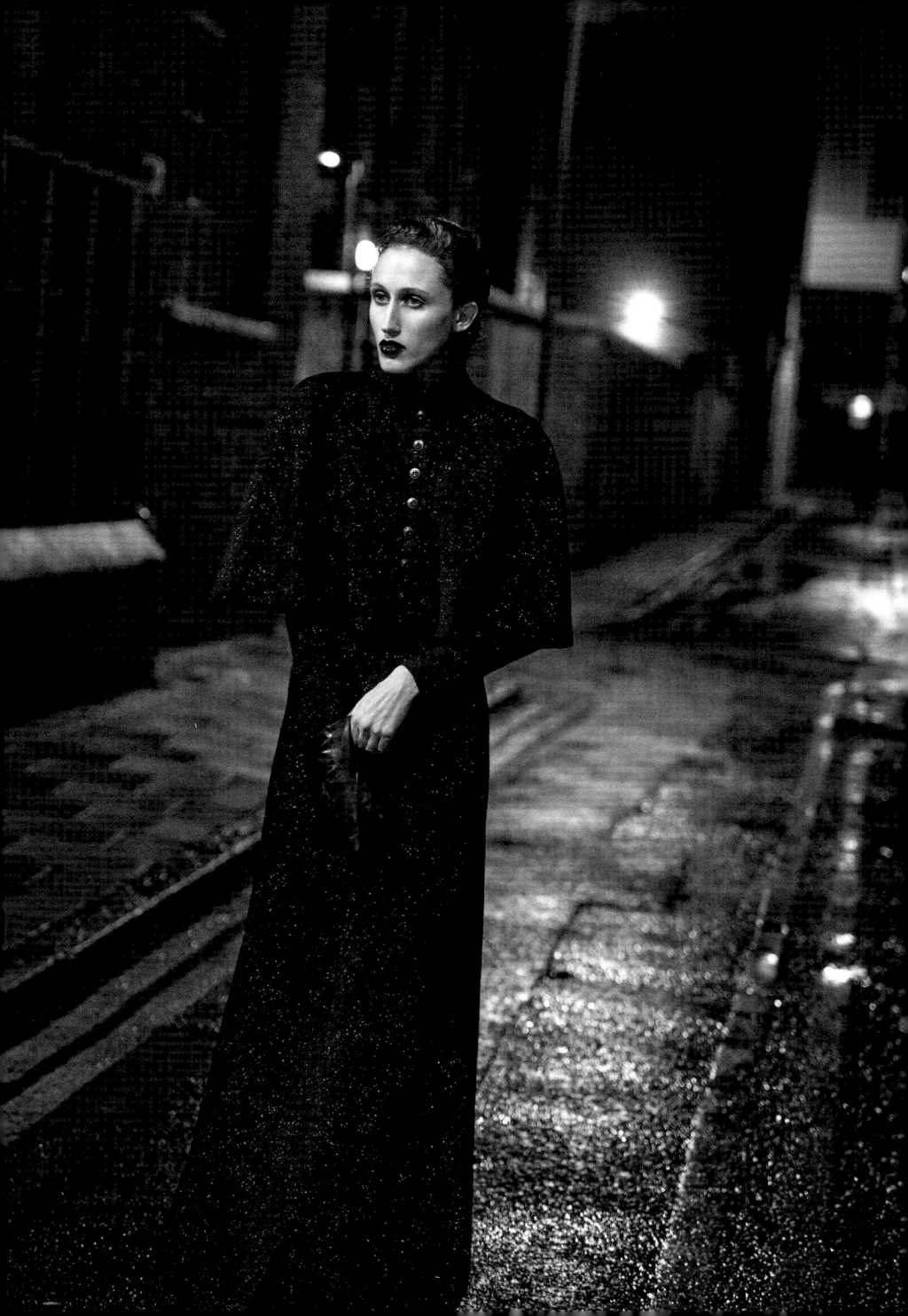

"Women are more open, courageous,
have more nerve, and take on
far more risks compared with men.
I look at them for what they really
are, perhaps this is what leads them
to abandon themselves to me.**"**
Peter Lindbergh

(Previous spread) Anna Cleveland, *London*, 2015
Cape, *Haute Couture Winter* 2015. Short cape and dress, *Winter* 2015
(Opposite) Ariane Koizumi, *Duisburg*, 1985. Pants and belt, *Winter* 1985

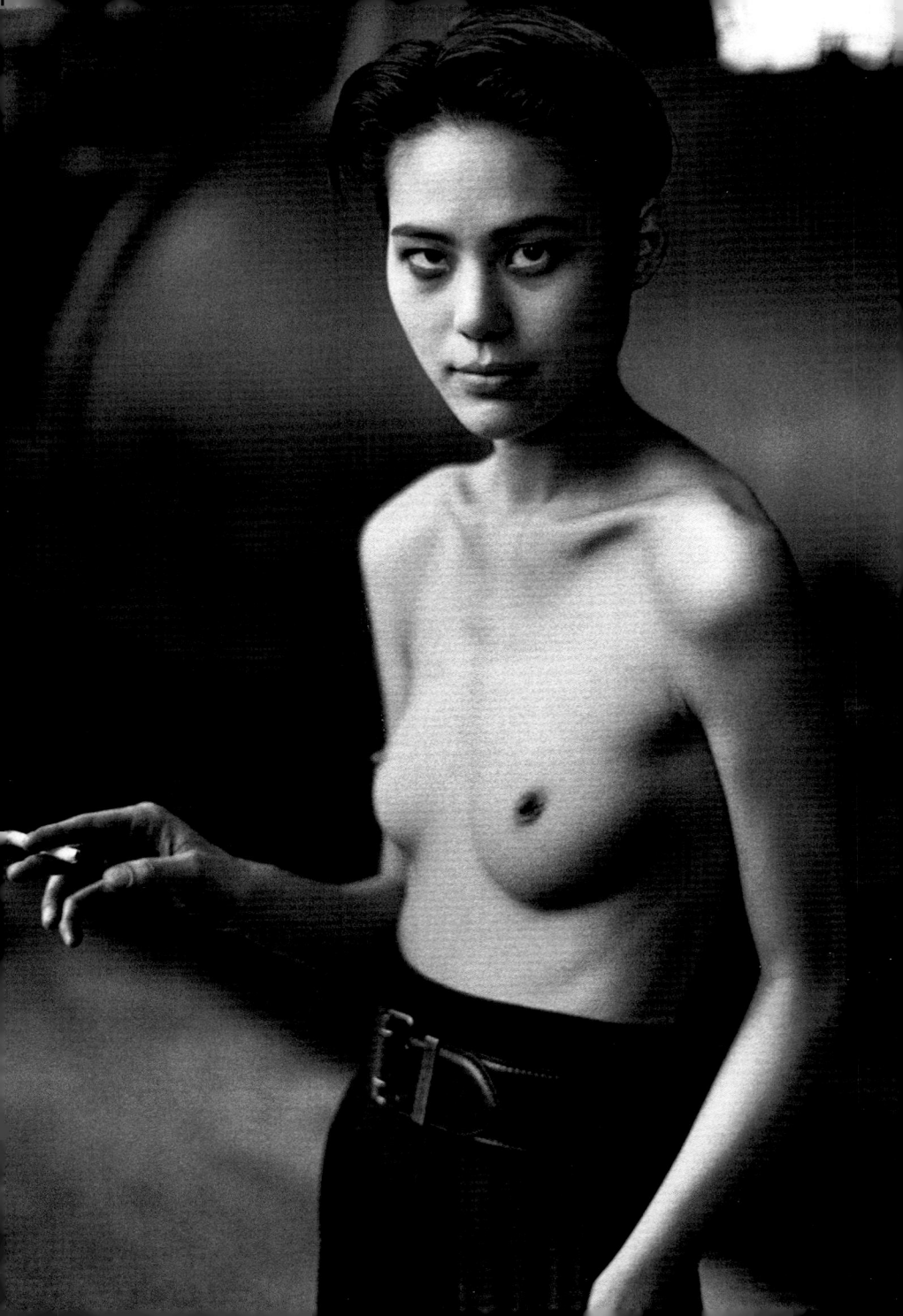

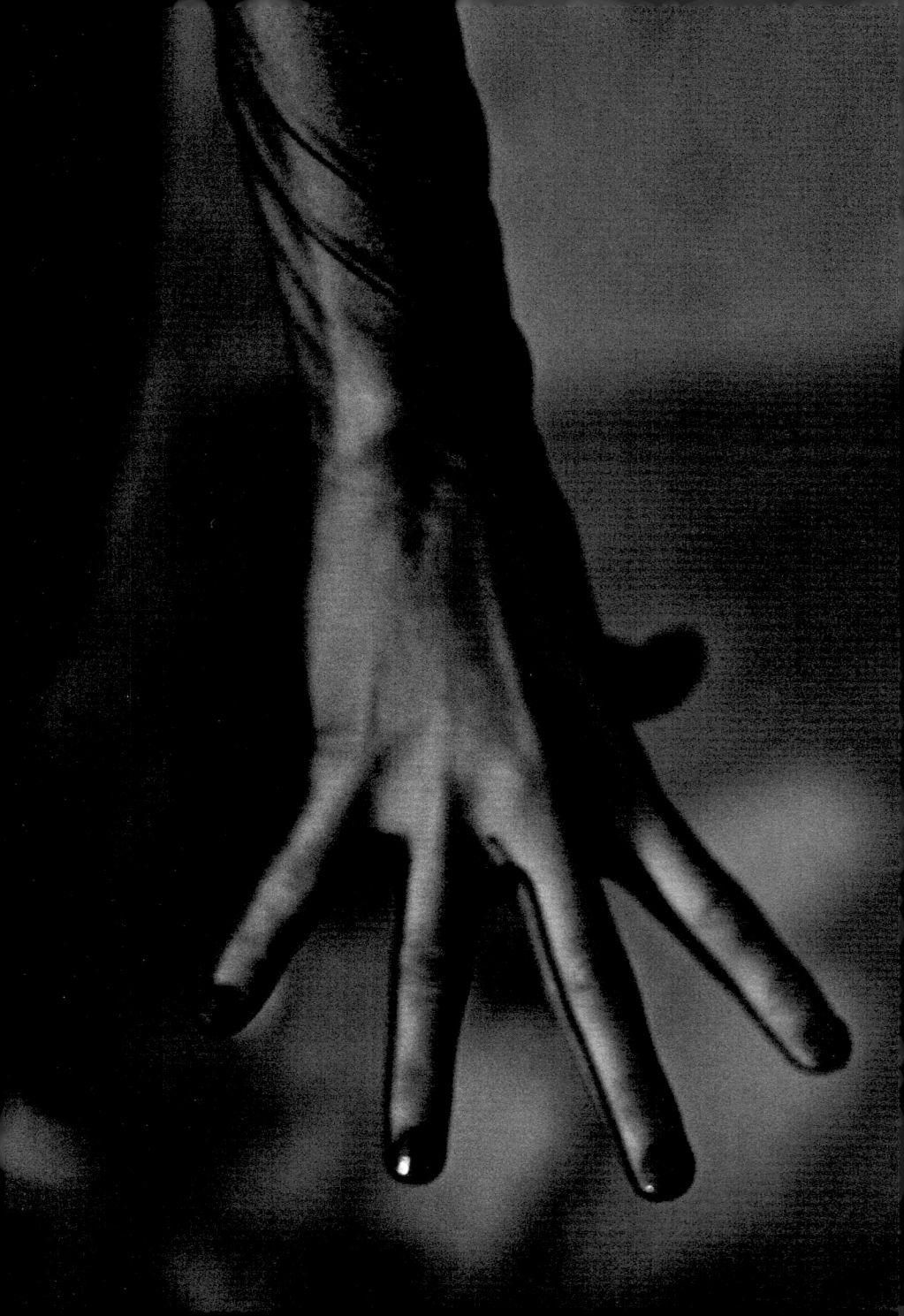

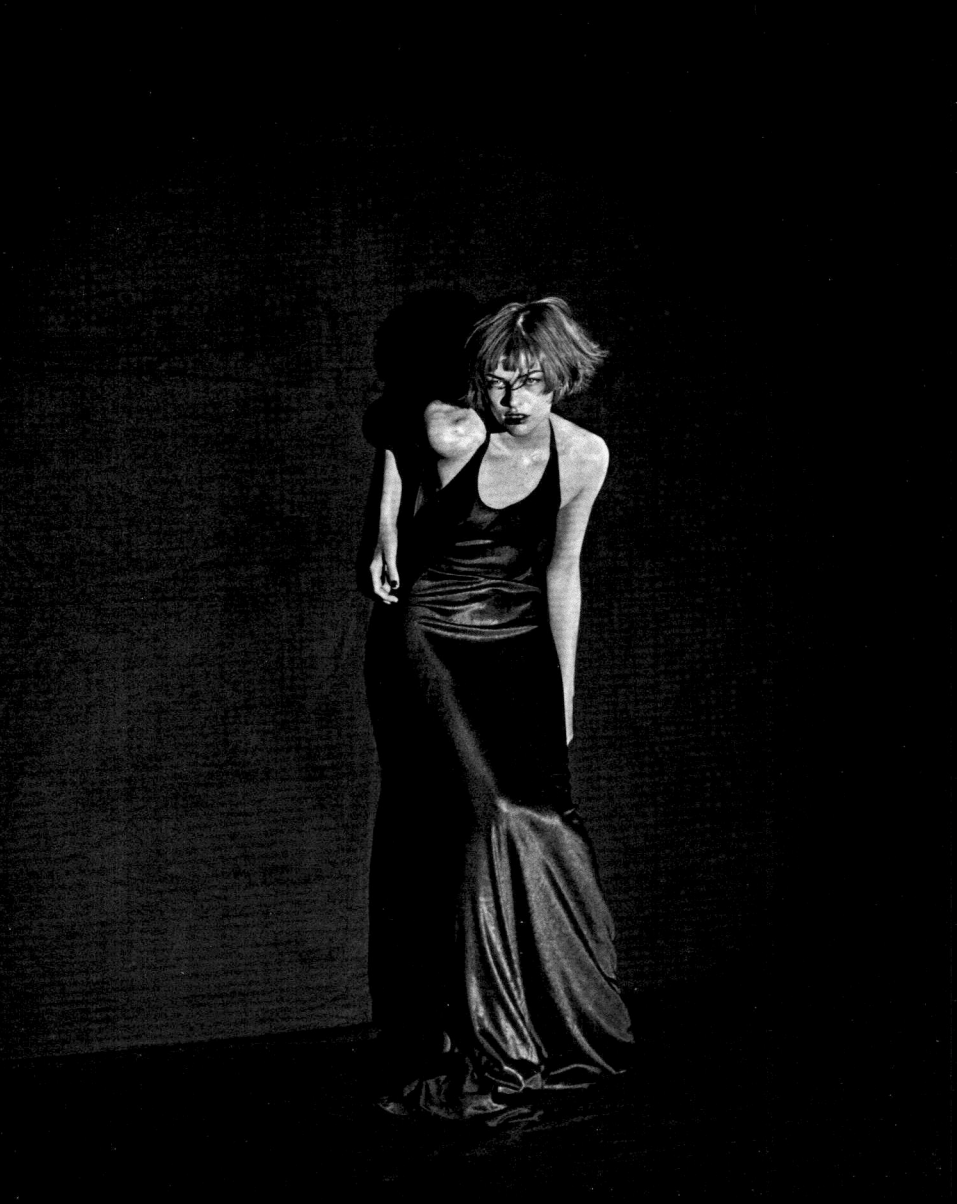

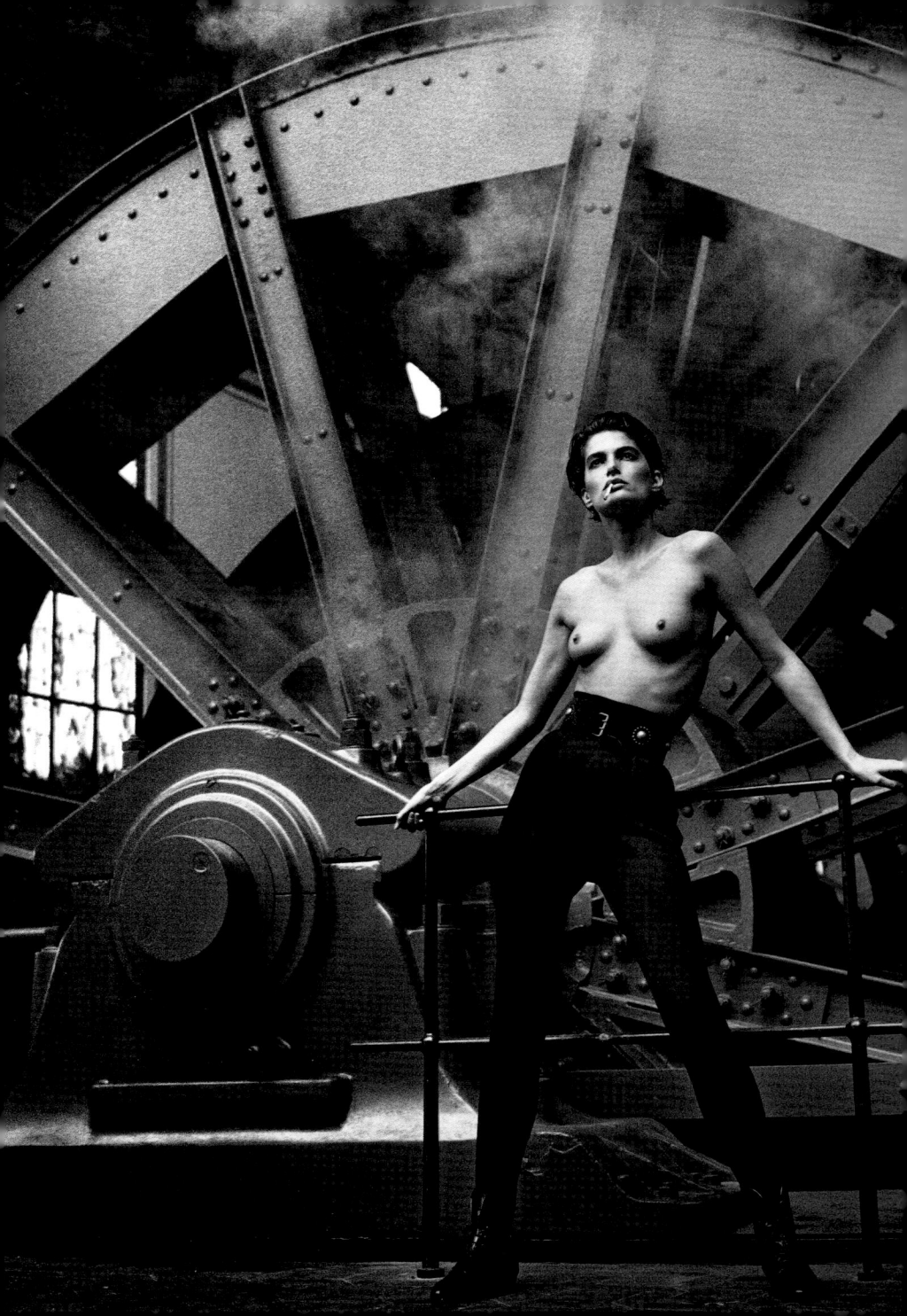

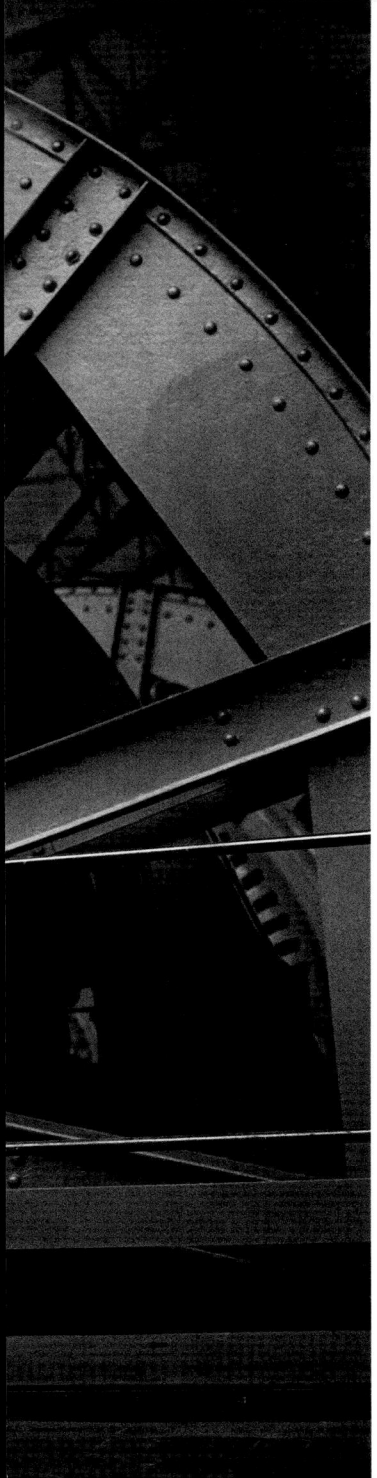

(Previous spread) Kristen McMenamy, *Beauduc*, 1990
Milla Jovovich, *Paris*, 1998
Dress, *Haute Couture Winter* 1997
(Opposite) Lynne Koester, *Duisburg*, 1985
Pants and belt, *Winter* 1985

" I like that a woman's face, body, and legs are her sole accessories. **"**
Azzedine Alaïa

Lynne Koester, *Duisburg*, 1986. Dress, *Summer* 1986

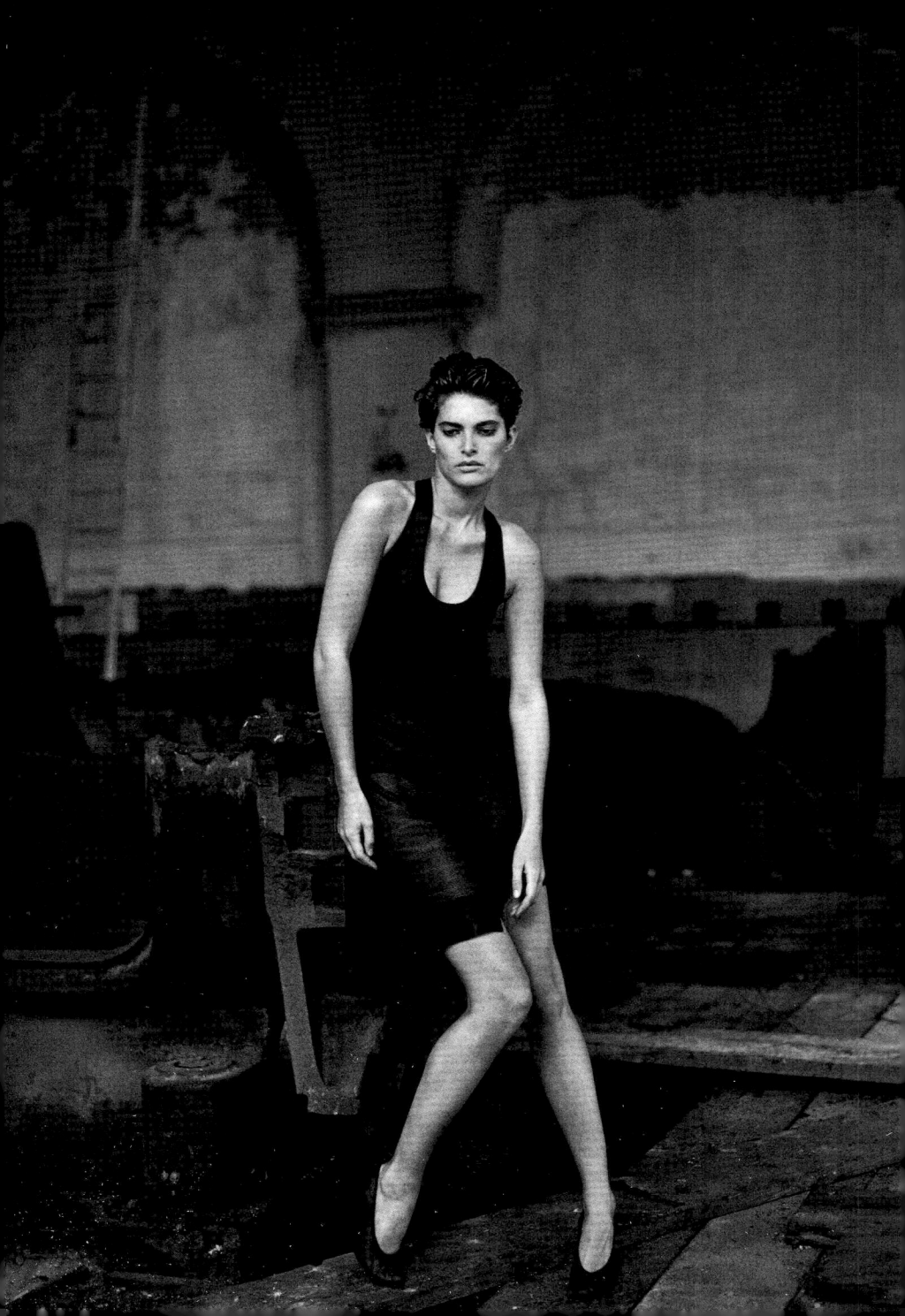

Lynne Koester, *Duisburg*, 1985
Coat, *Winter* 1985

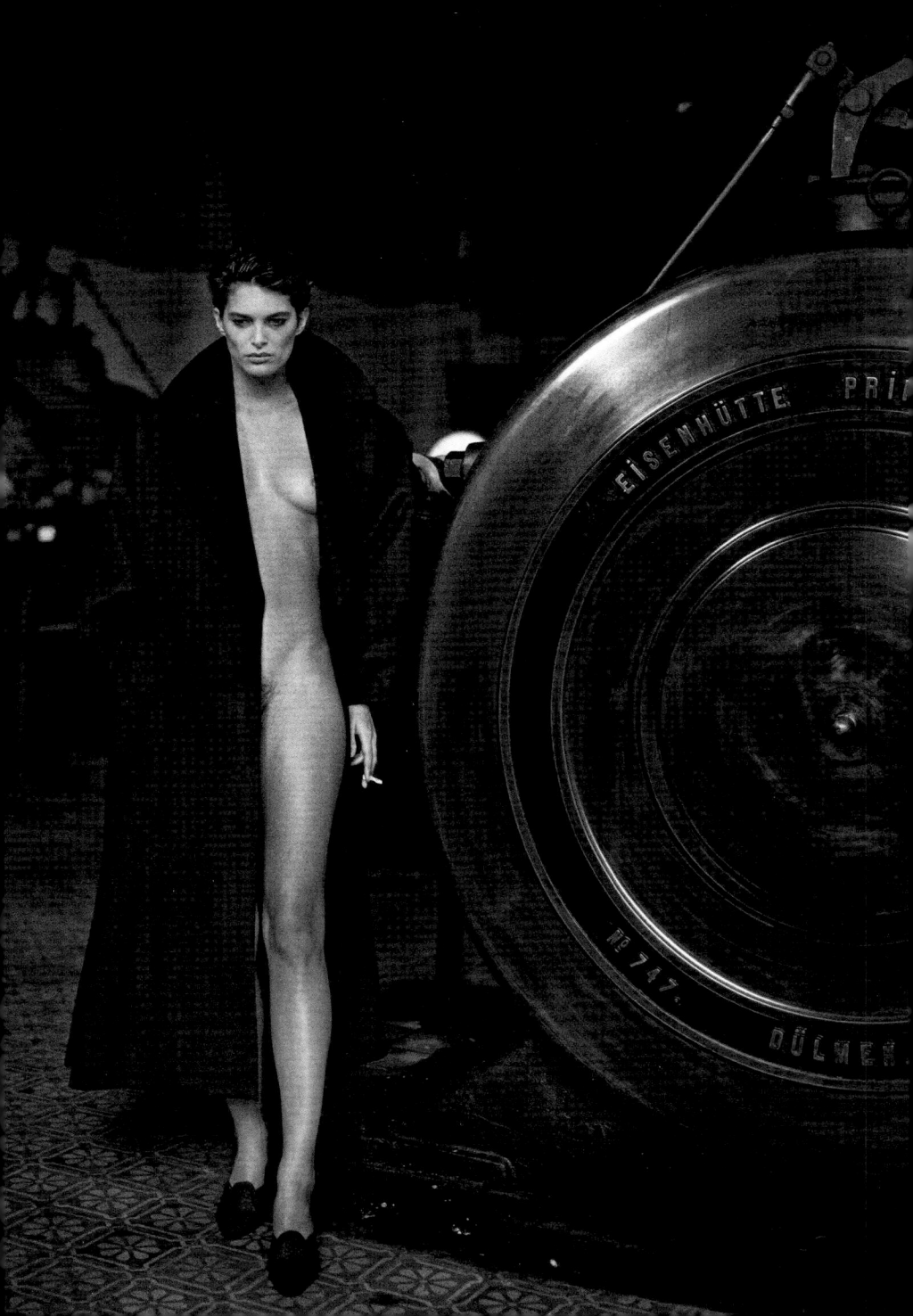

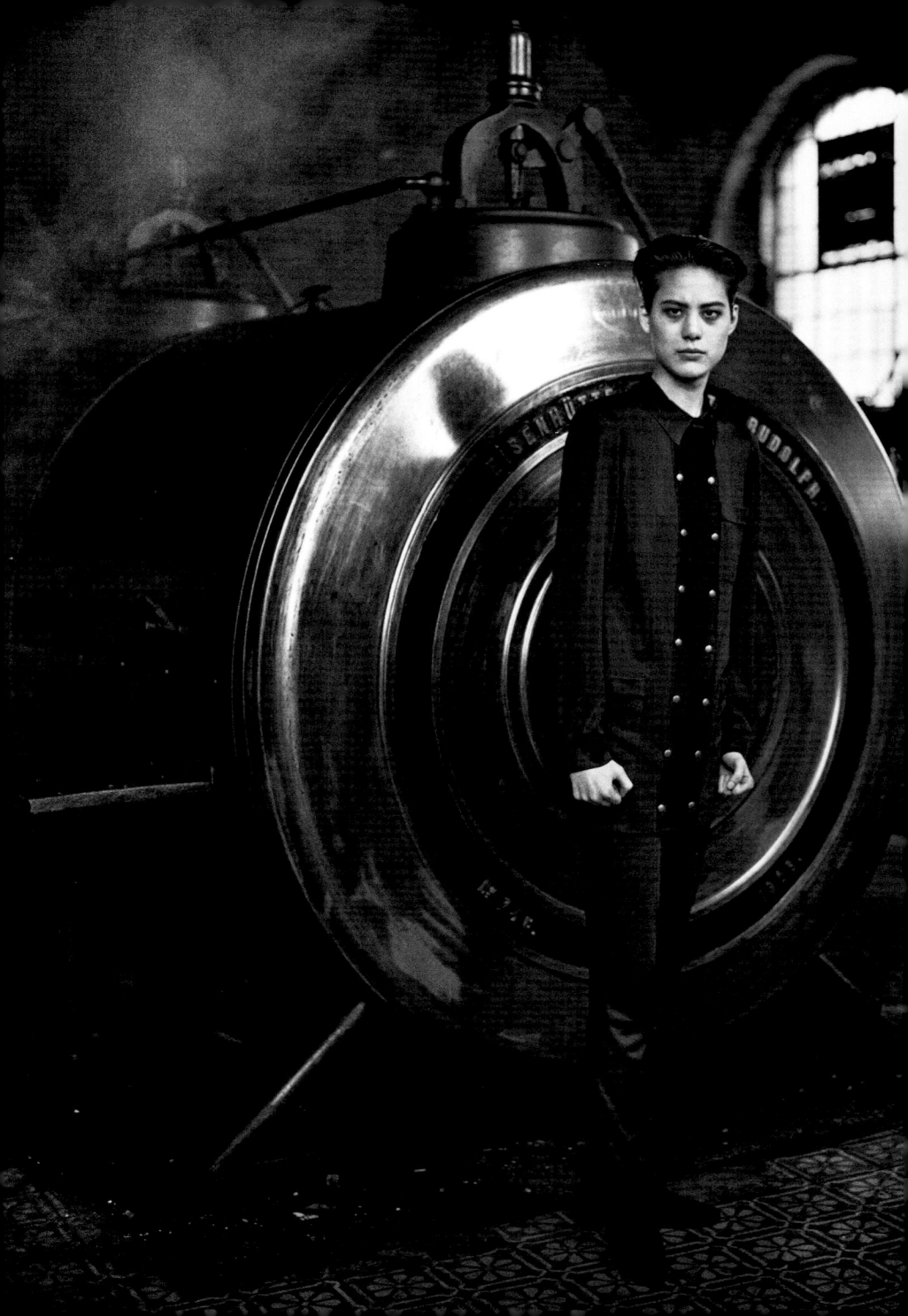

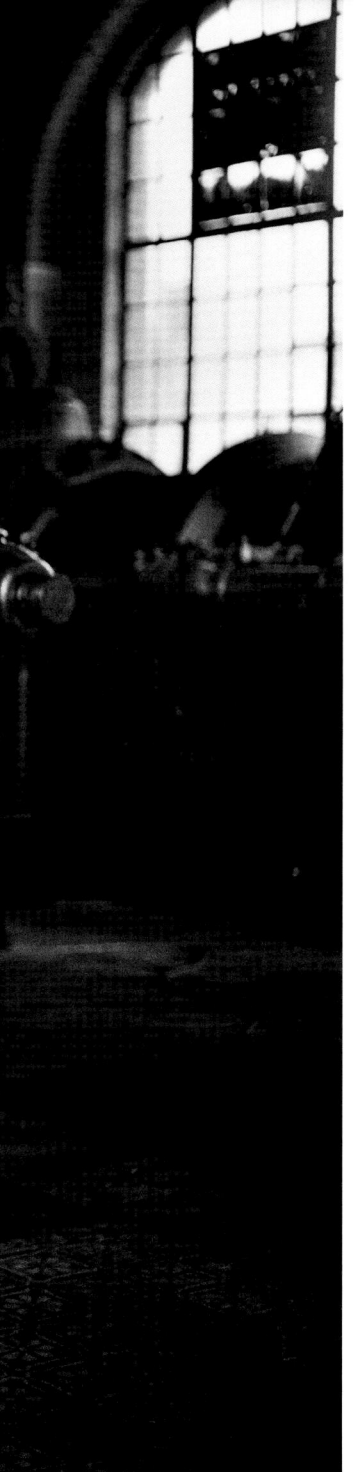

Ariane Koizumi, *Duisburg*, 1985. Ensemble, *Summer* 1986
(Following spread) Lynne Koester, *Duisburg*, 1985
Pants, *Winter* 1985

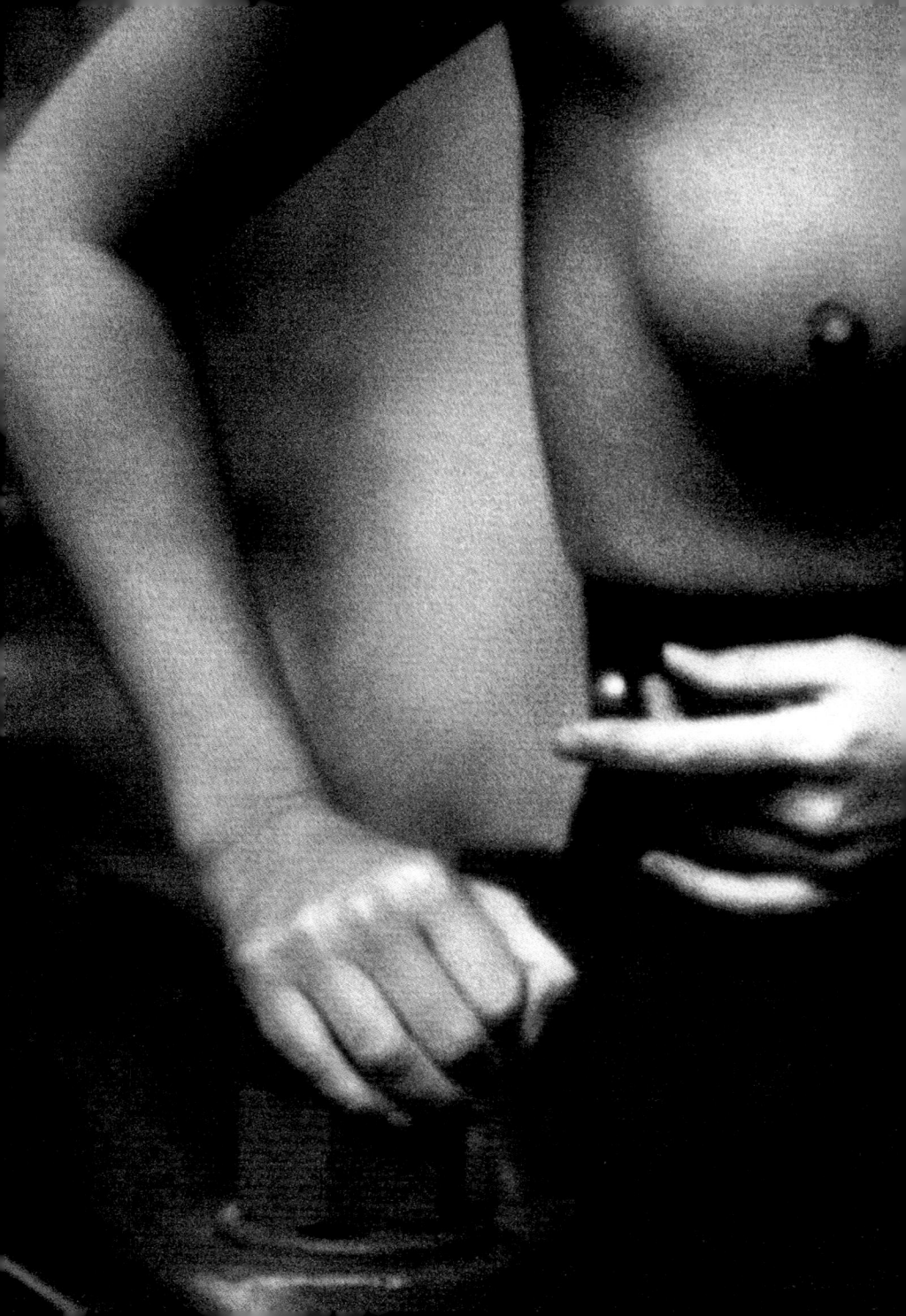

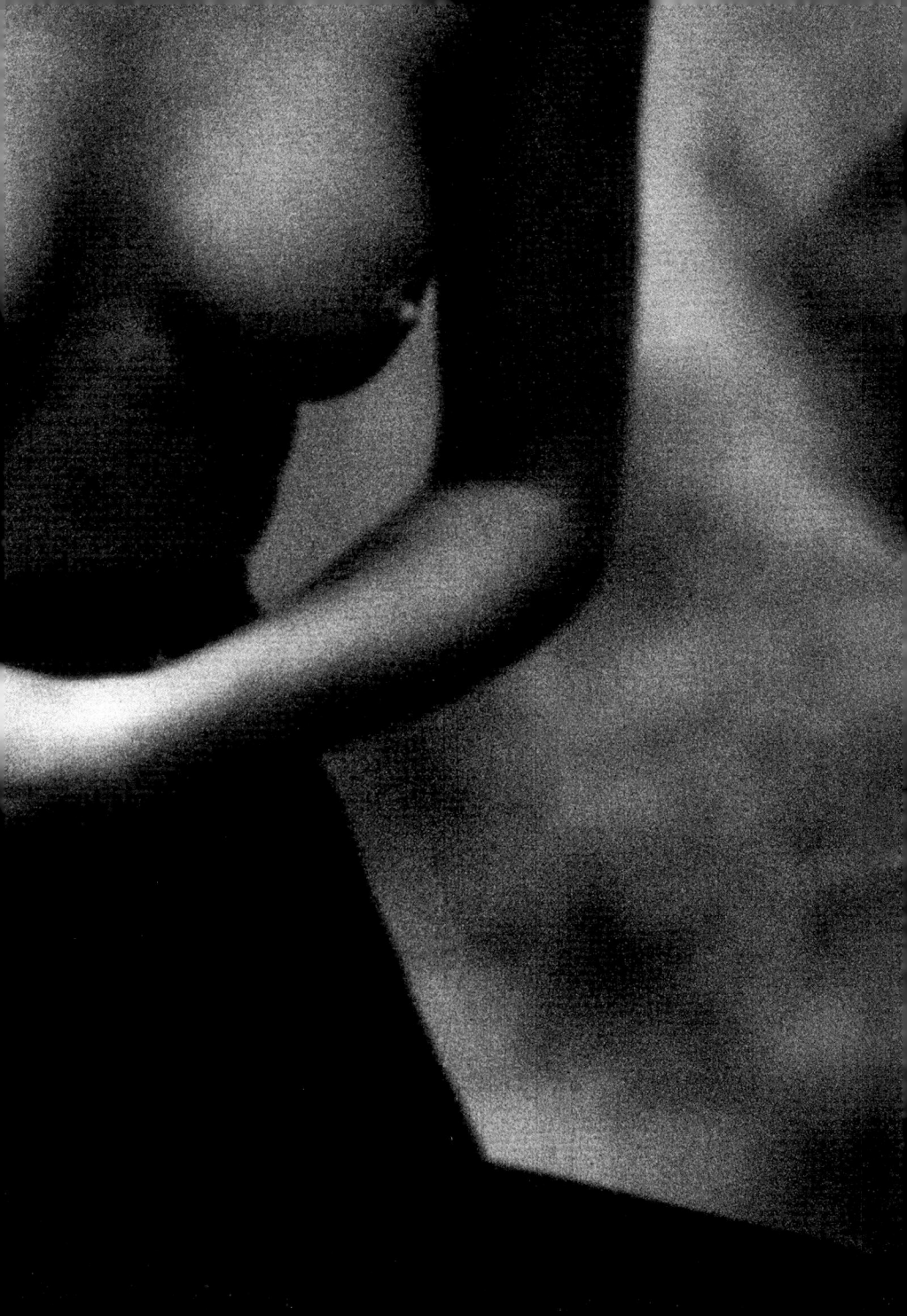

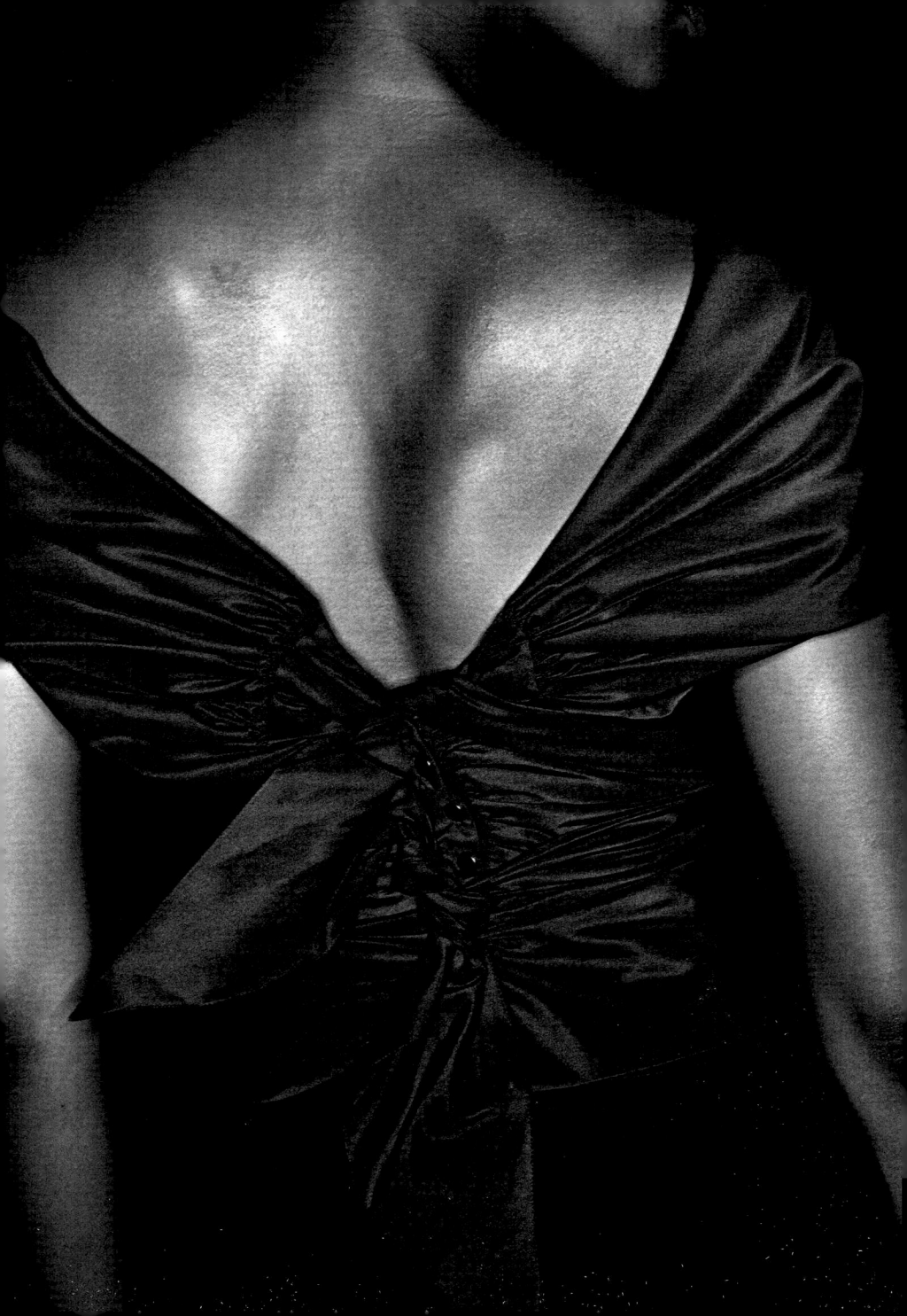

Naomi Campbell, *Paris*, 2001. Top, *Haute Couture* 2001
(Following spread) Helene Fischer, *Paris*, 2018. Skirt, *Haute Couture Summer* 2017

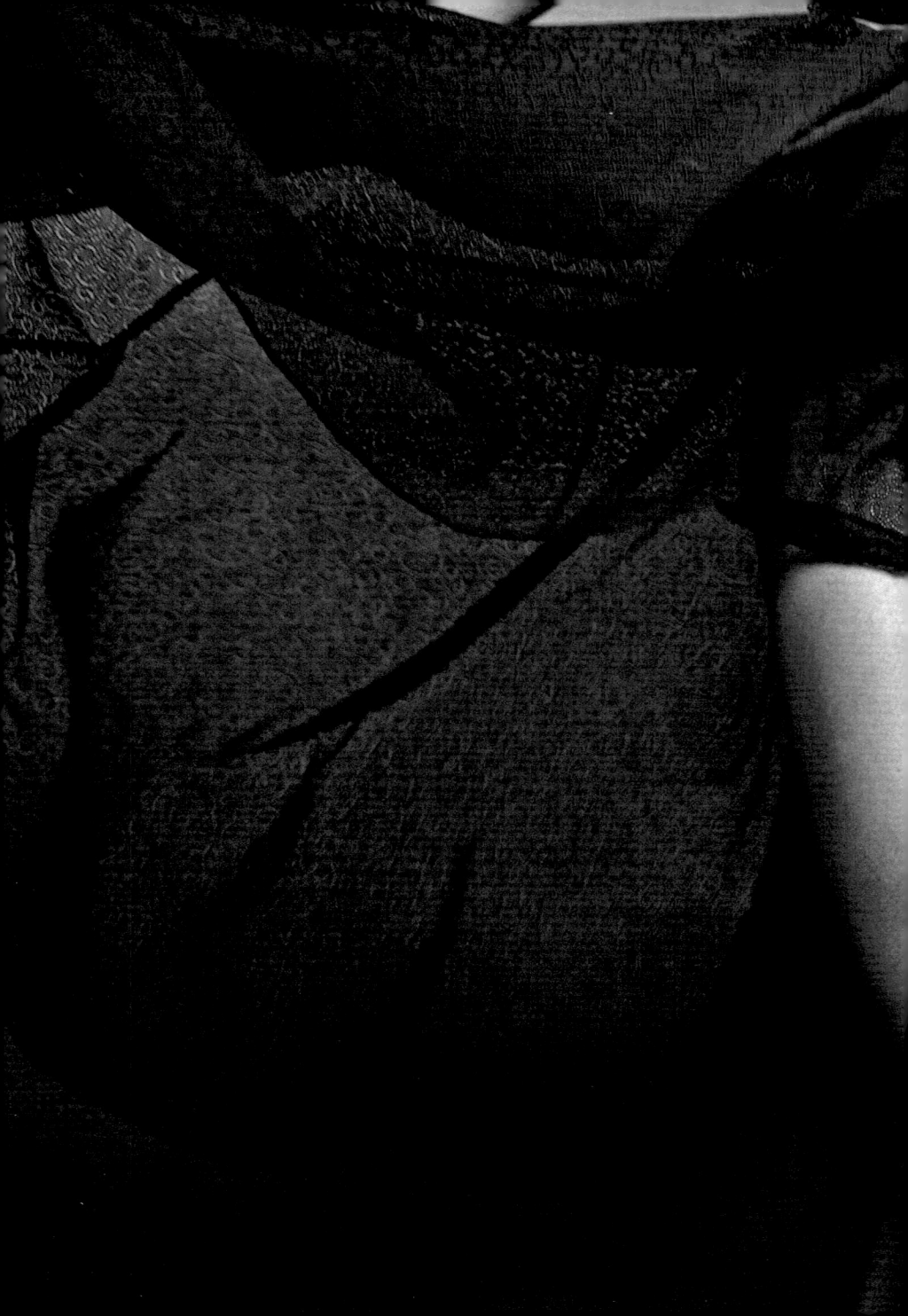

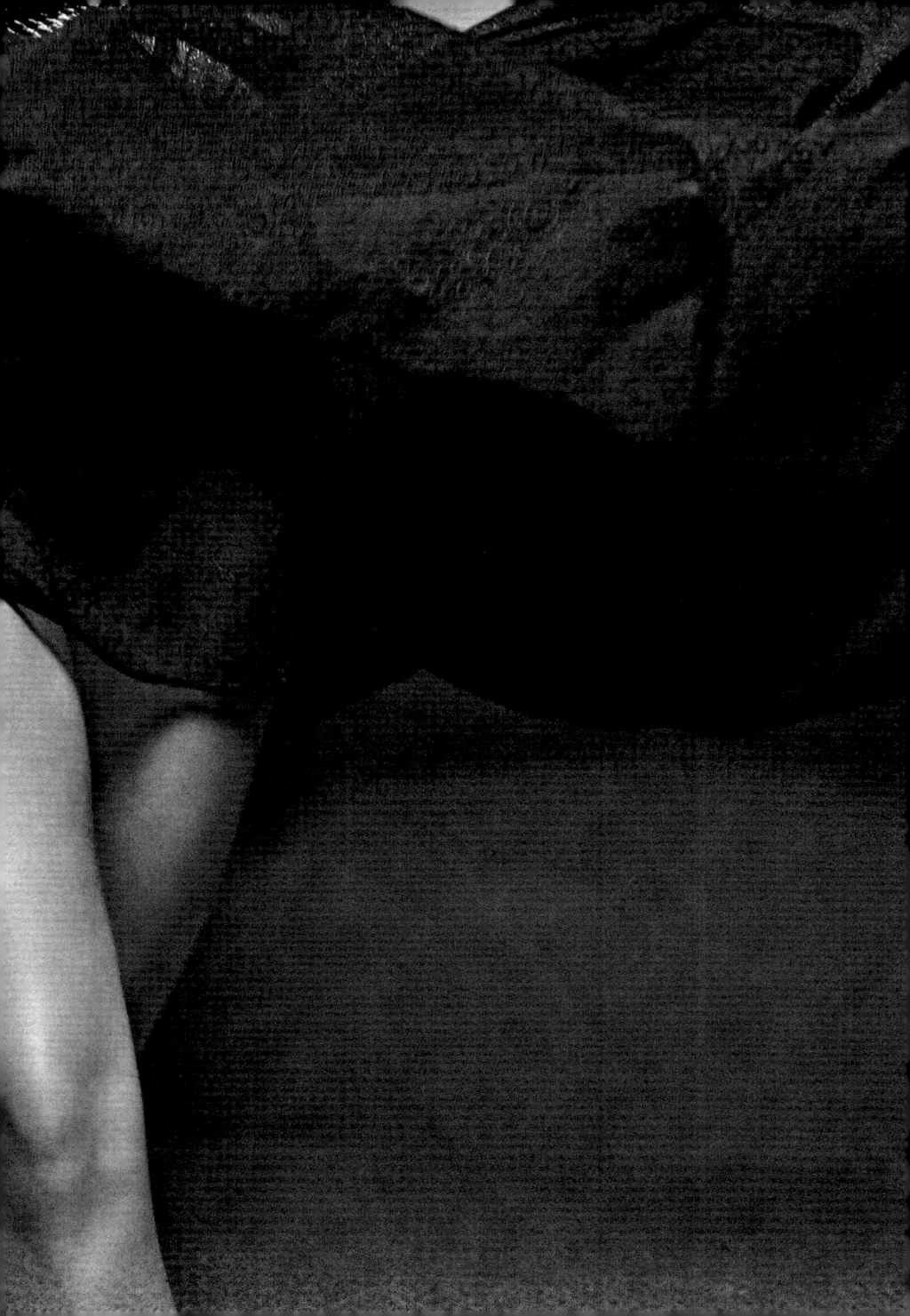

" I have always wanted women to be free. I hope my dresses give them that lightness. The finest compliment is when they look at themselves and say to me, 'I feel free.'**"**
Azzedine Alaïa

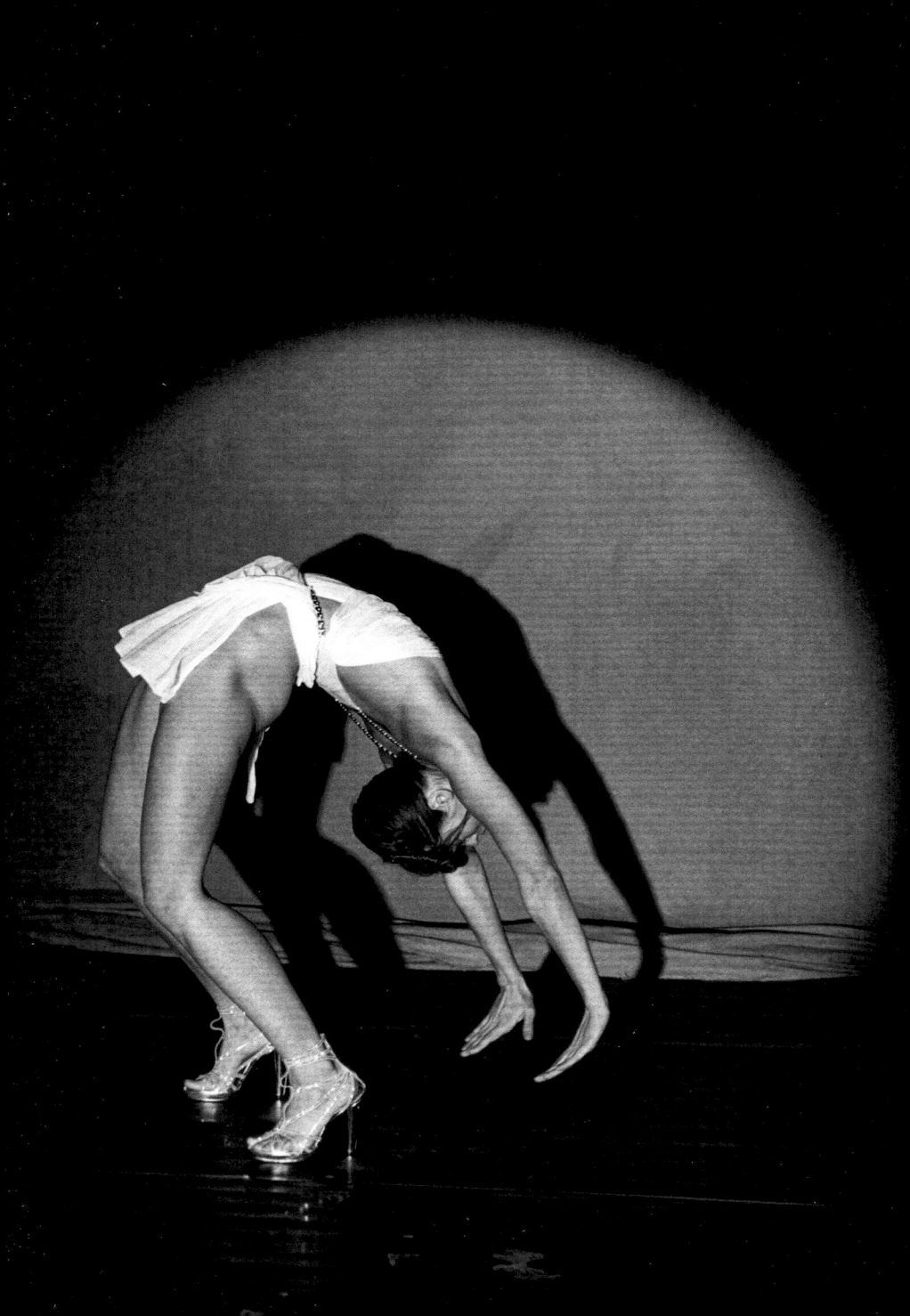

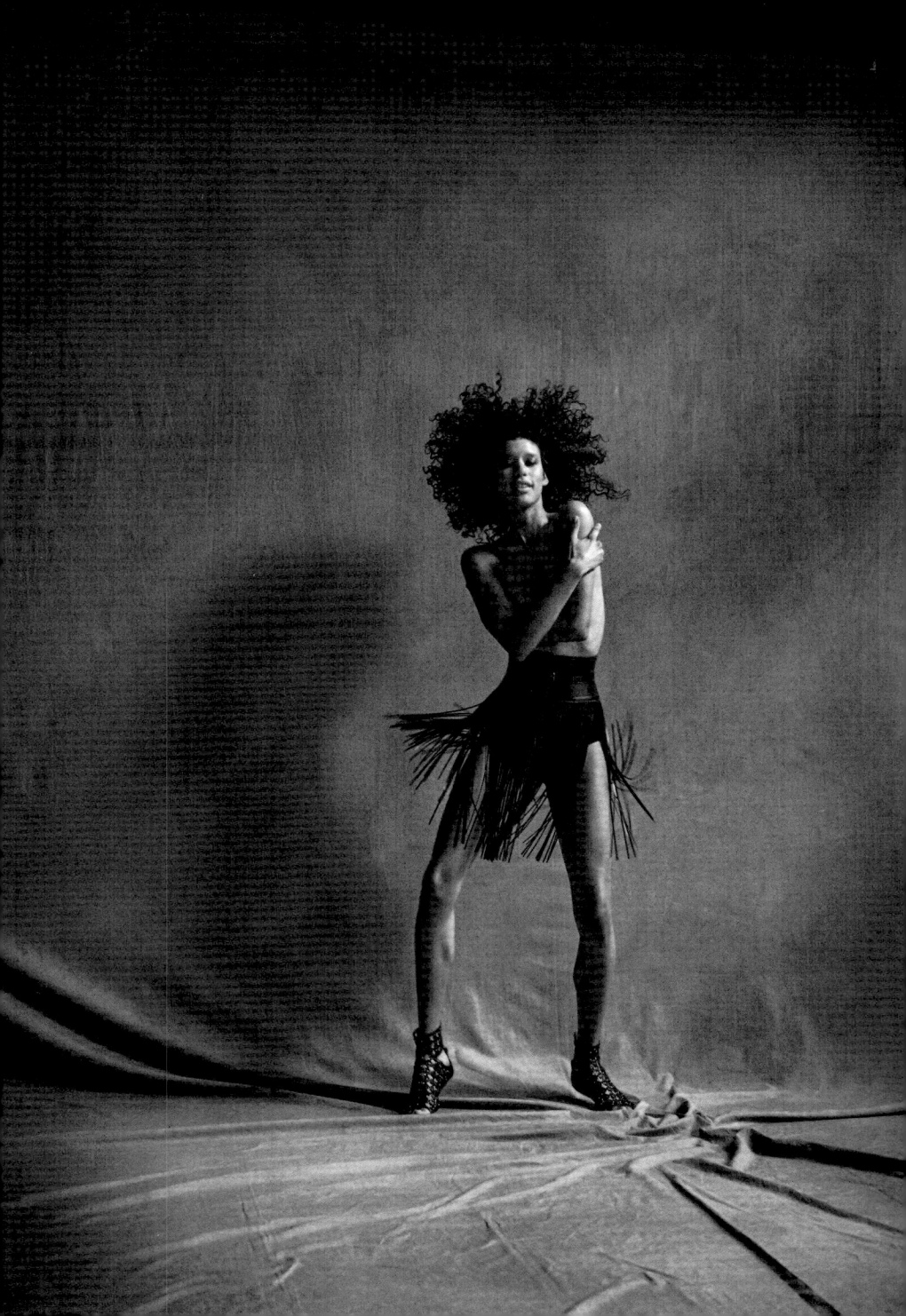

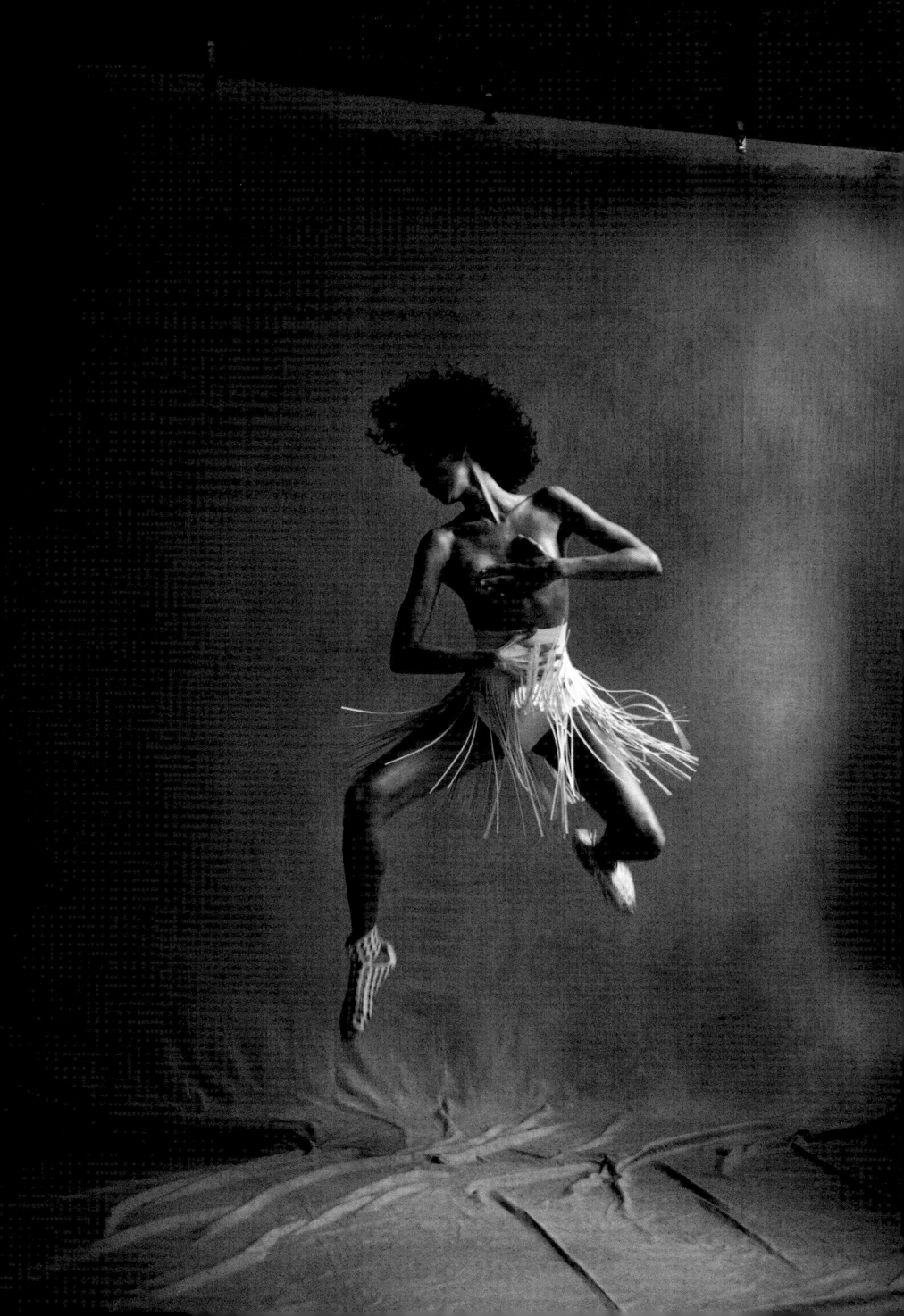

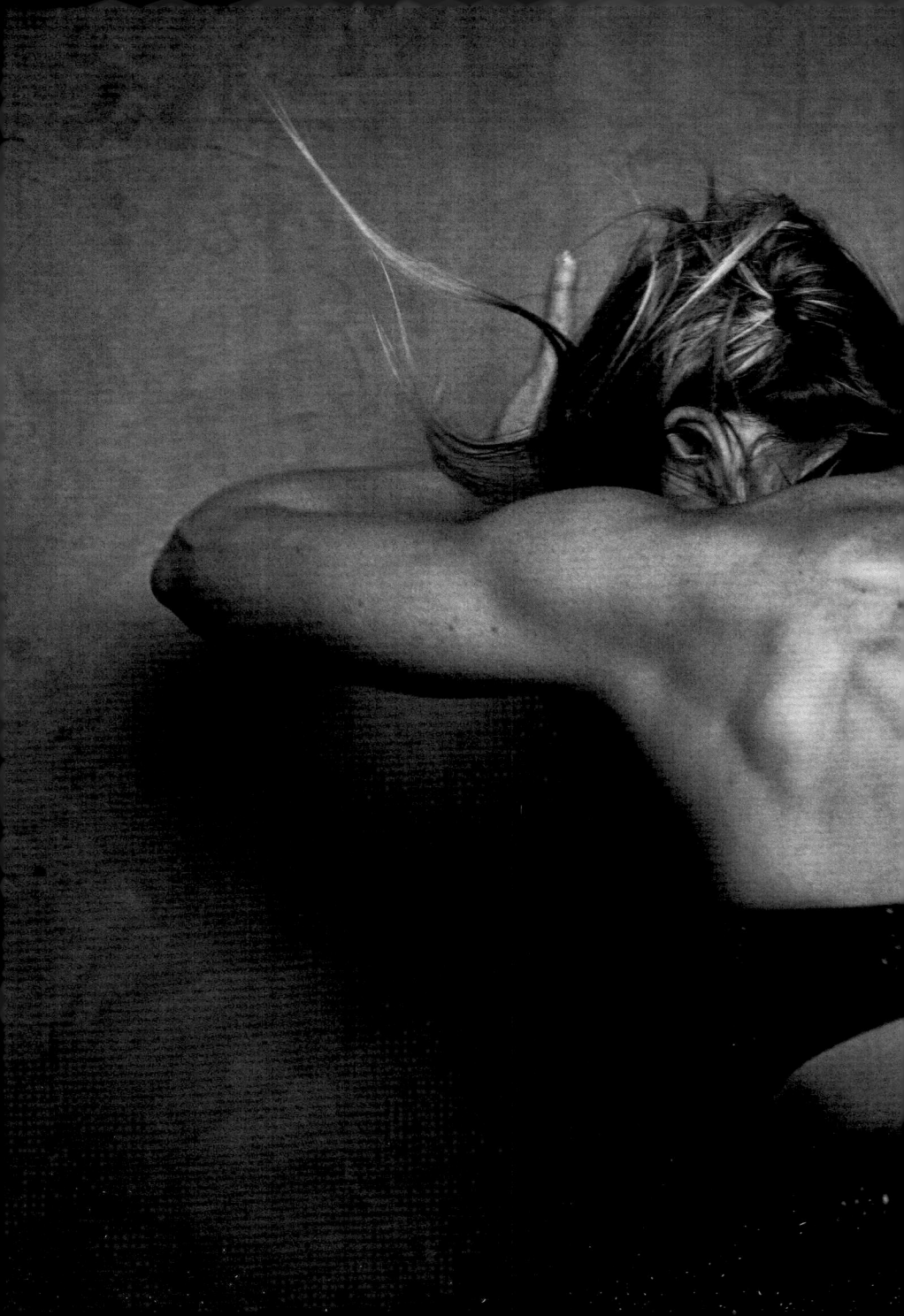

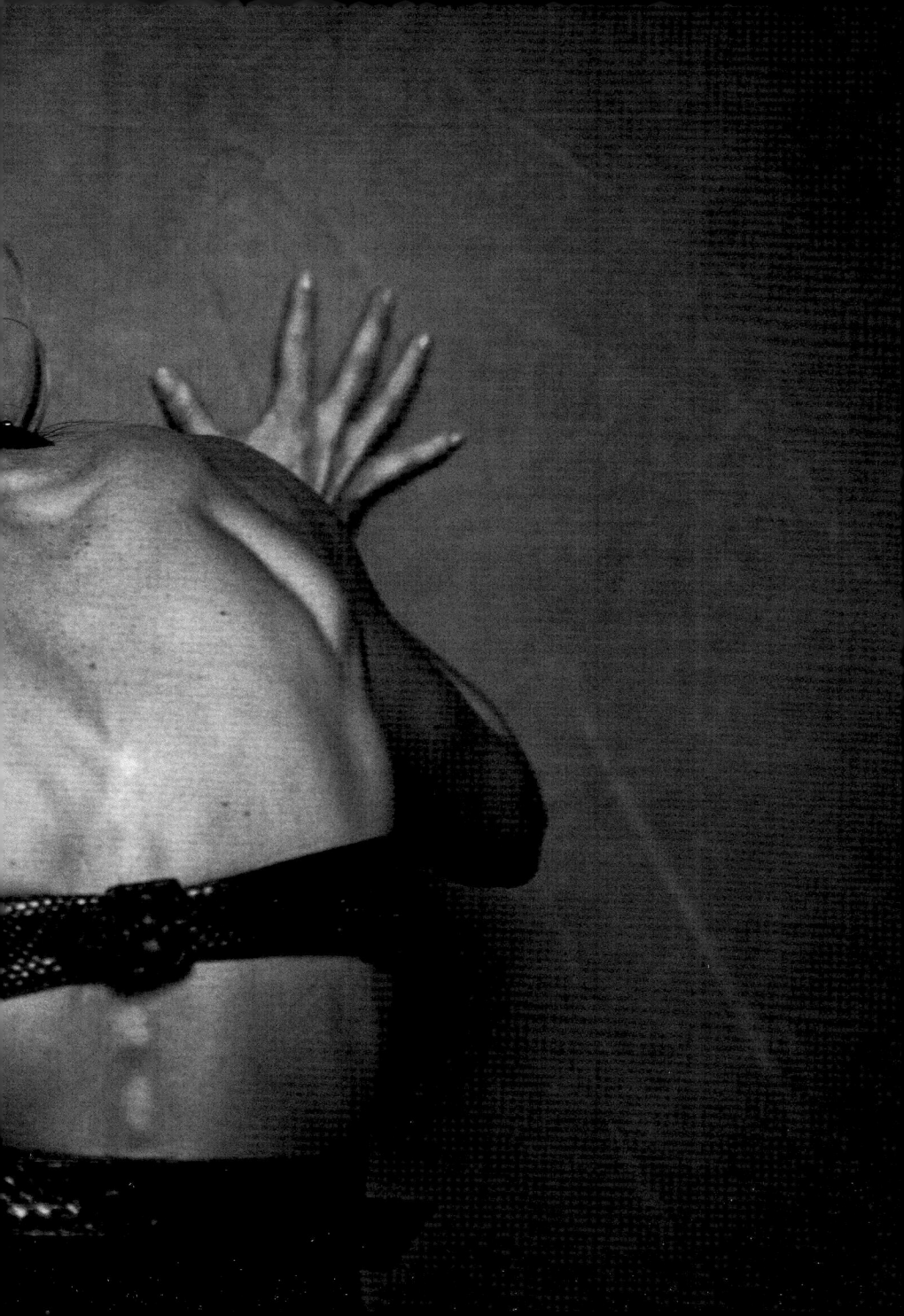

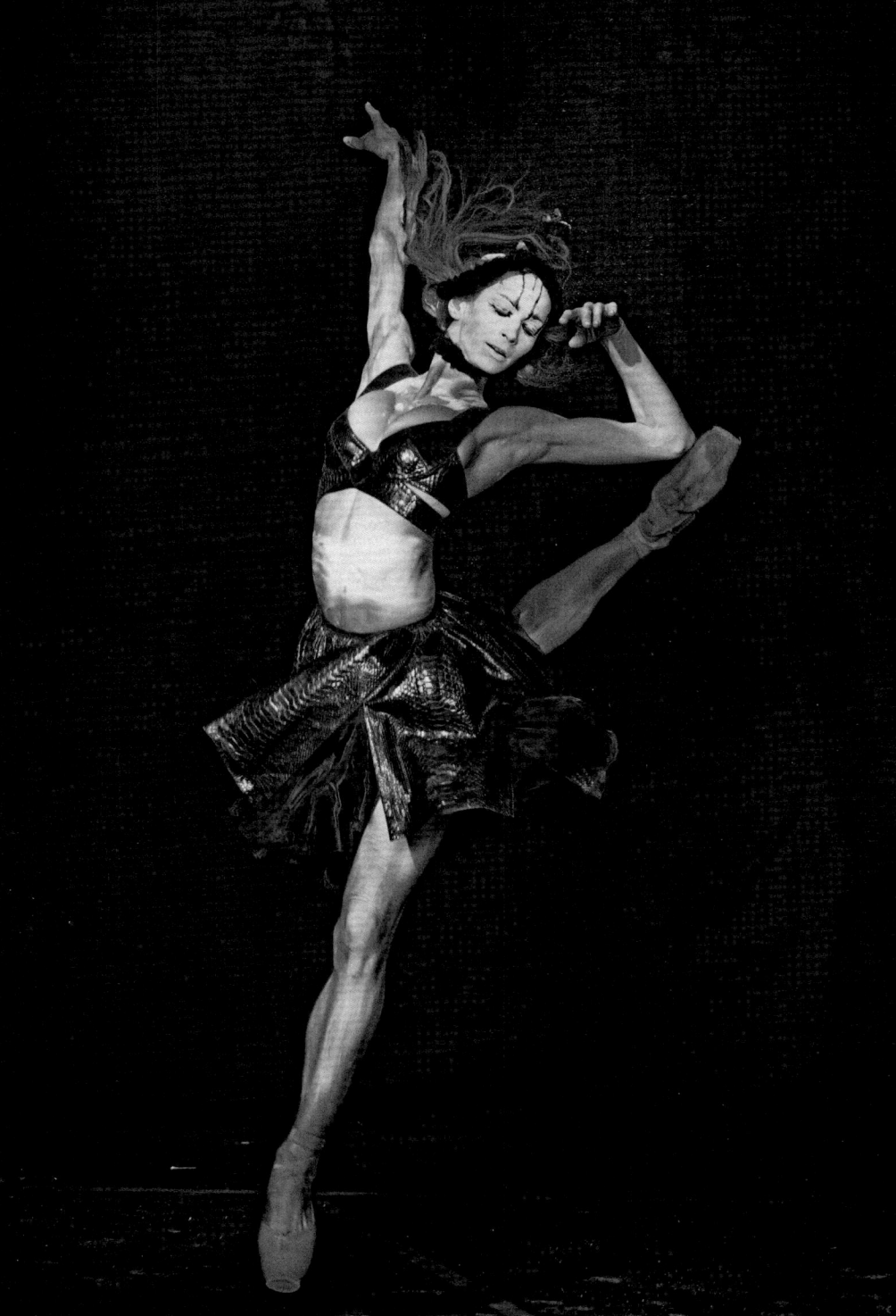

(Previous spread) Helene Fischer, *Paris*, 2018. Bra and skirt, *Haute Couture Summer* 2017
(Opposite) Polina Semionova, *Berlin*, 2010. Bra and skirt, *Summer* 2010

Helene Fischer, *Paris*, 2017. Bra and skirt, *Haute Couture Summer* 2017
(Following spread) Mariacarla Boscono, *Paris*, 2017
Dress and belt, *Haute Couture Summer* 2017

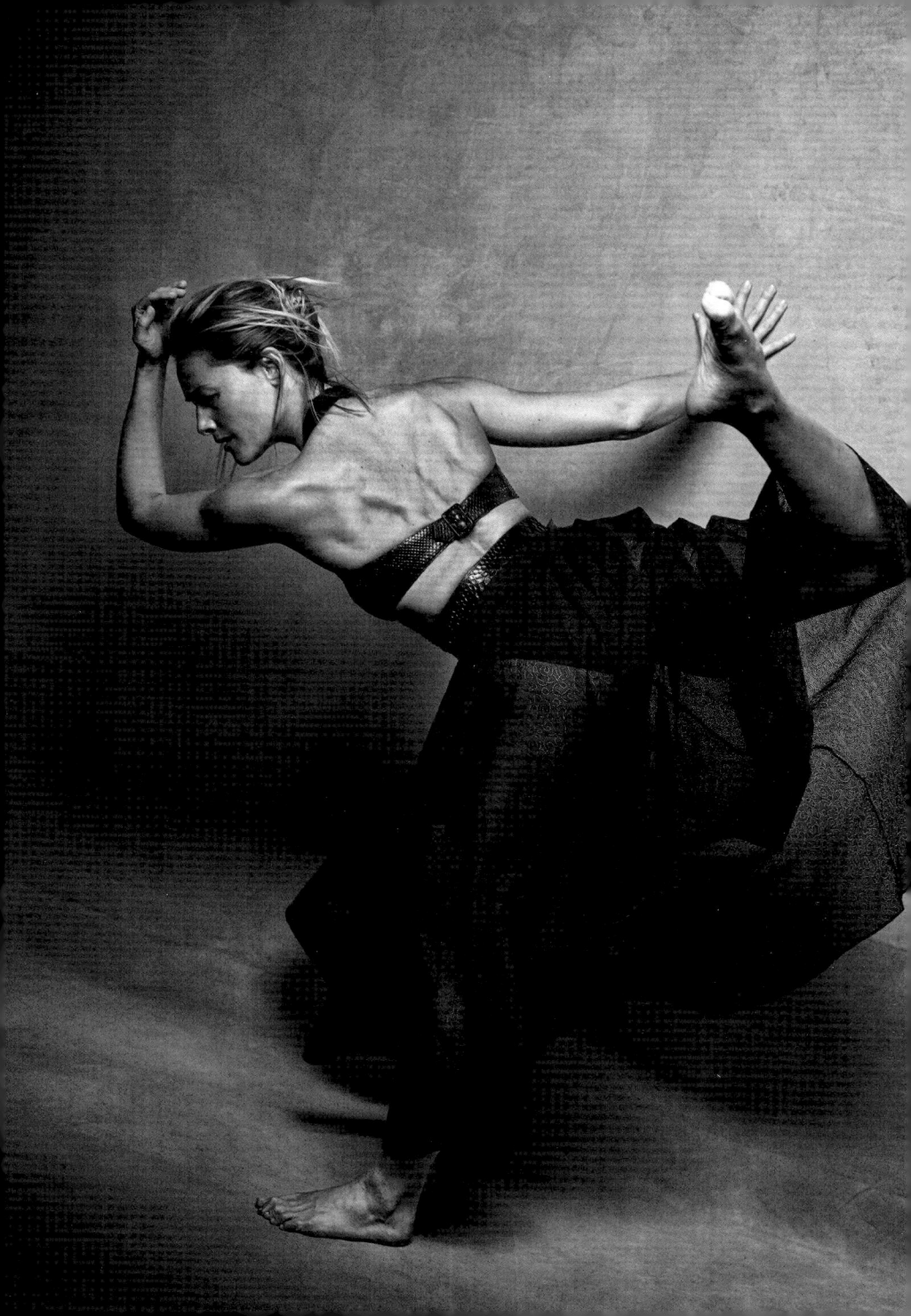

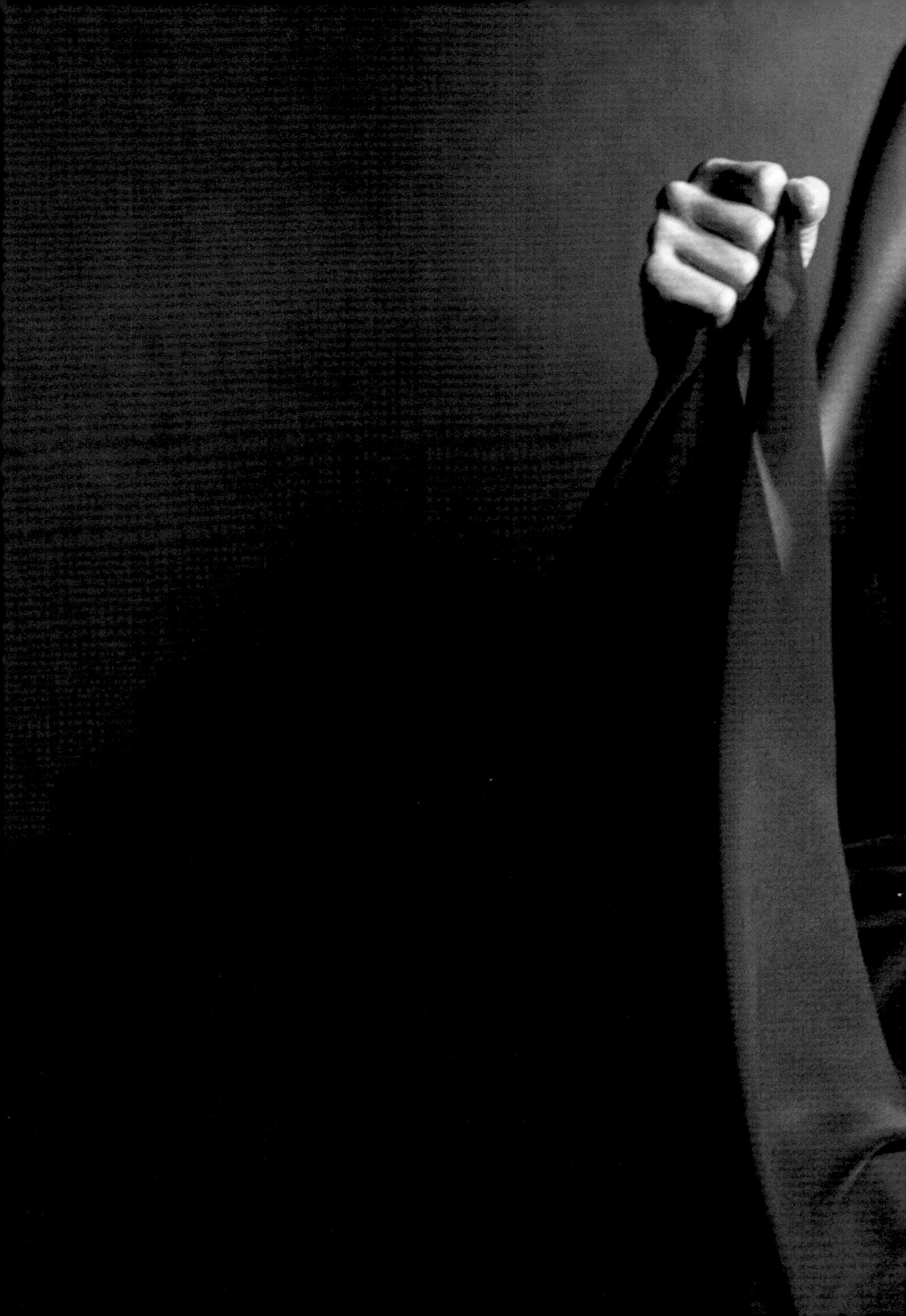

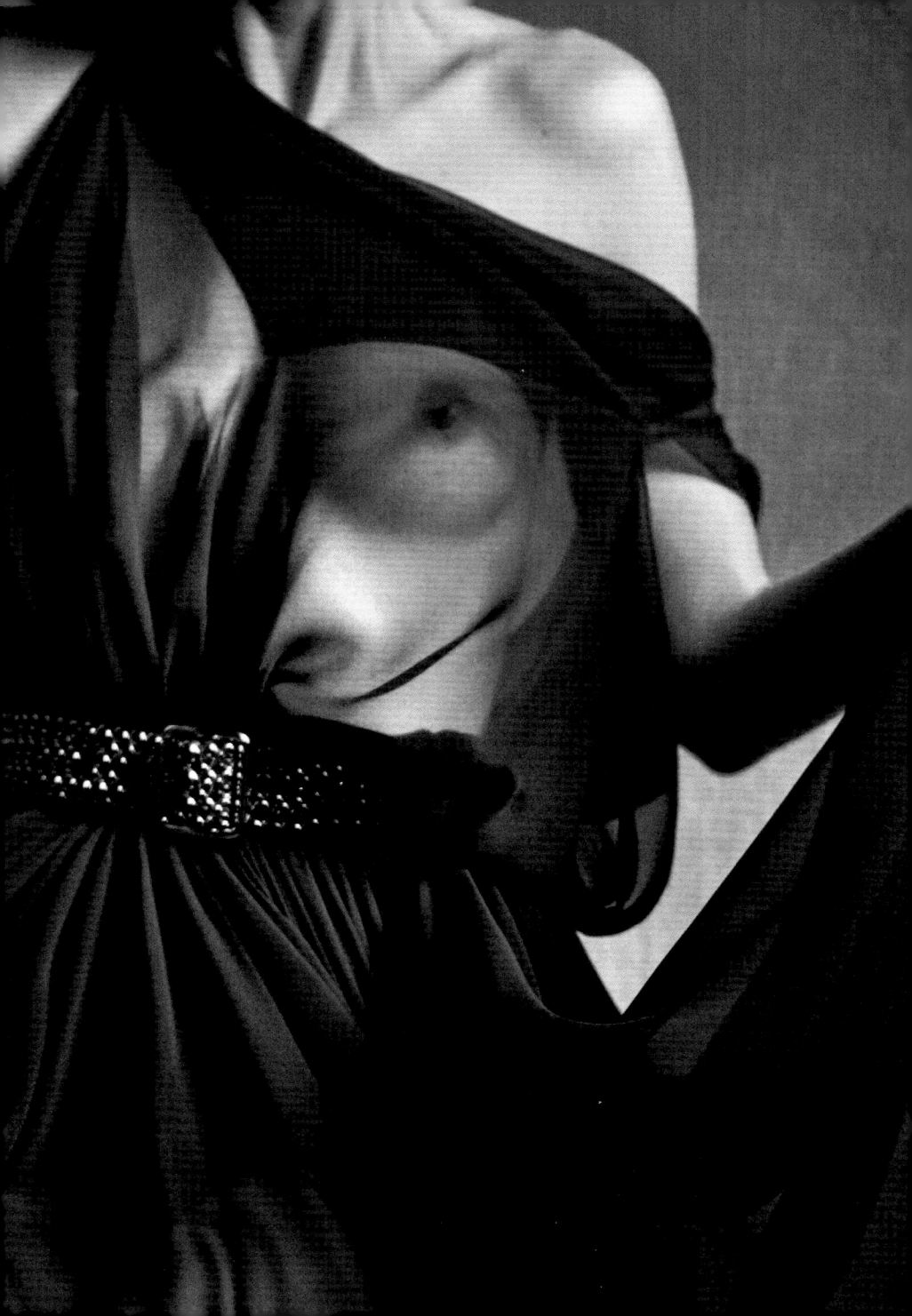

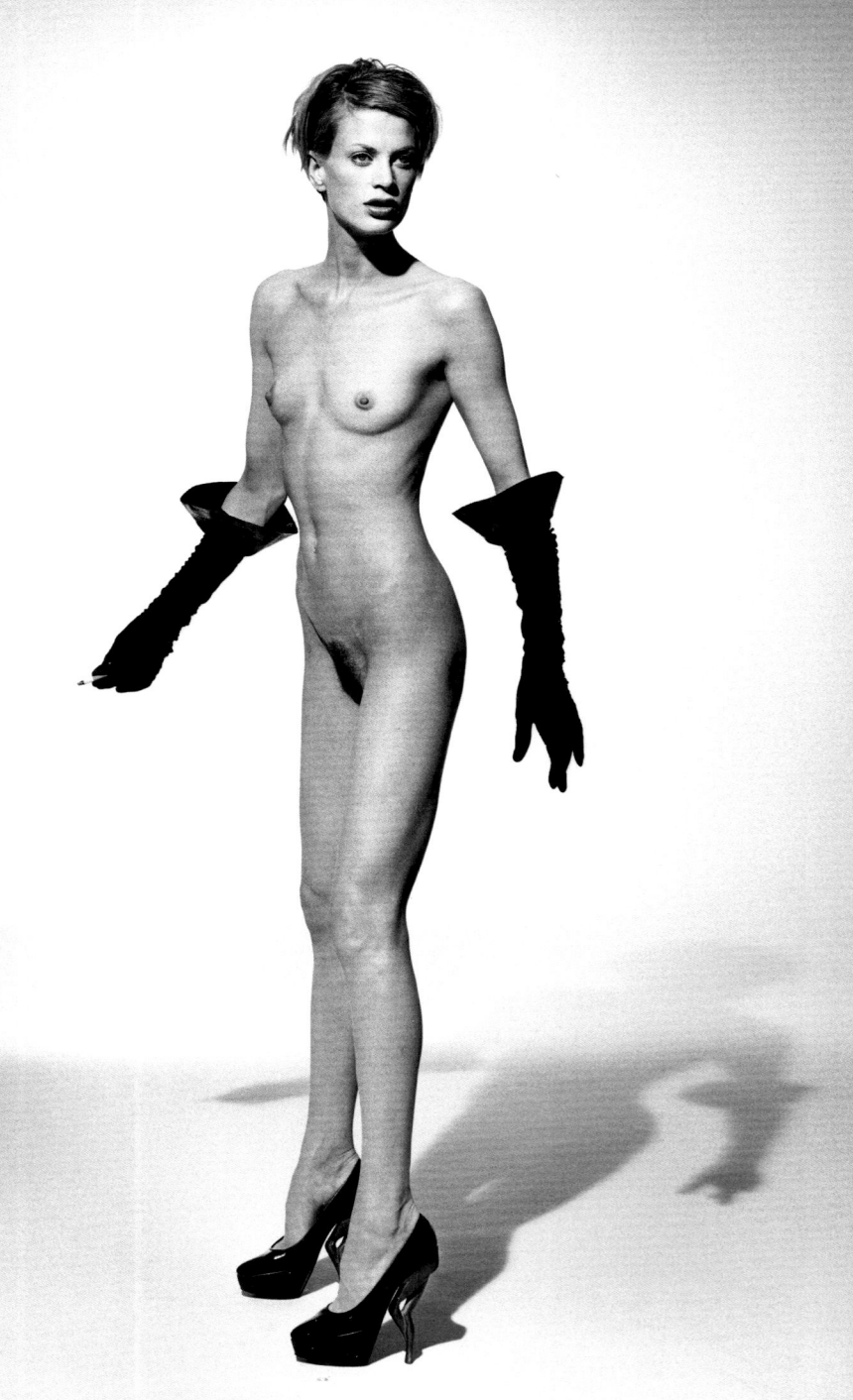

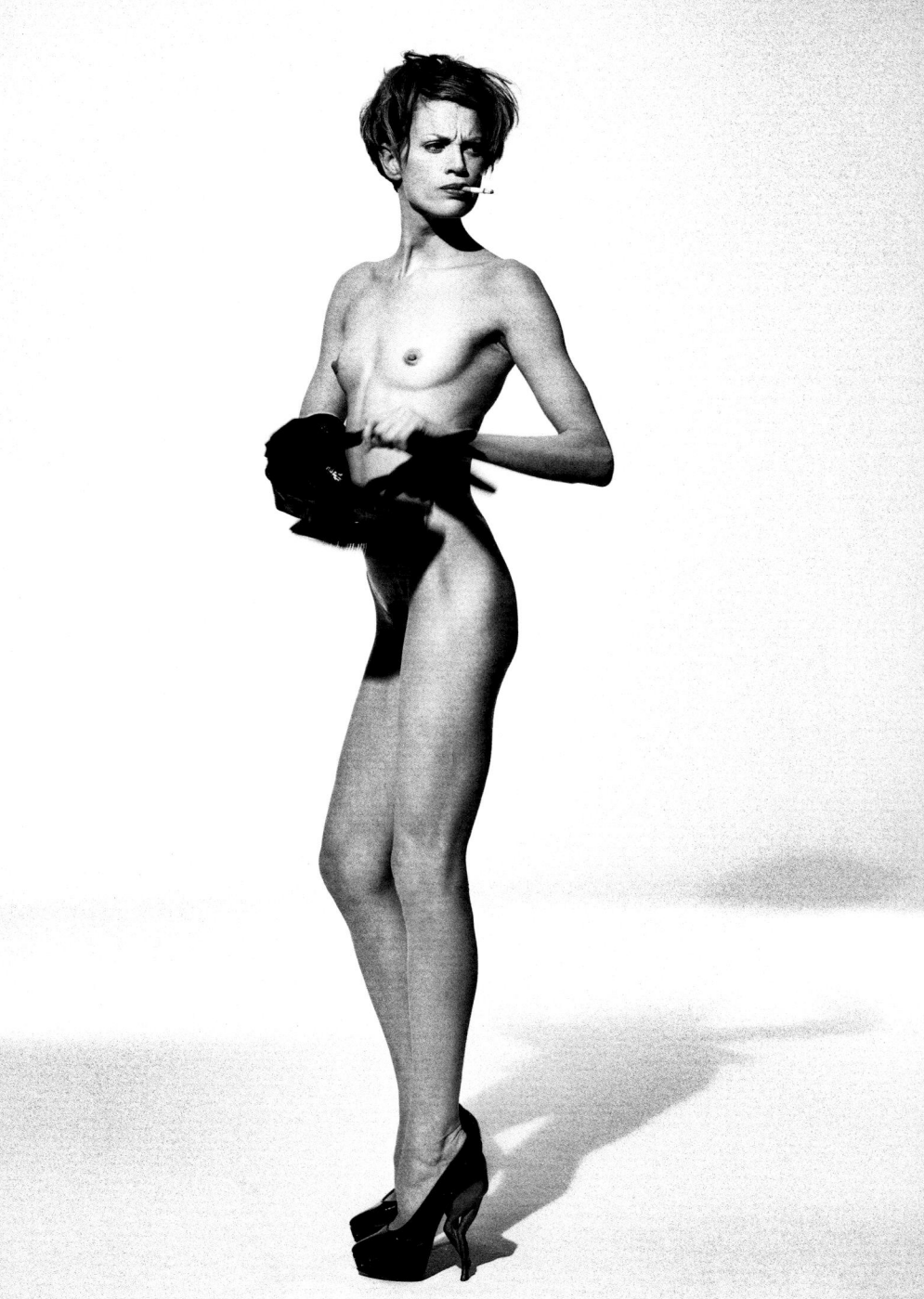

" I do fitting after fitting
until I am satisfied. **"**
Azzedine Alaïa

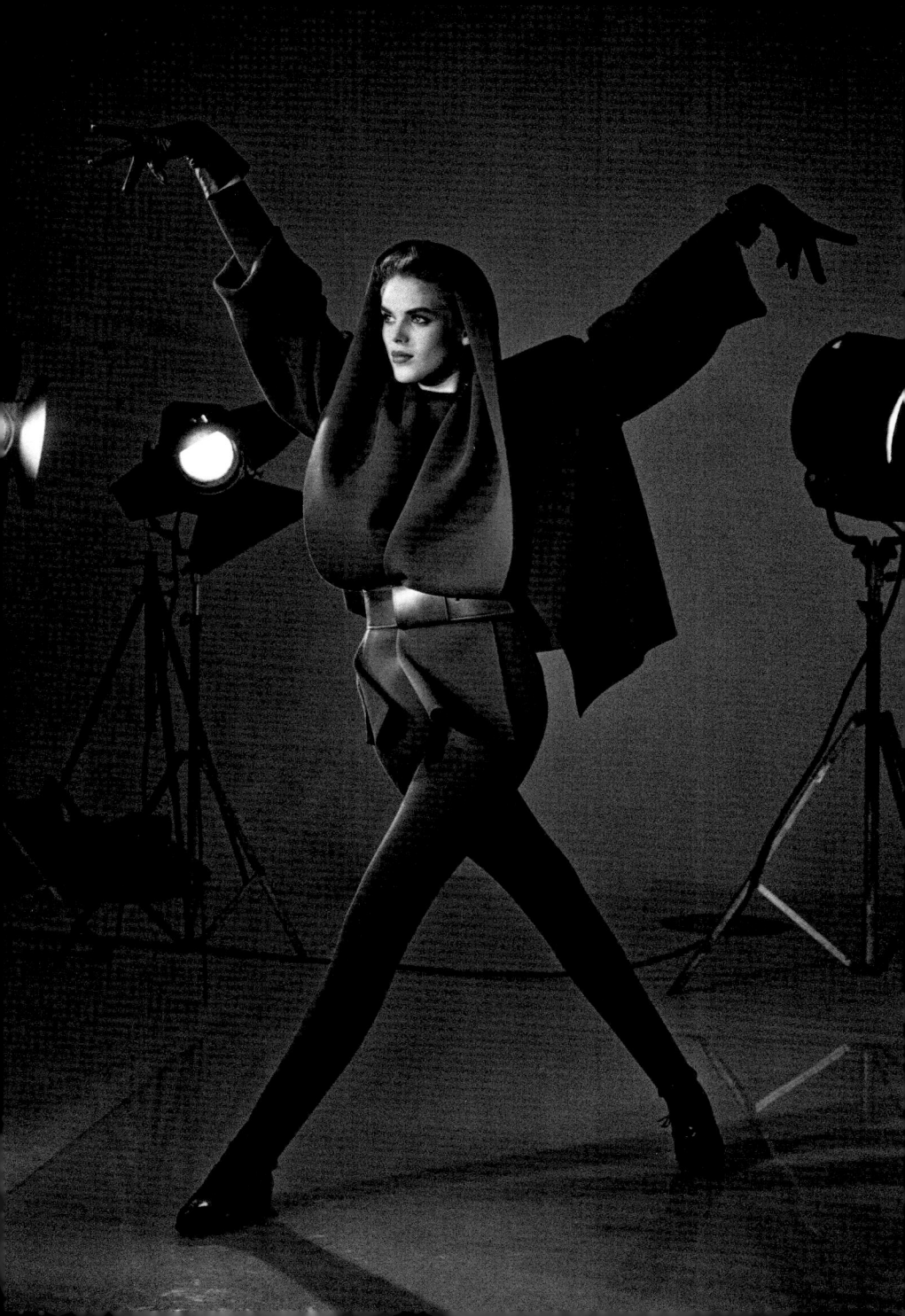

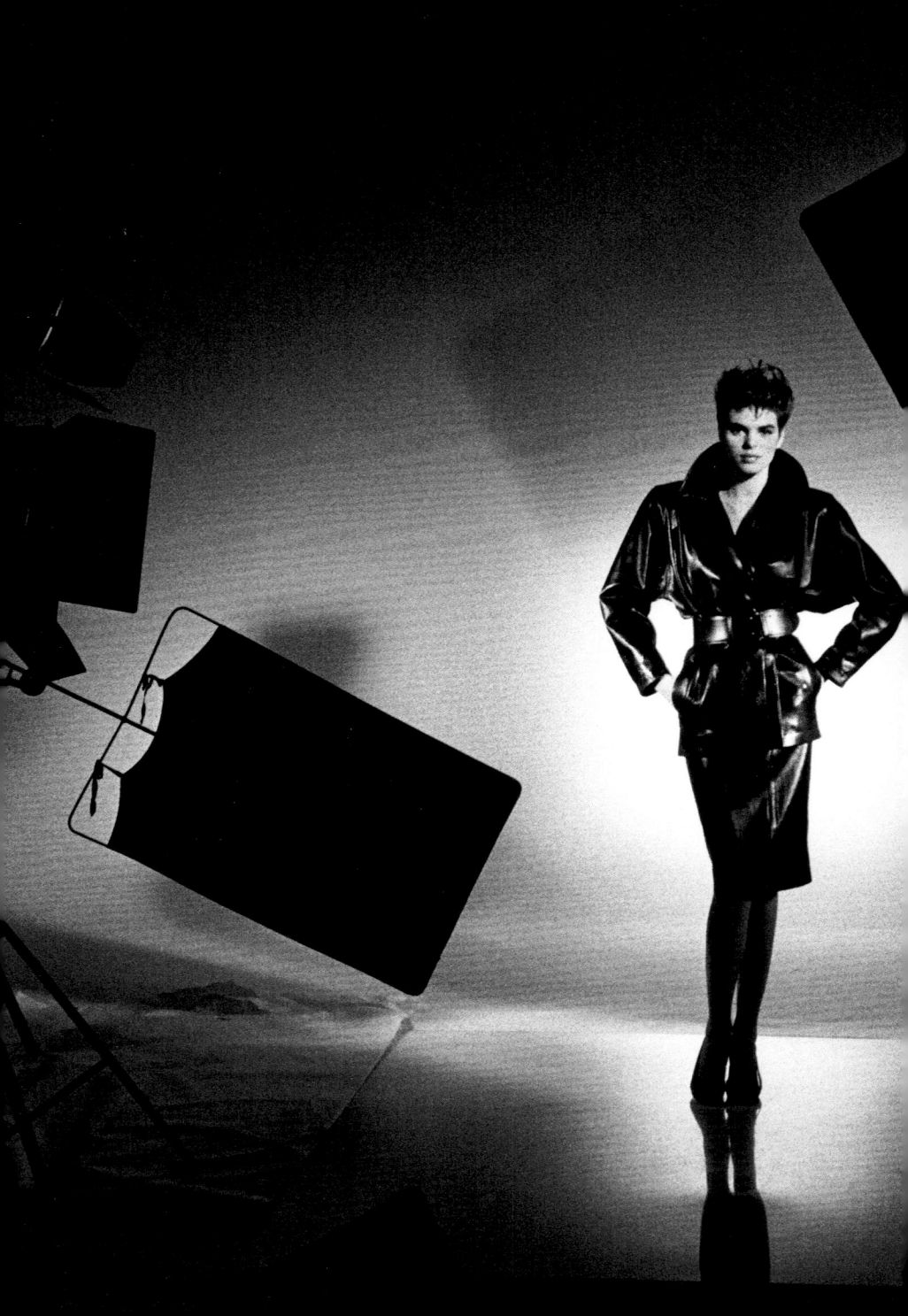

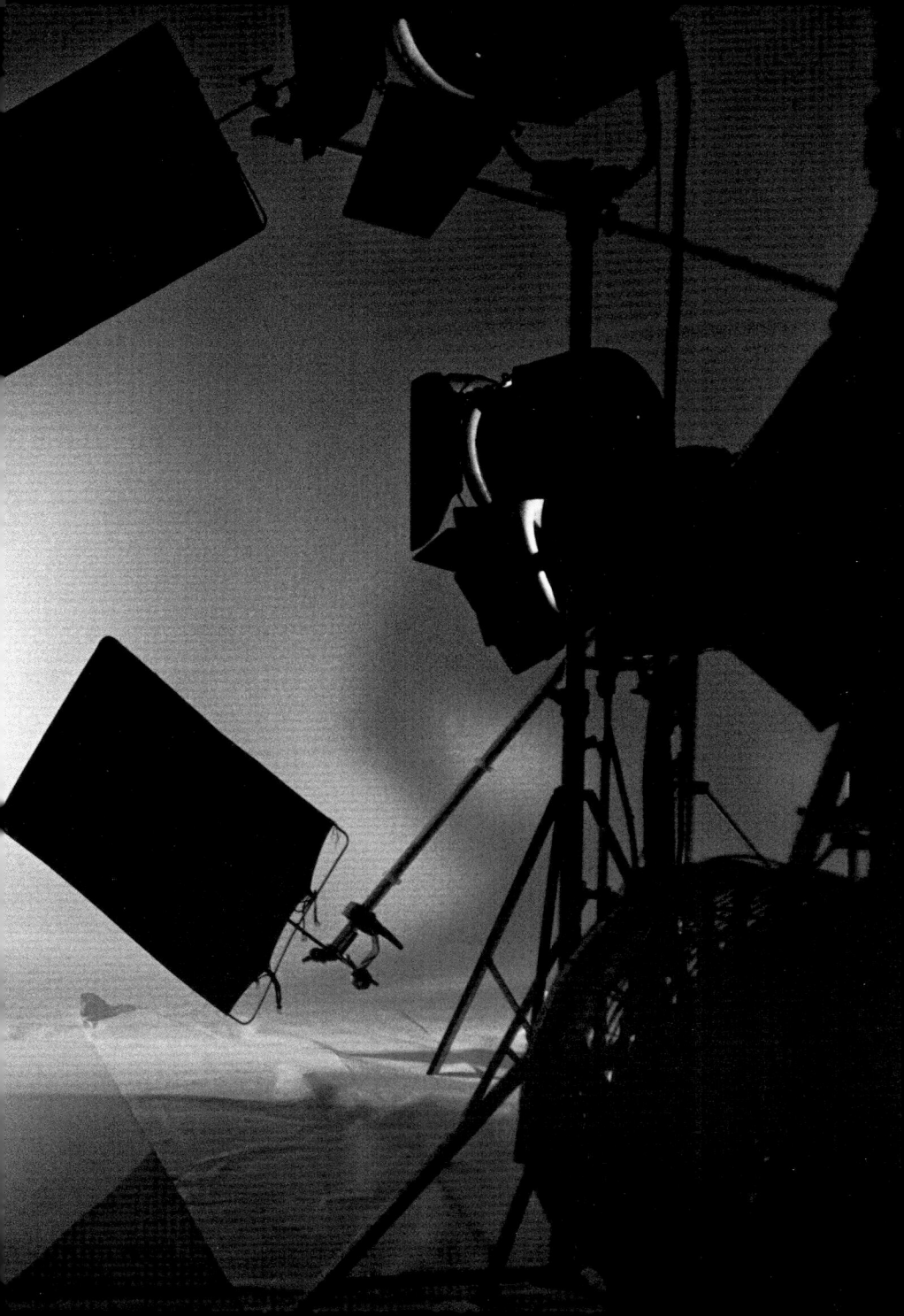

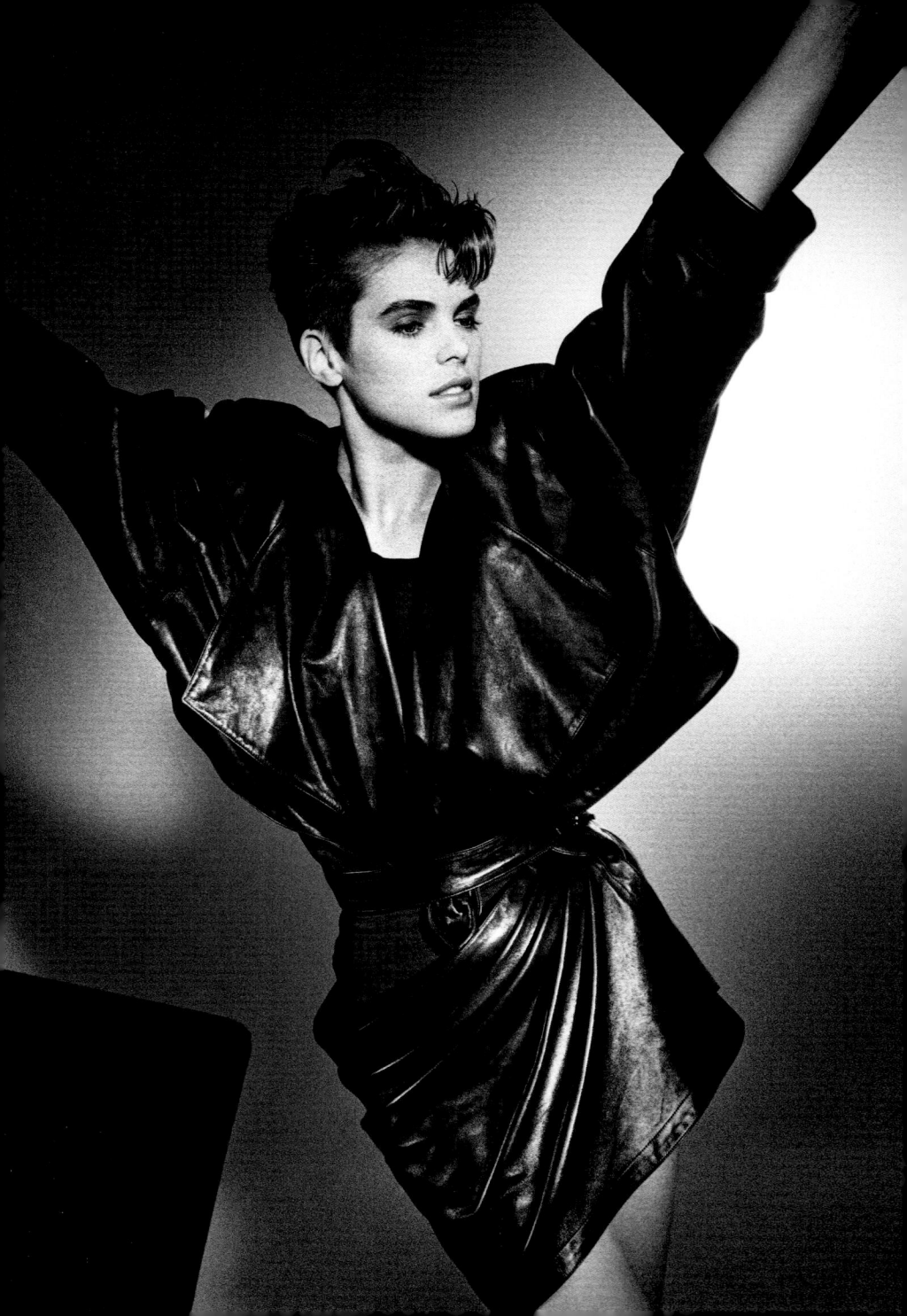

(Previous spread) Maria Johnson, *Paris*, 1984. Jacket and skirt, *Summer* 1984
(Opposite) Maria Johnson, *Paris*, 1984. Jacket and skirt, *Summer* 1984

" I only think about women when I create. And I owe it all to the women, all my success. **"**
Azzedine Alaïa

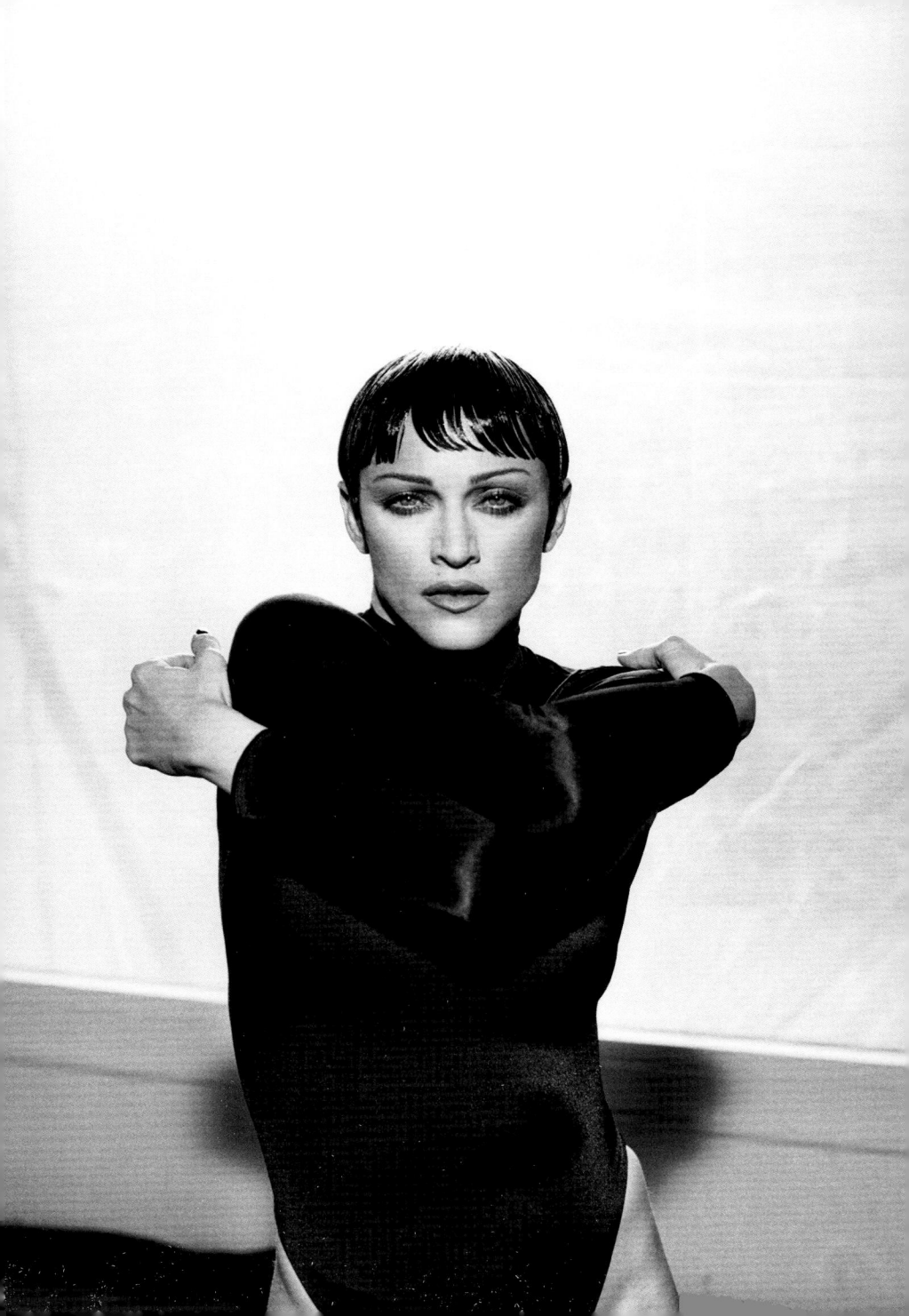

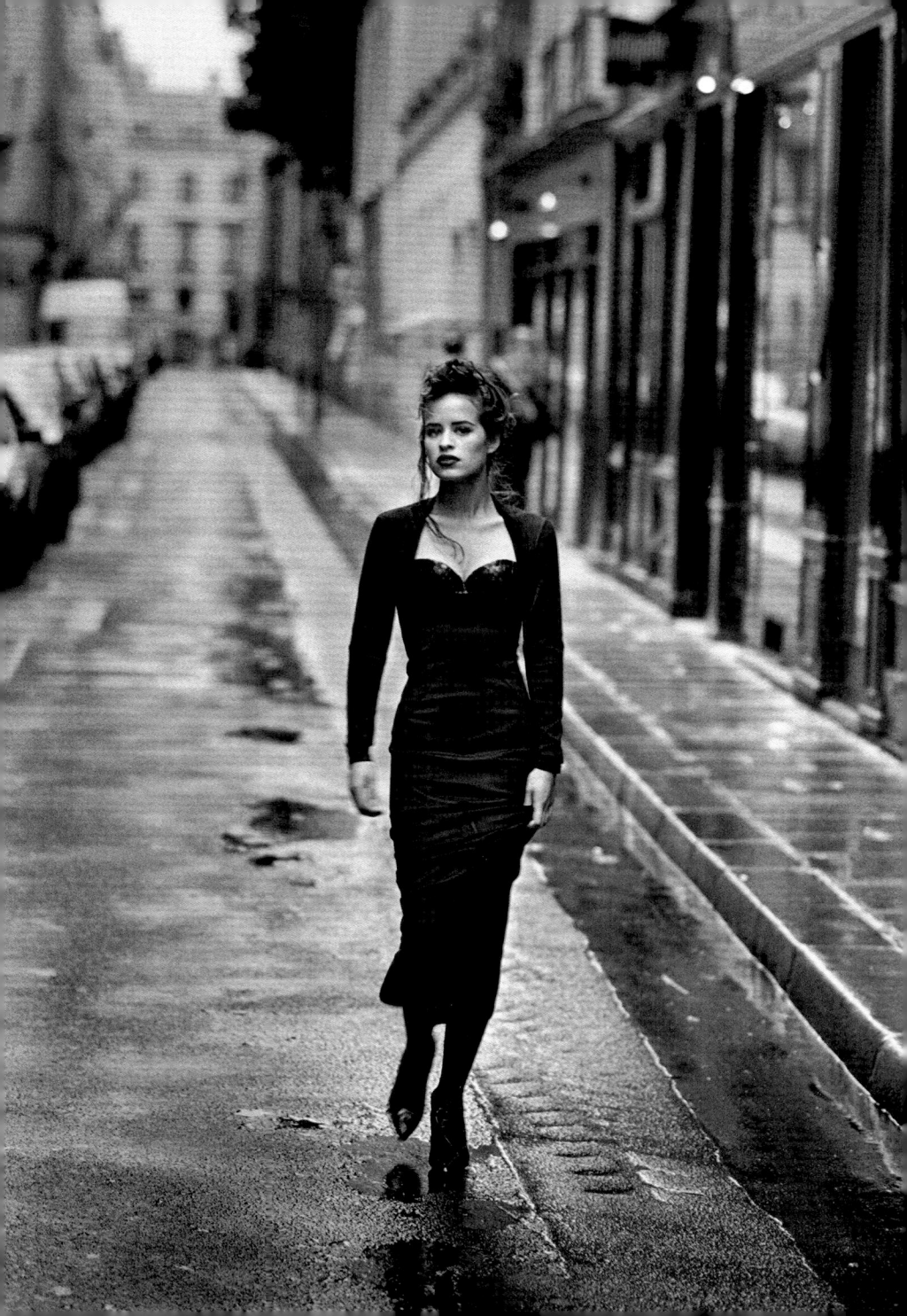

" I rid myself of color.
I only want black. Black is
the most important color for me.
It is what I start with when
I create a model: it makes
the silhouette appear better. **"**
Azzedine Alaïa

Yasmin Le Bon, *Paris*, 1985. Knitted jacket and pants, *Winter* 1985
(Following spread) Yasmin Le Bon, *Paris*, 1985. Jacket and leggings, *Winter* 1985
Veronica Webb, *Paris*, 1986. Dress, *Winter* 1986

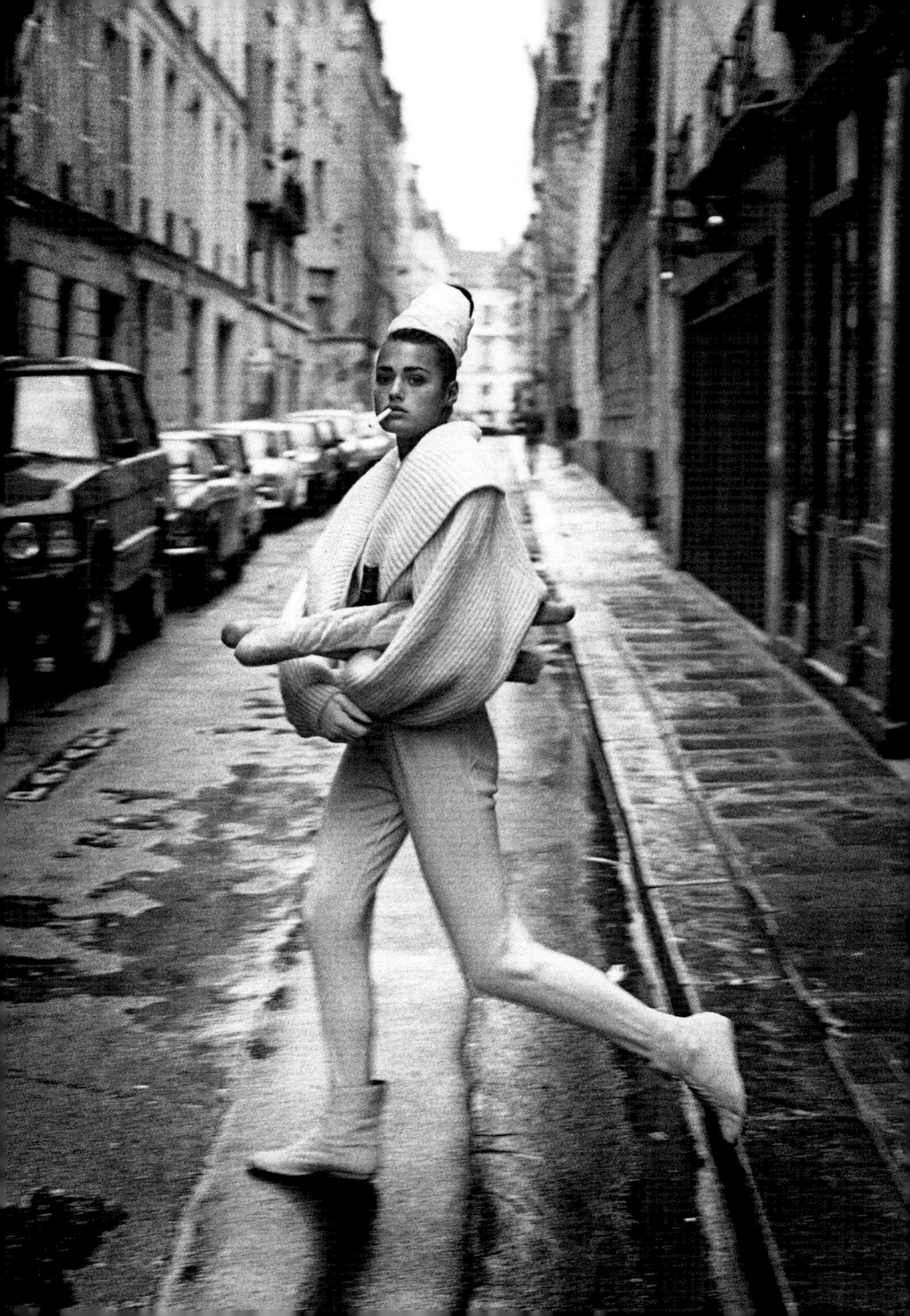

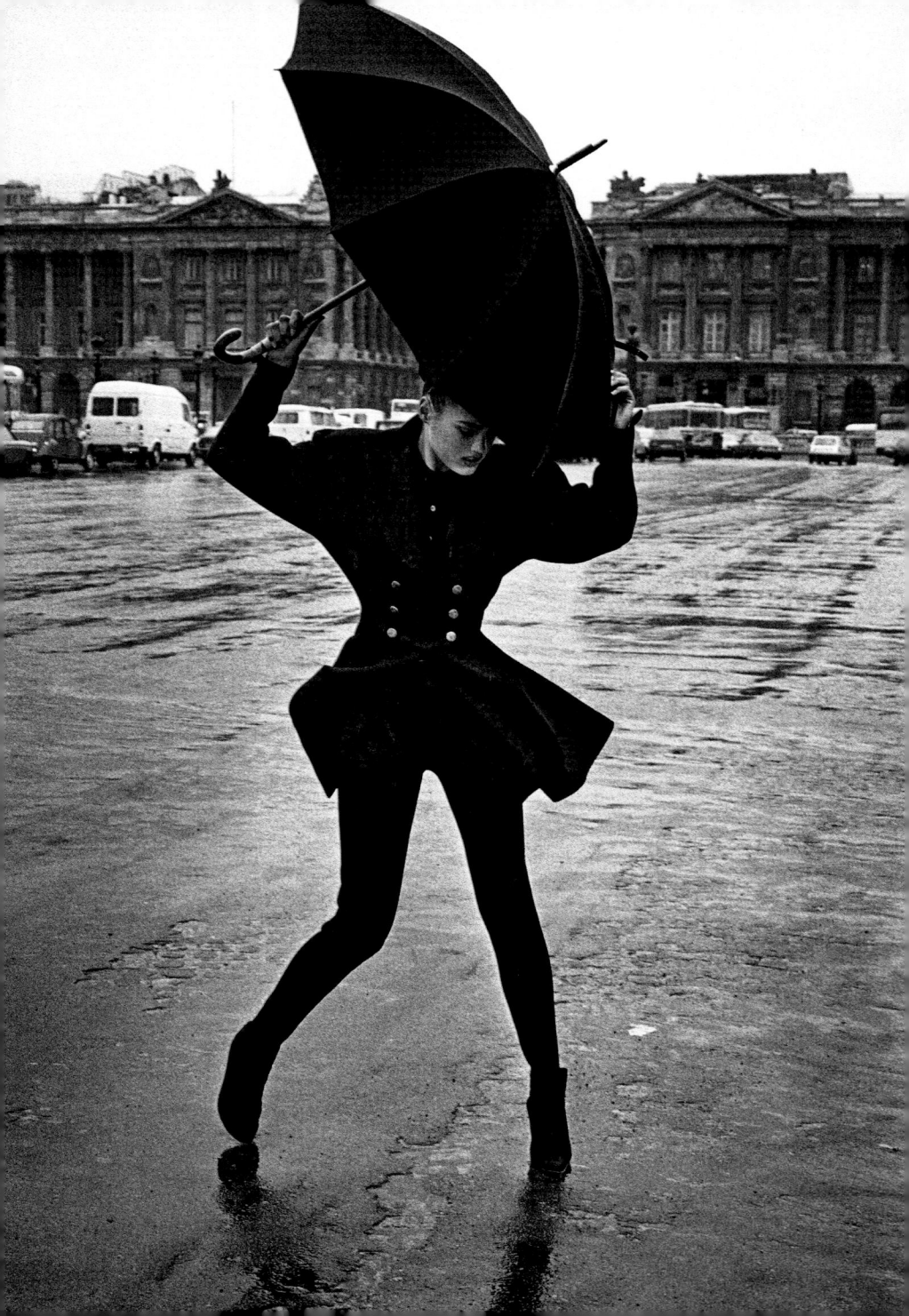

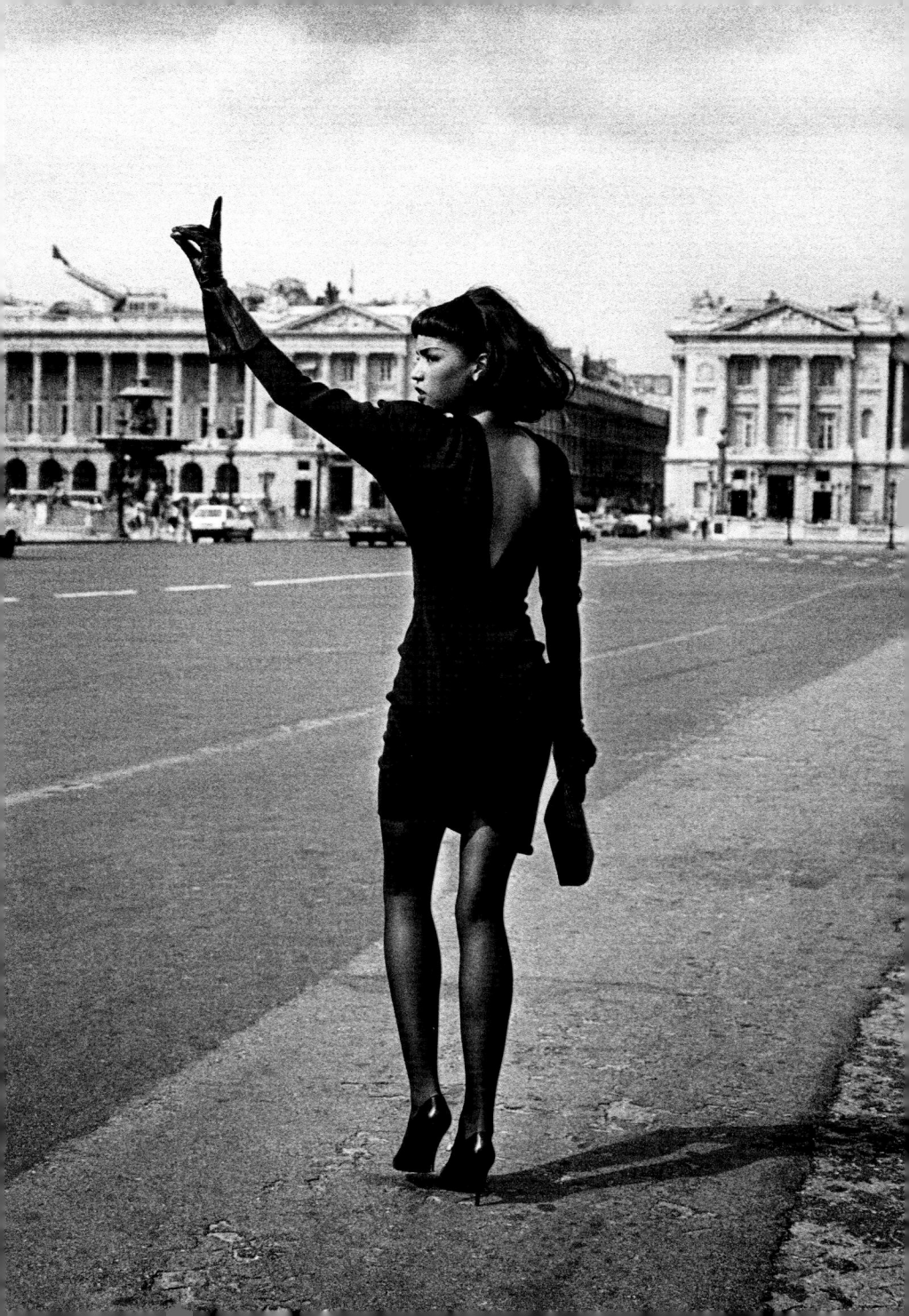

" When she did her first series for Vogue in 1988, I was stunned by her incredible beauty. But she was much more than just a sublime black girl. Out there on the beach in Deauville she had an incredible, tangible presence rarely seen in other models. **"**

Peter Lindbergh

Naomi Campbell, *Deauville*, 1988. Suit, *Winter* 1988

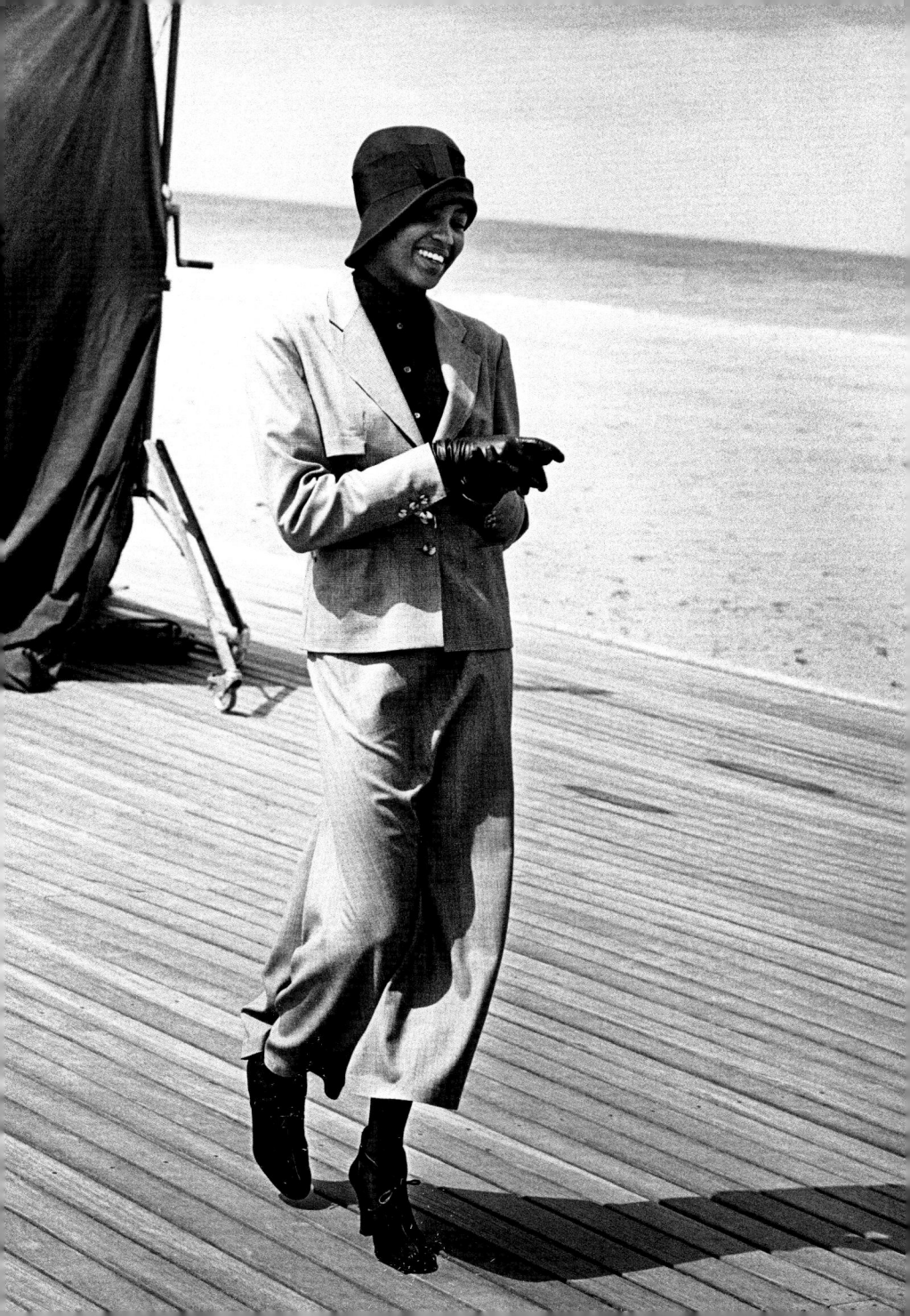

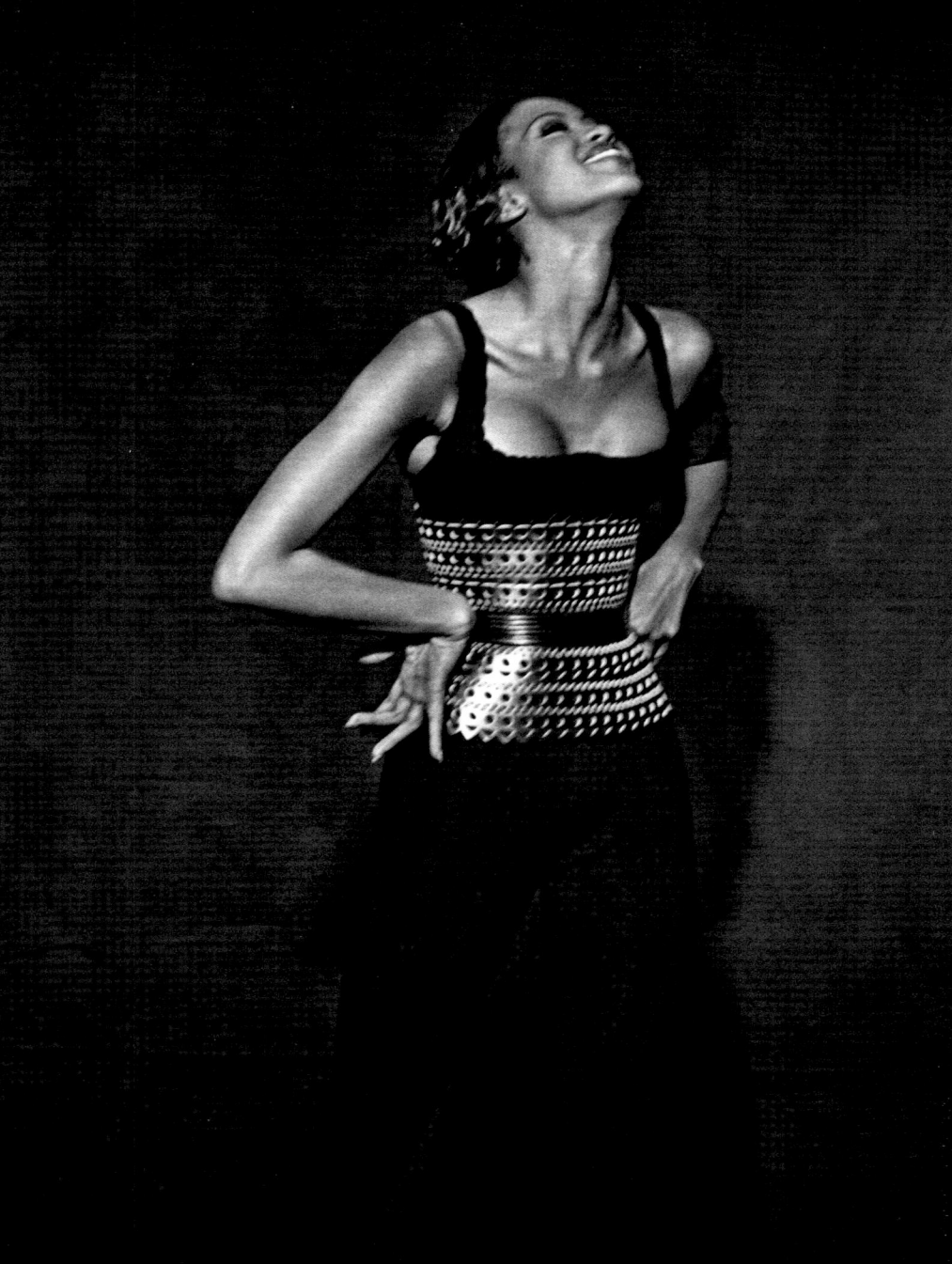

“ I saw her metamorphose,
become the huge personality
that she still is today,
still on top of the world.”
Peter Lindbergh

Naomi Campbell, *Paris*, 1992. Body, leggings, and belt, *Summer* 1992
(Following spread) Naomi Campbell, *Paris*, 1992. Top and panties, *Summer* 1992

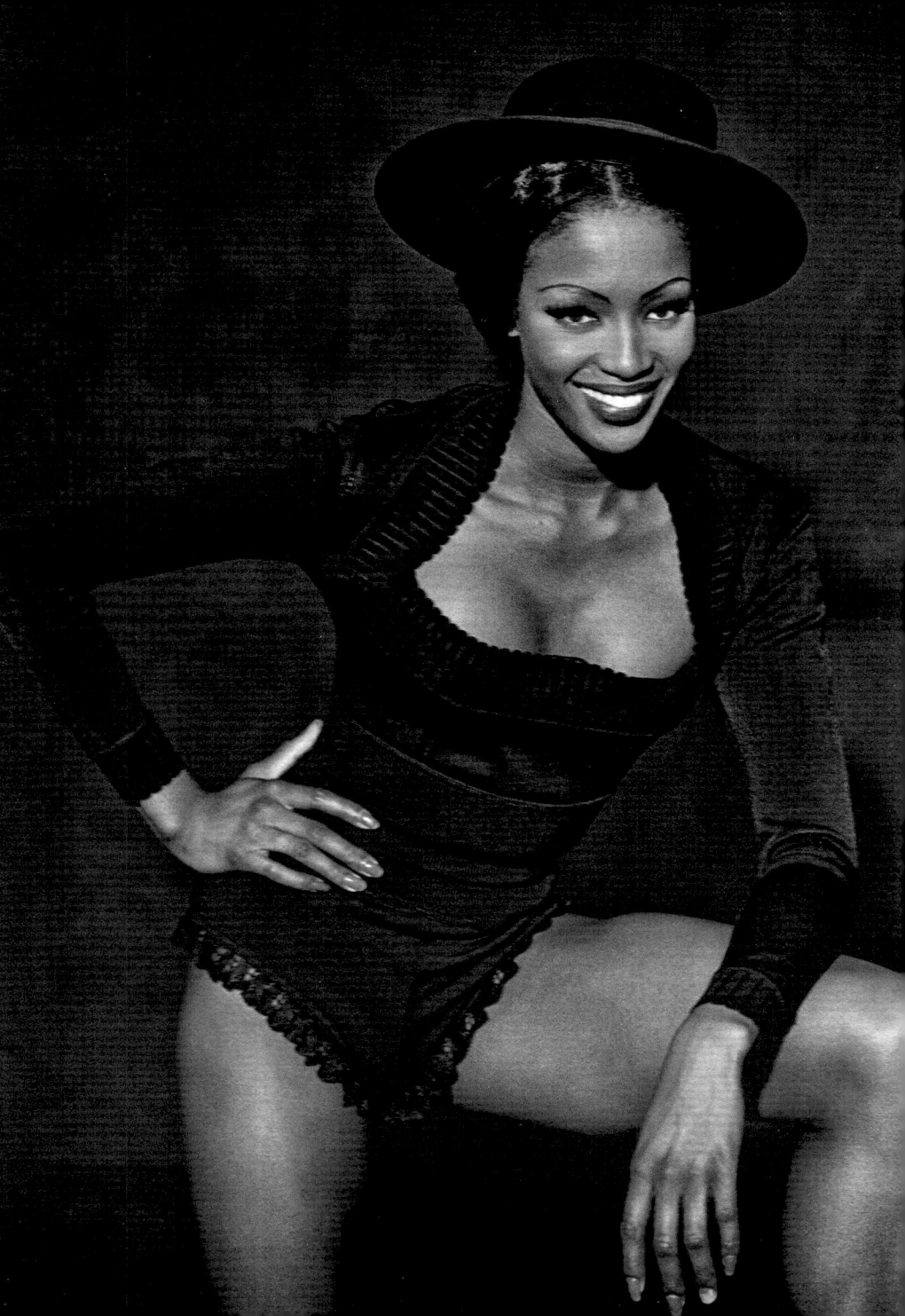

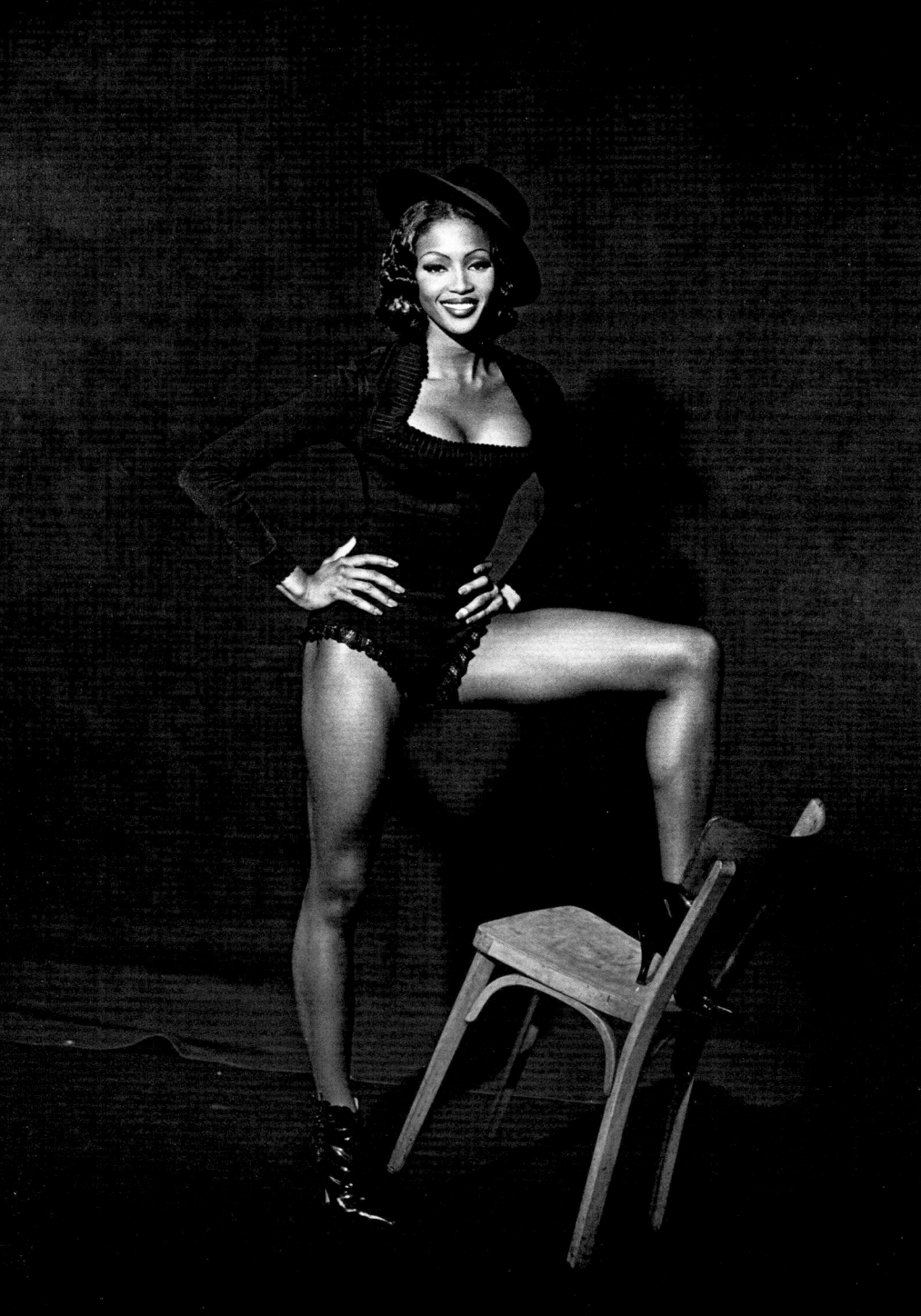

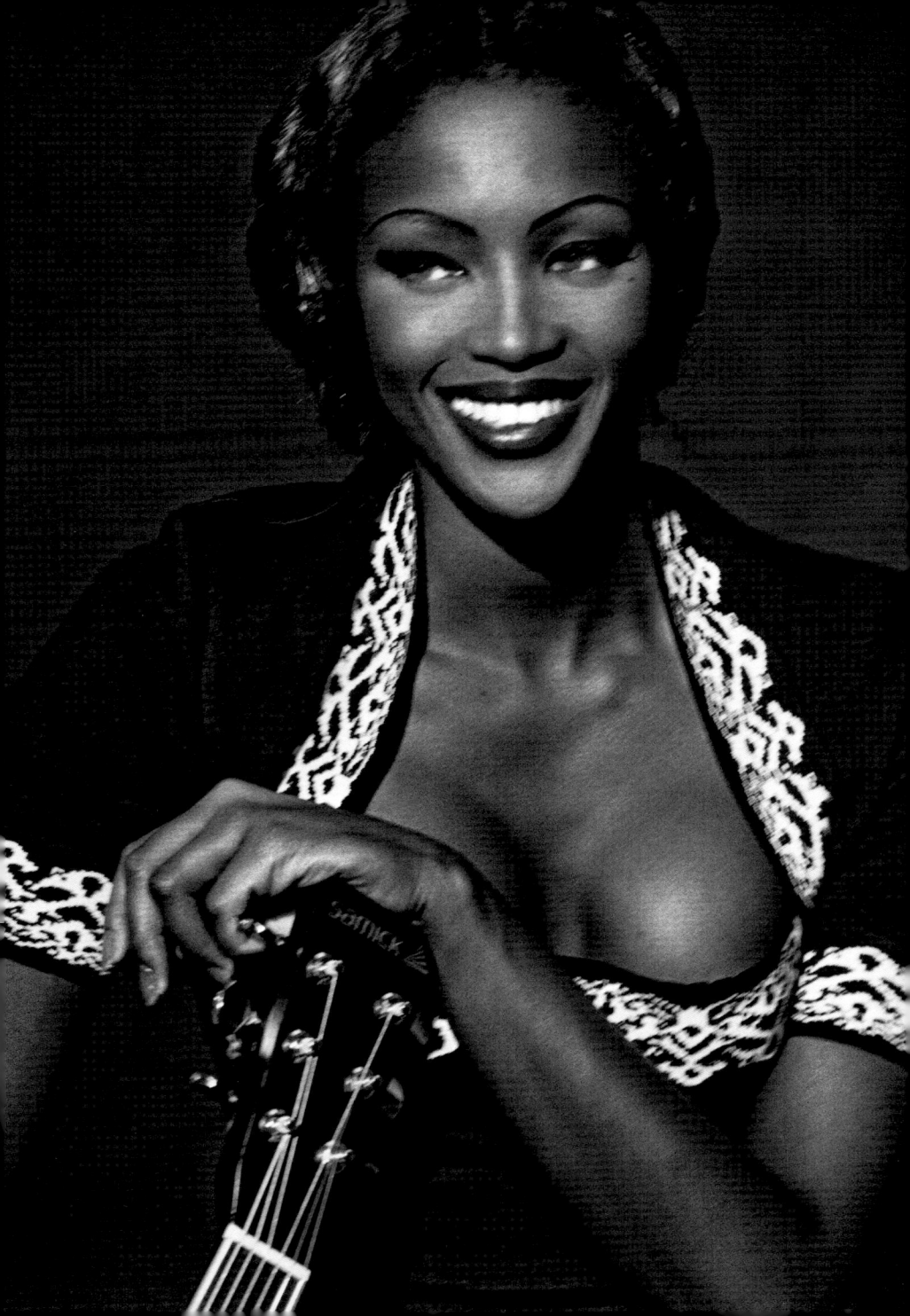

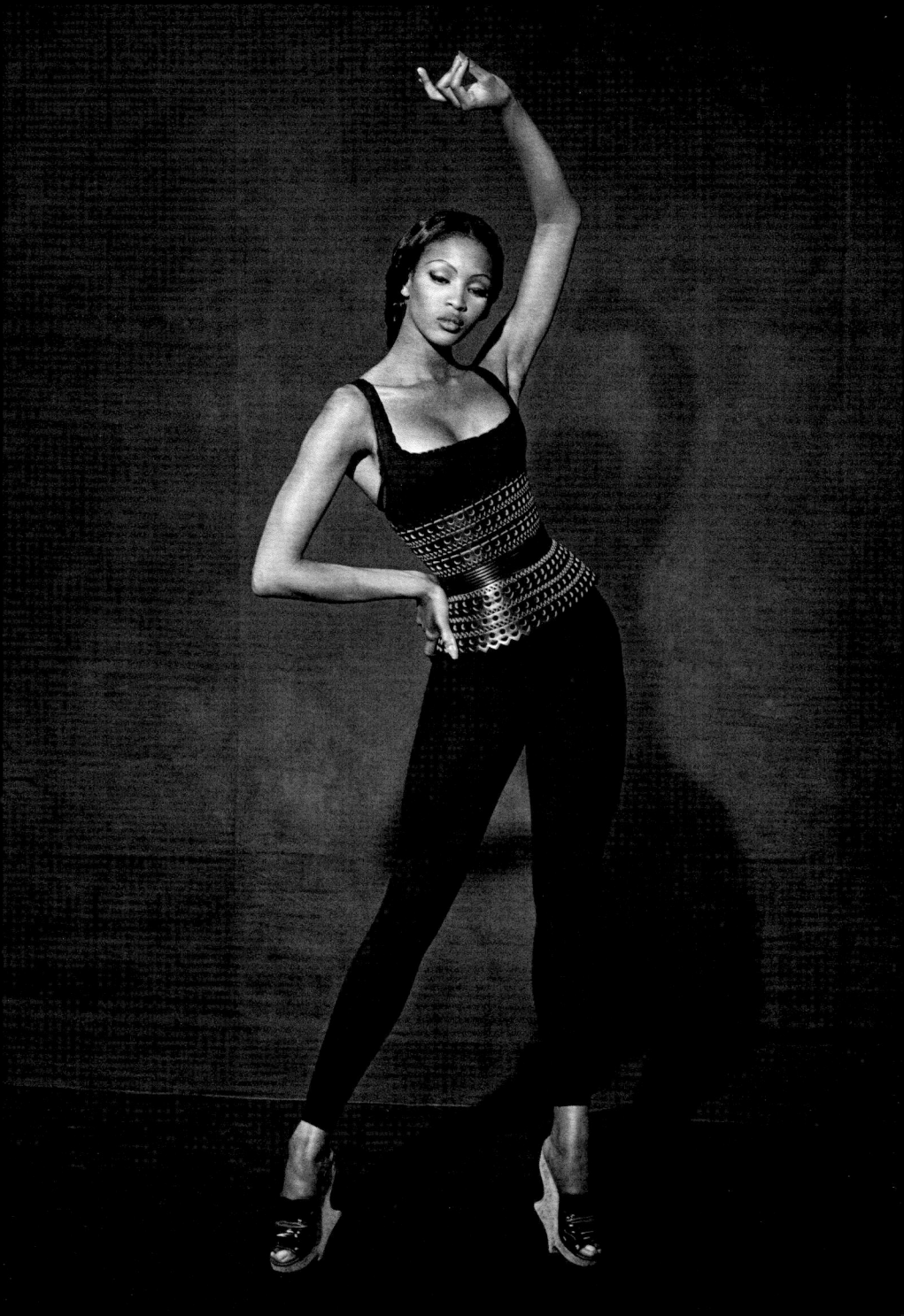

“She is touching because she is true. Capricious because she needs affection. Exhaustingly energetic. A small and divinely muscular boxer, an African statue: a beauty.”

Azzedine Alaïa

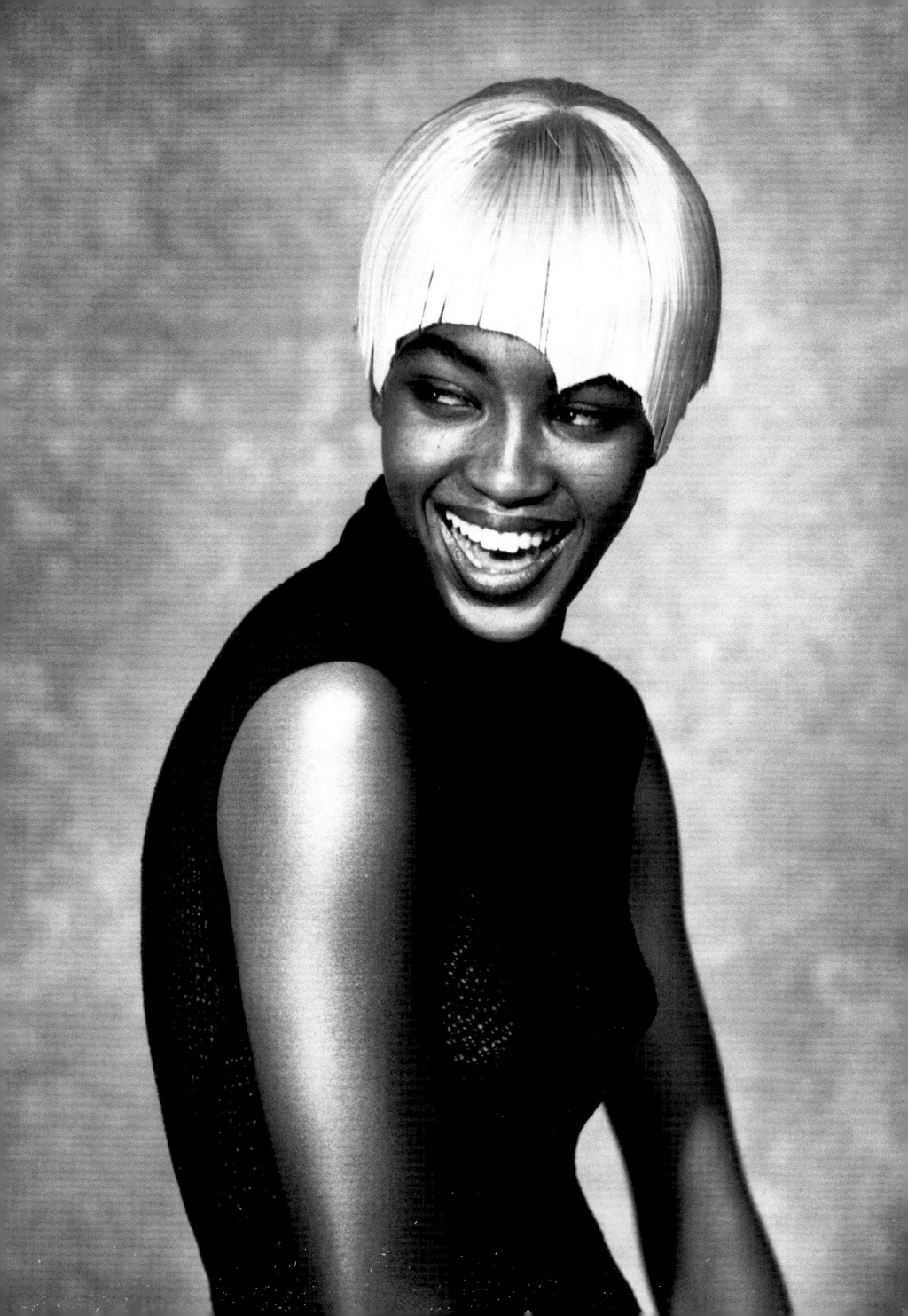

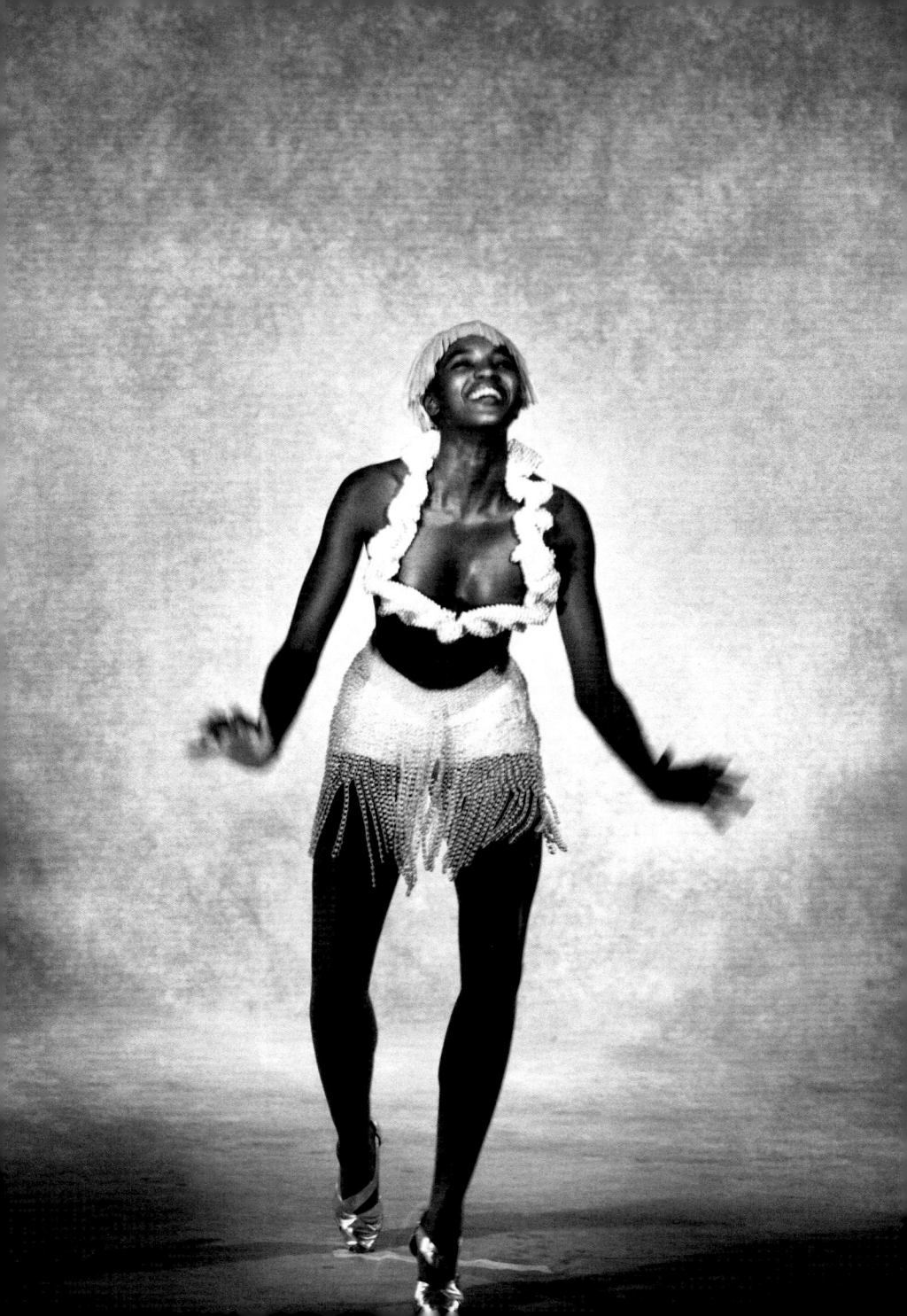

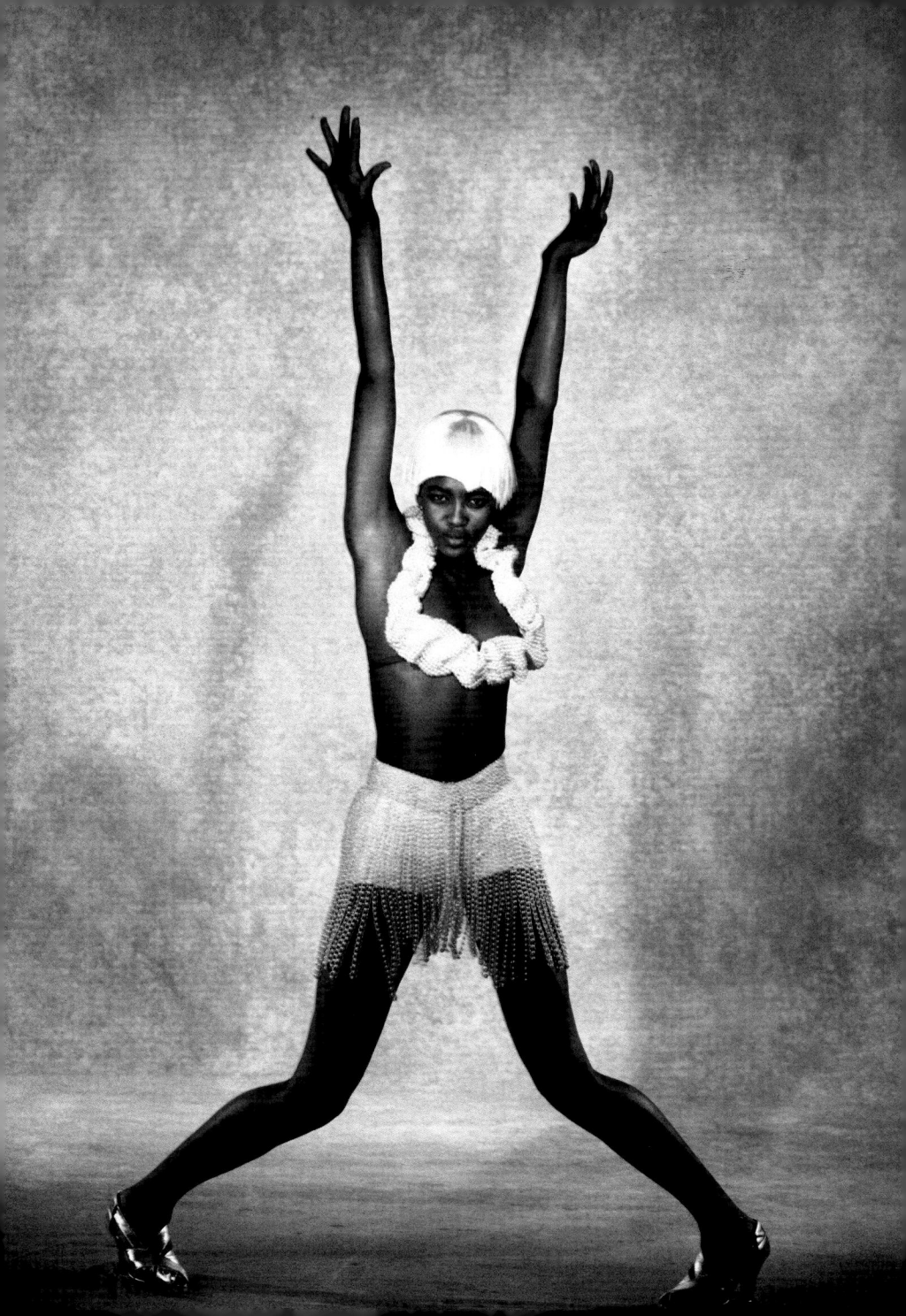

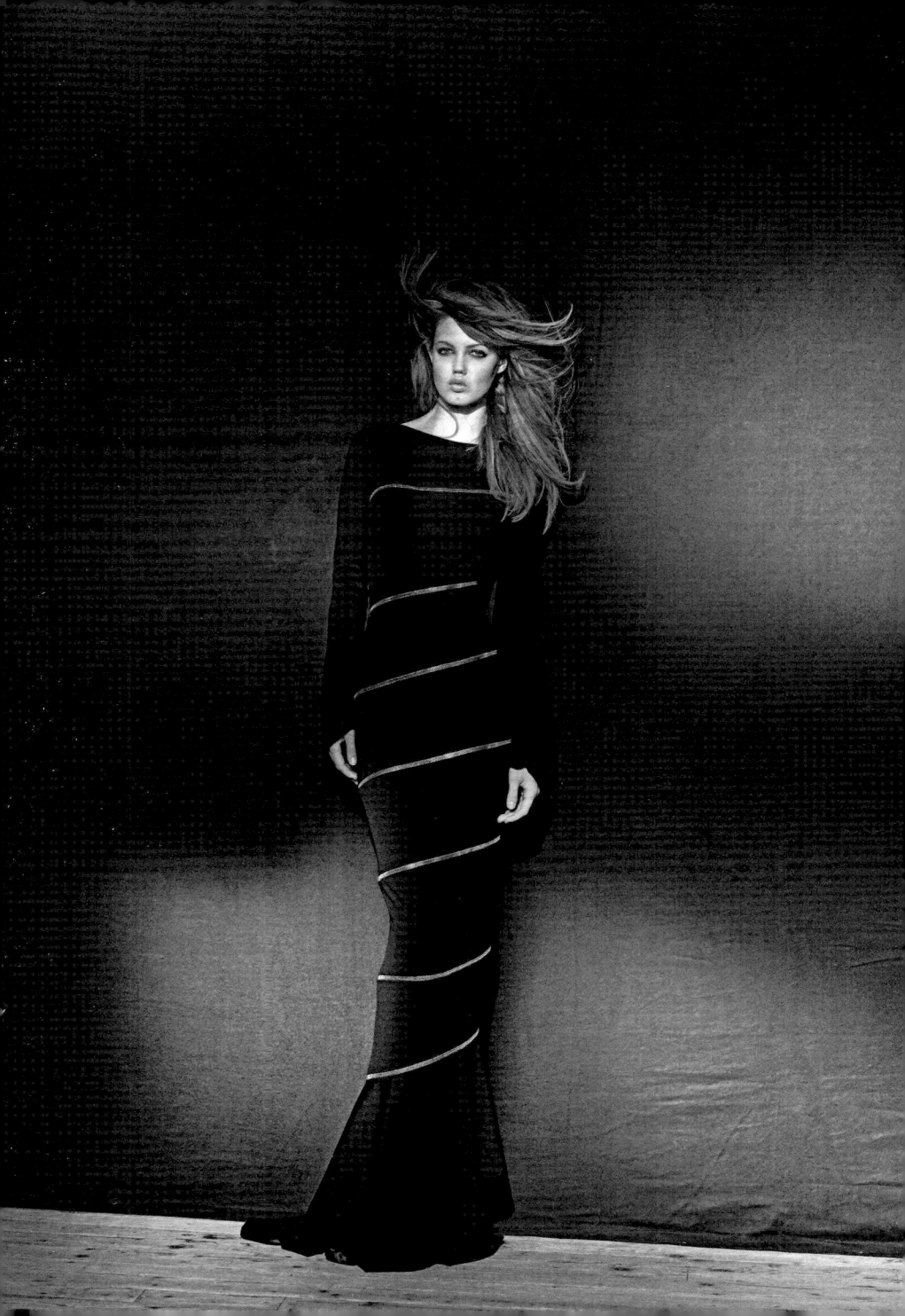

" This series of photos
is a gift for me. **"**
Azzedine Alaïa

Lindsey Wixson, *Paris*, 2013. Top and skirt, *Haute Couture Summer* 2010

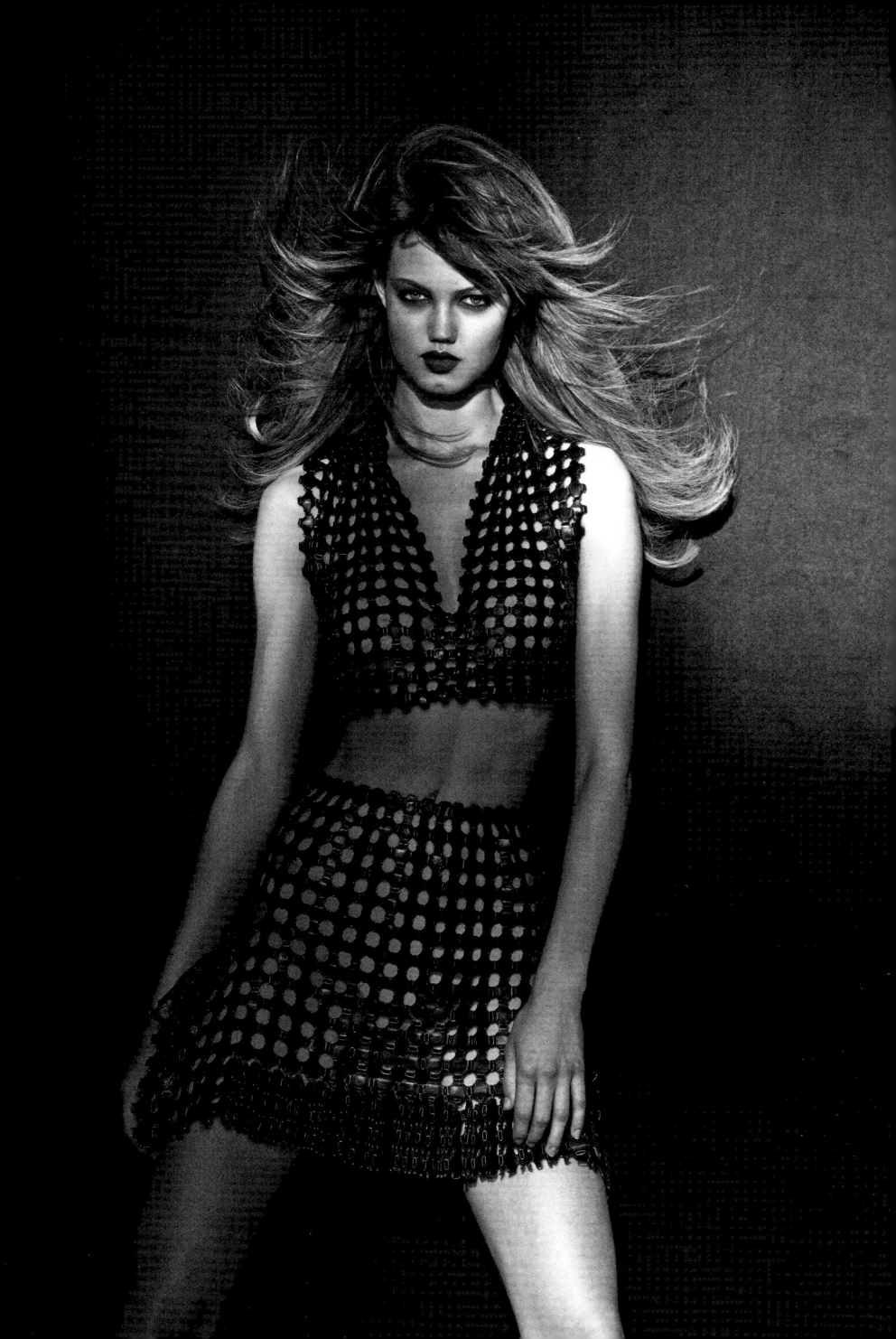

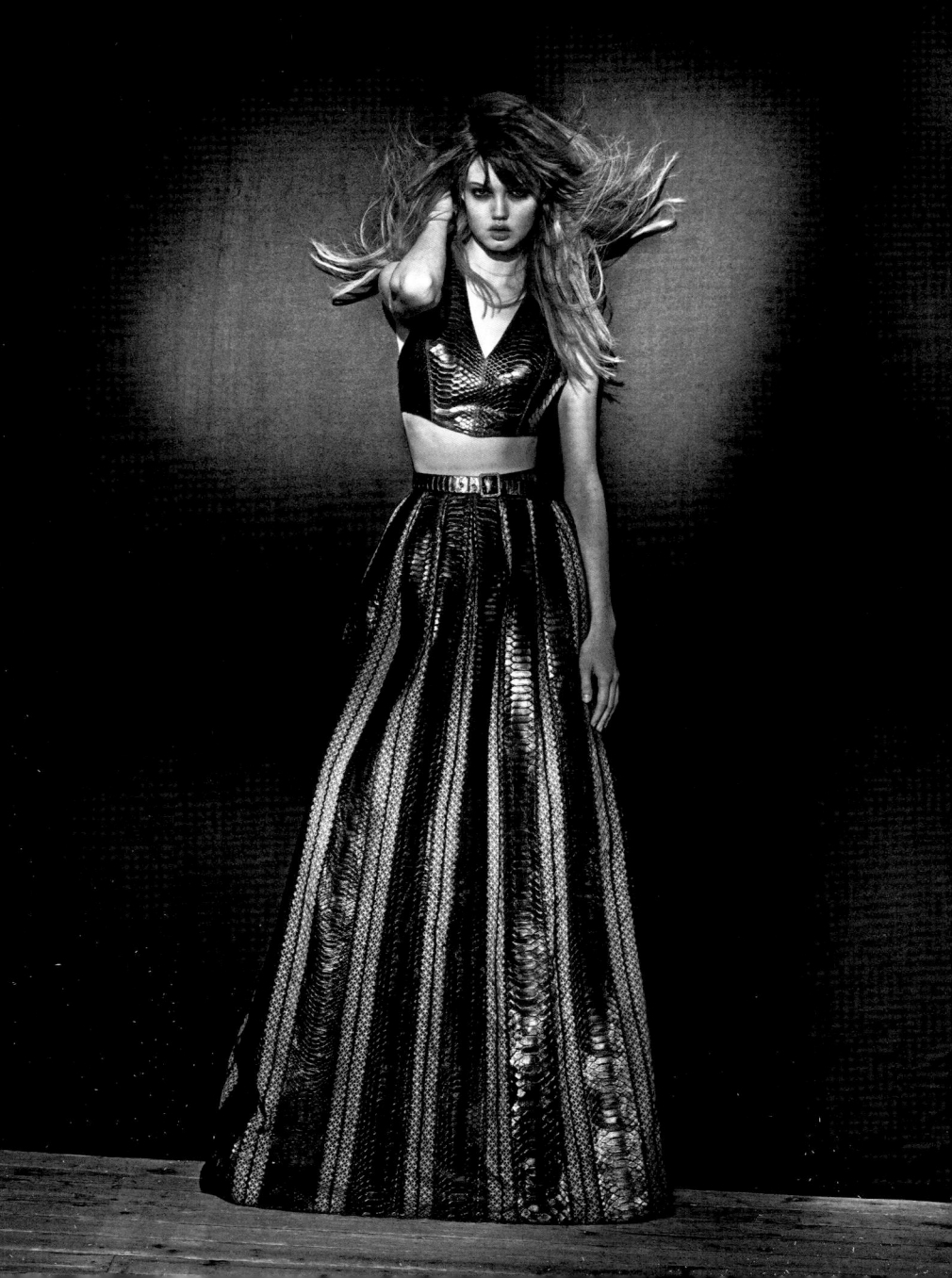

" For me, black and white
has always been connected to
the image's deeper truth,
to its most hidden meaning.**"**
Peter Lindbergh

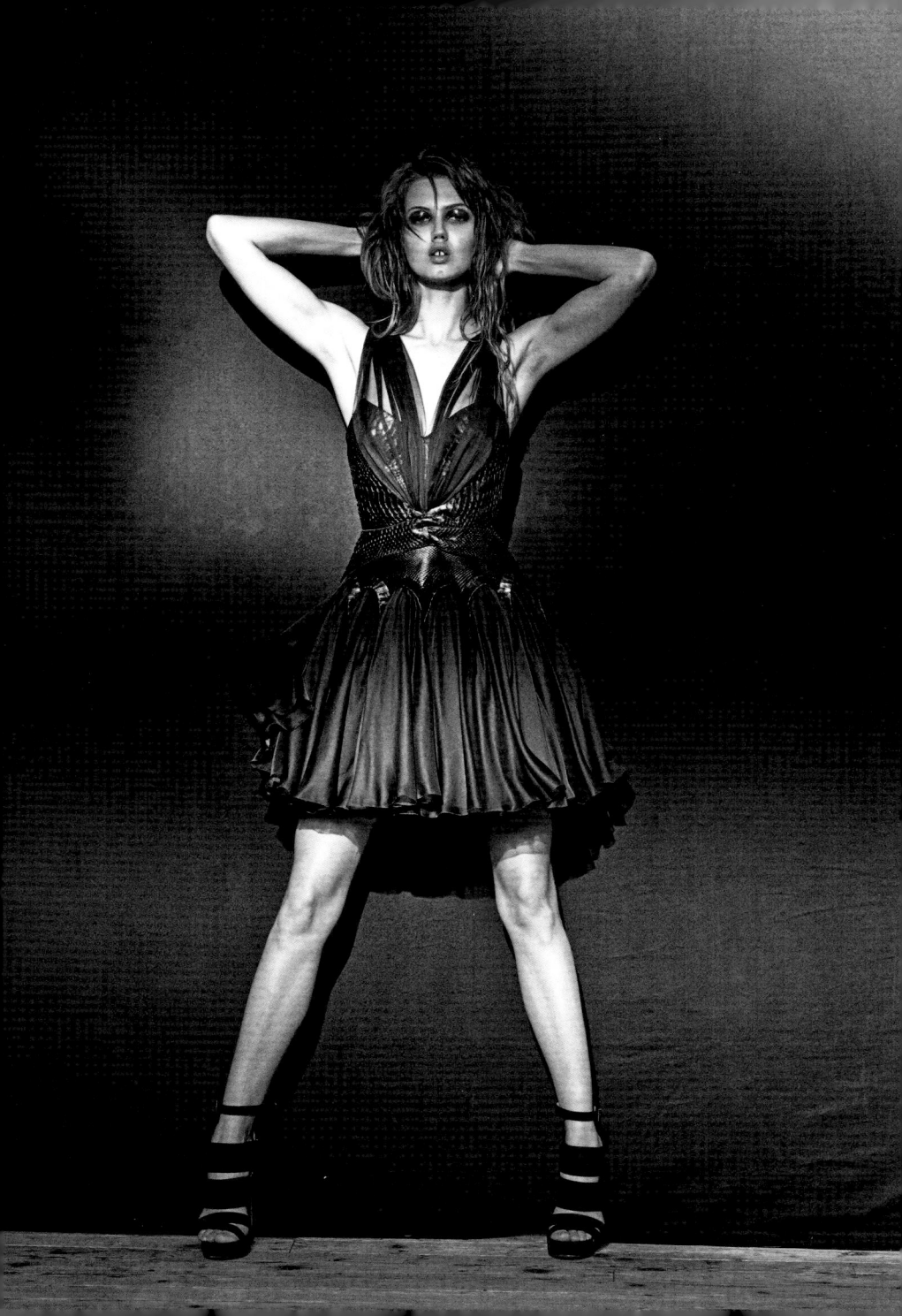

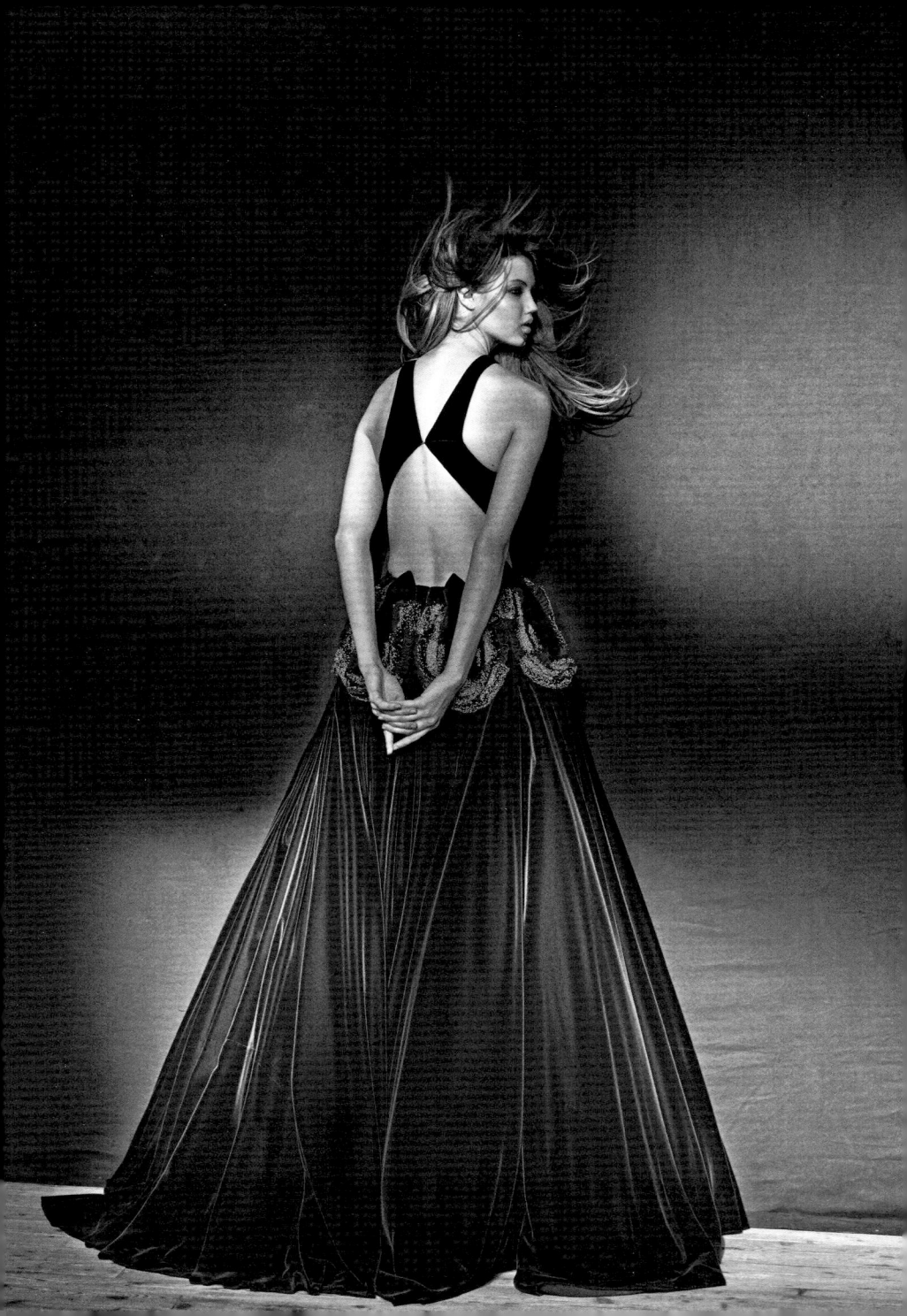

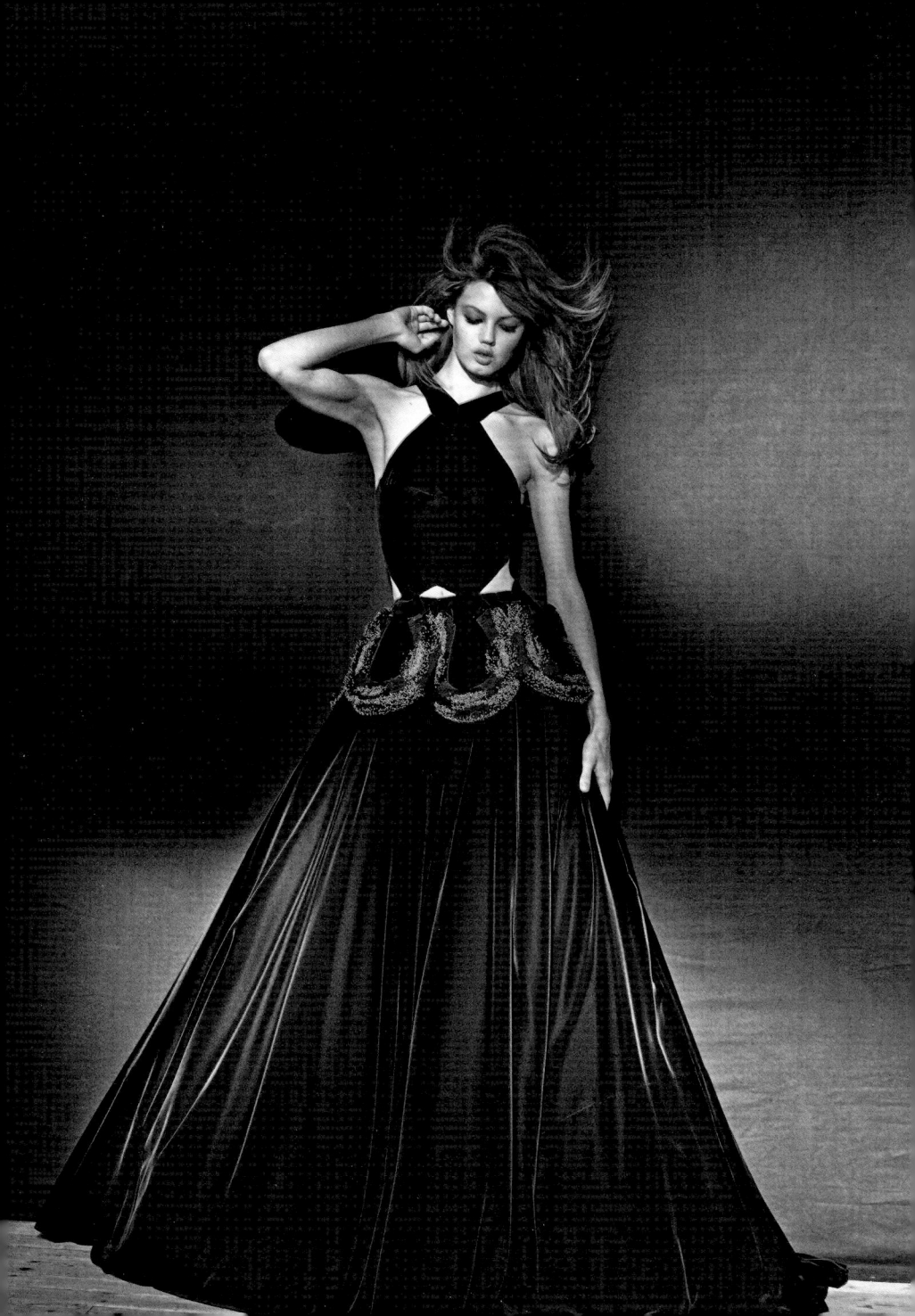

Lindsey Wixson, *Paris*, 2013. Dress, *Haute Couture Winter* 2011

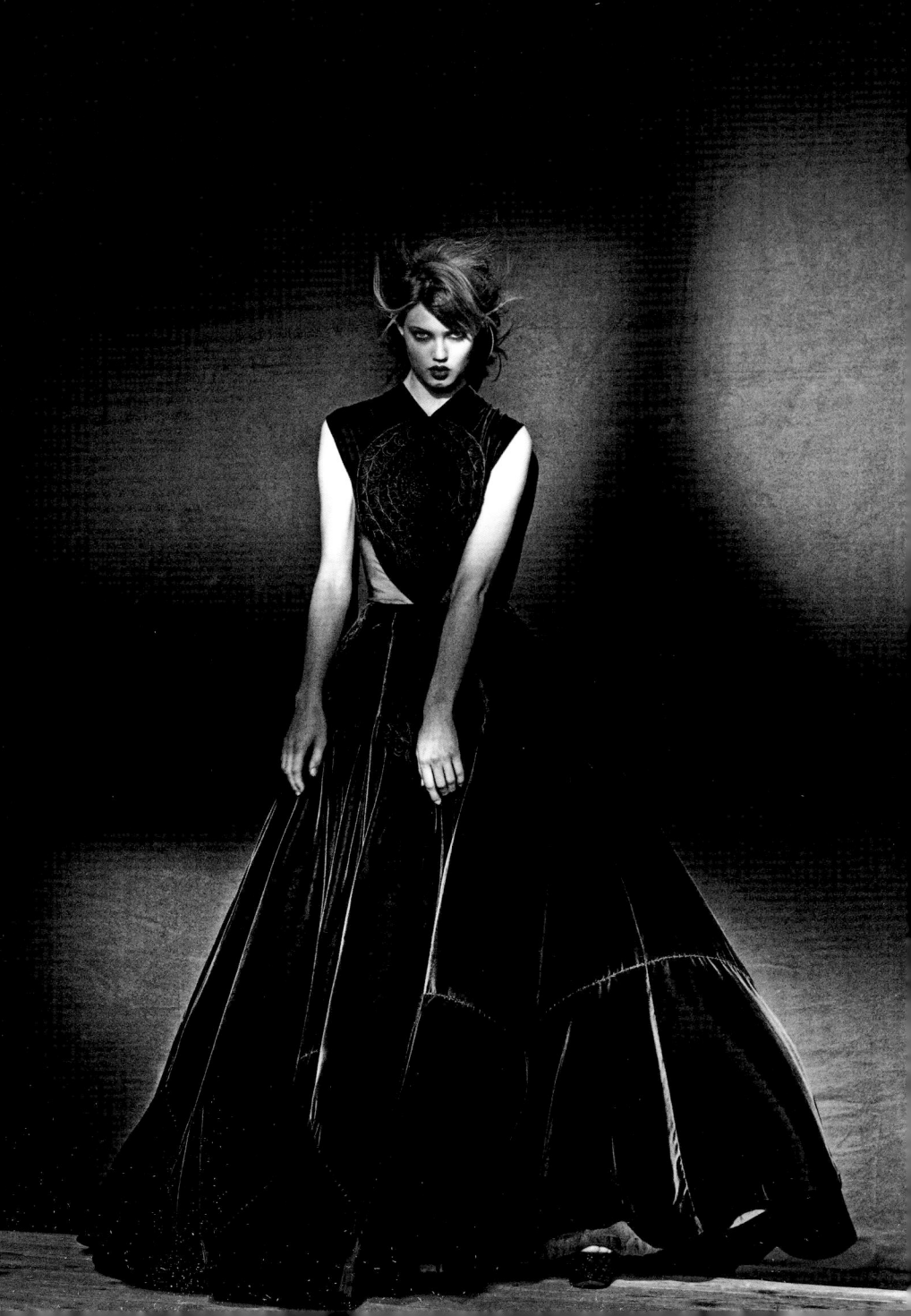

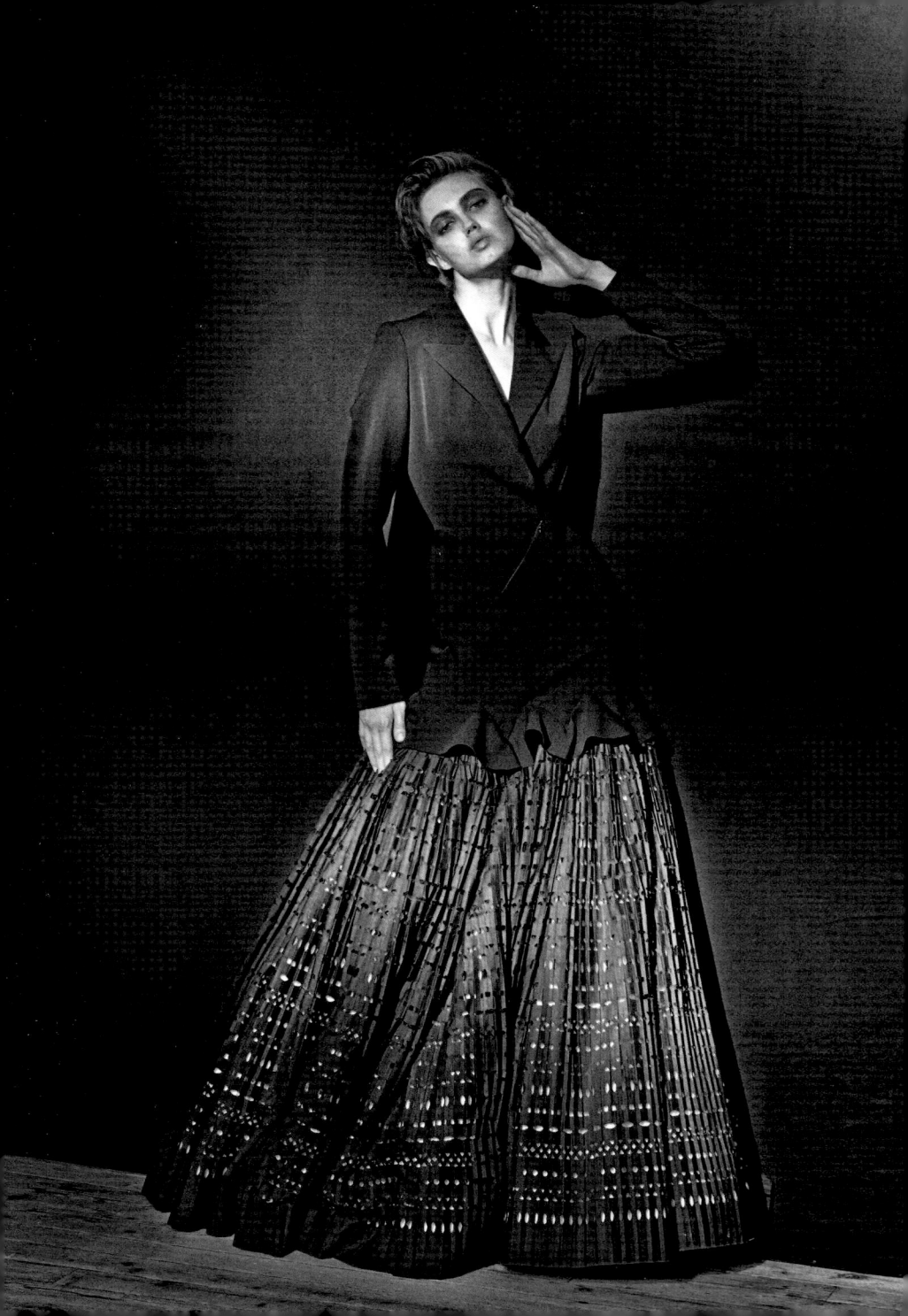

"I admire Azzedine Alaïa because he's definitely beyond fashion.
He is in his own fashion, a form of expression that is his and his alone."
Peter Lindbergh

Lindsey Wixson, *Paris*, 2013. Jacket and skirt, *Haute Couture Winter* 2009
(Following spread) Lindsey Wixson, *Paris*, 2013. Dress, *Haute Couture Winter* 2009

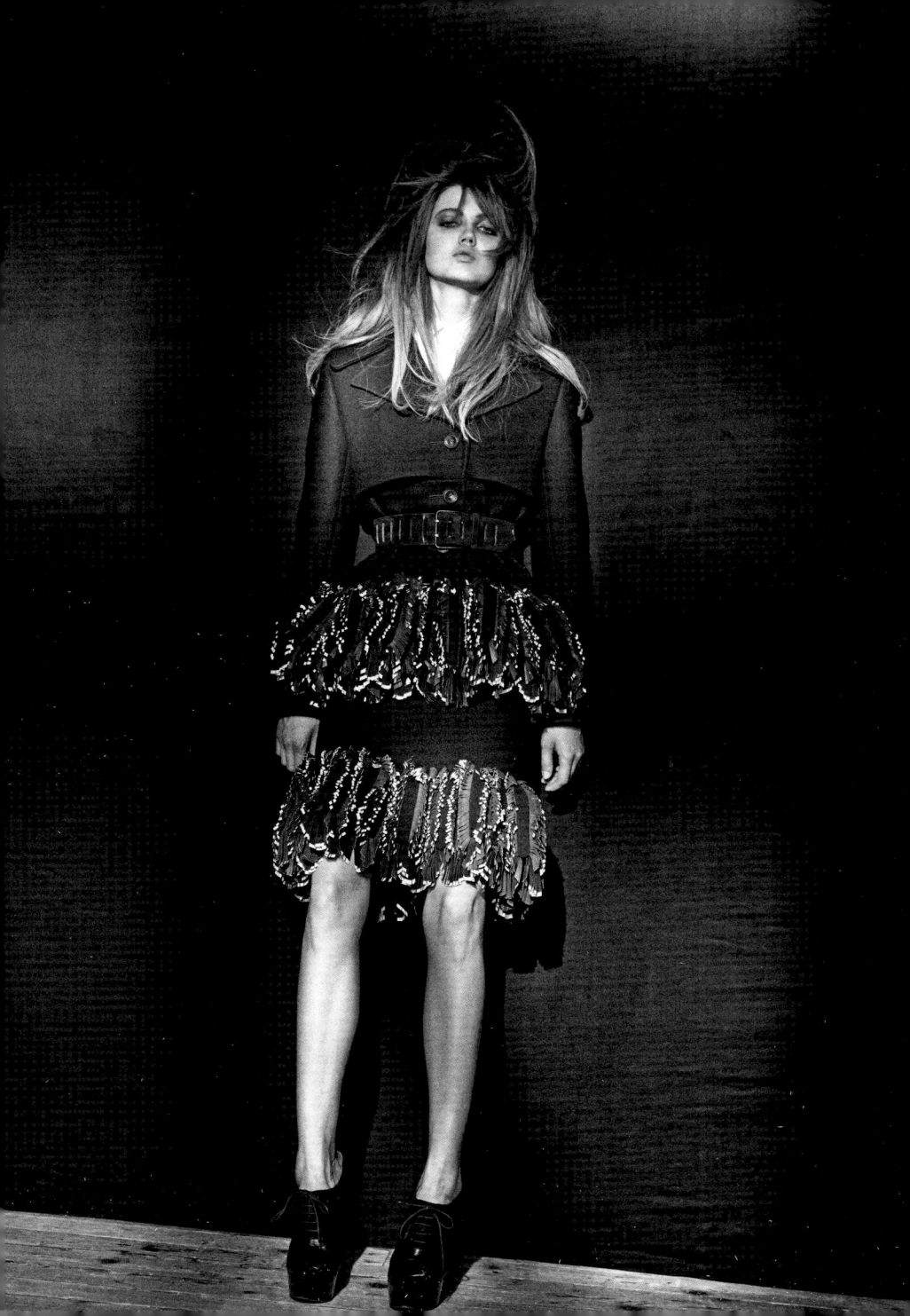

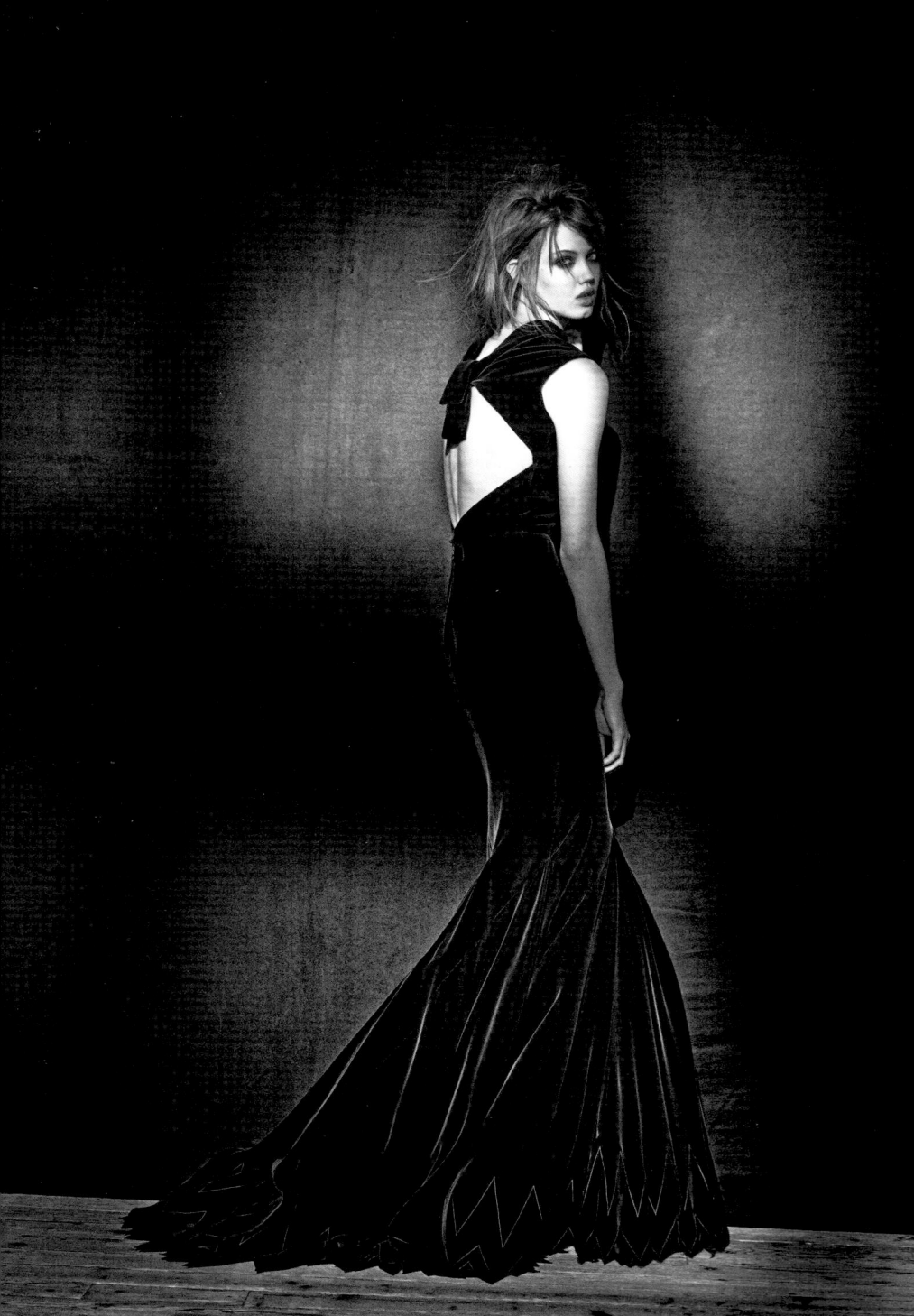

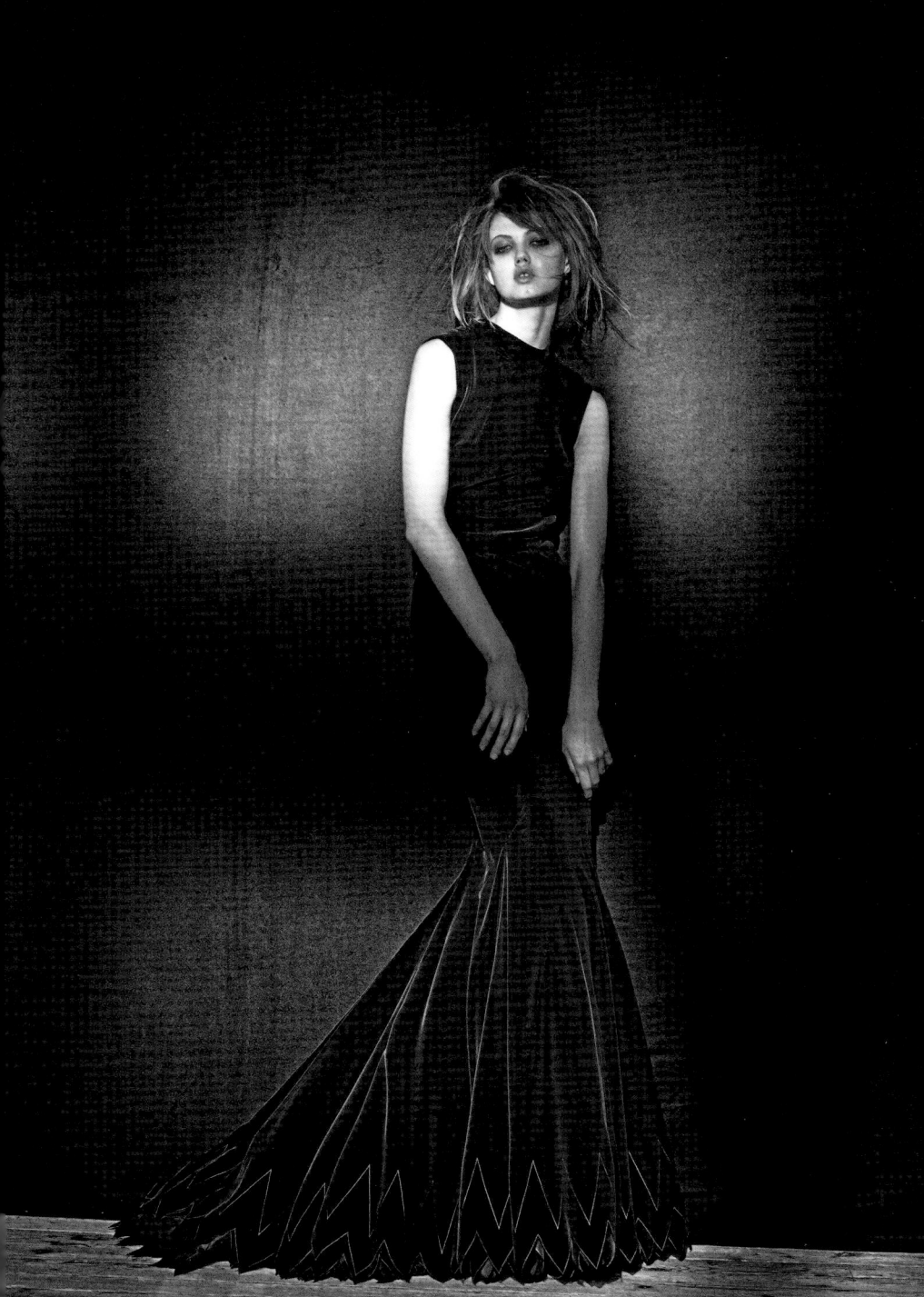

" I like women. I never think about doing new things, about being creative, but about making clothing that will make women beautiful. **"**
Azzedine Alaïa

Lindsey Wixson, *Paris*, 2013. Dress, *Haute Couture Winter* 2009

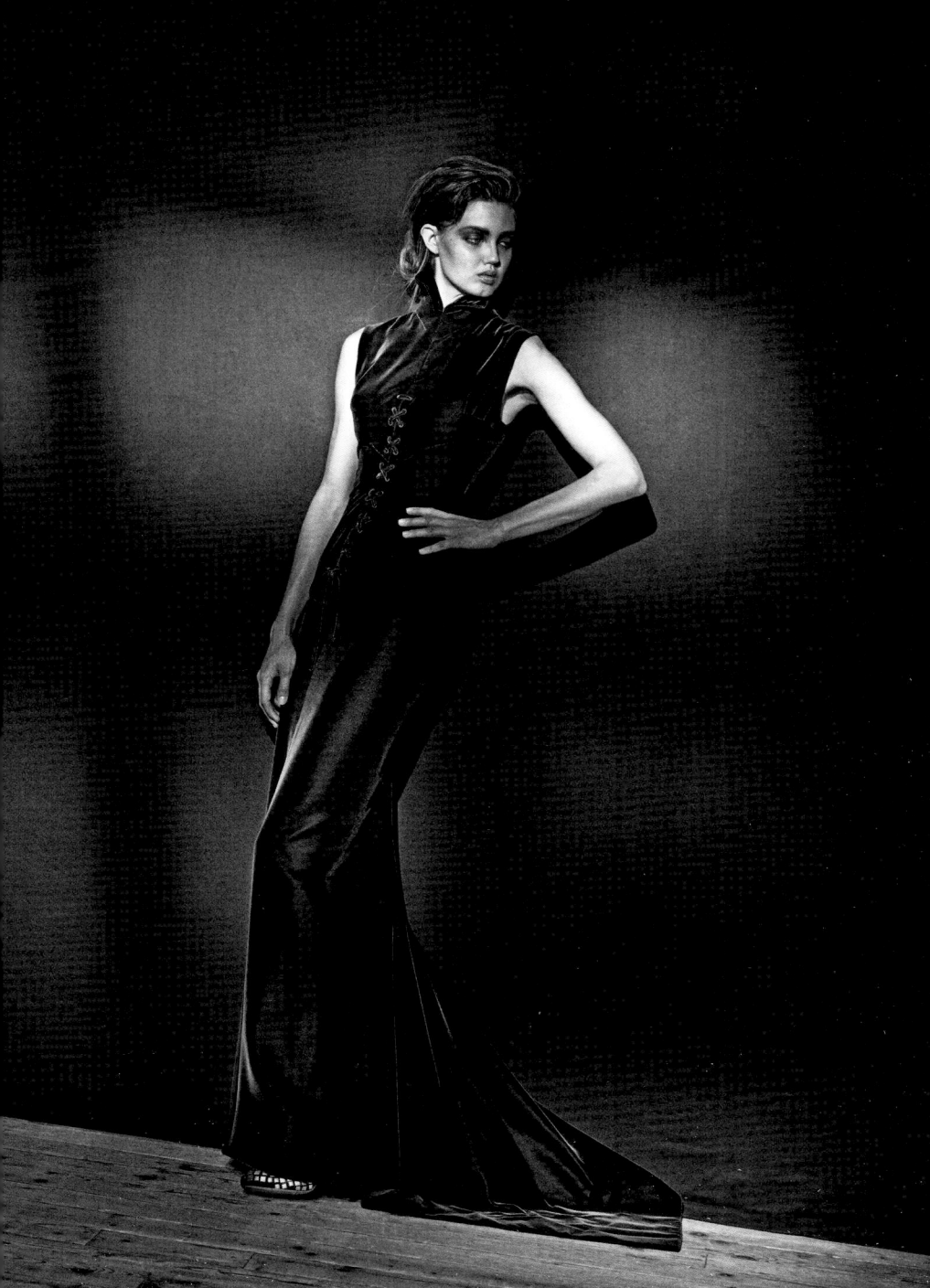

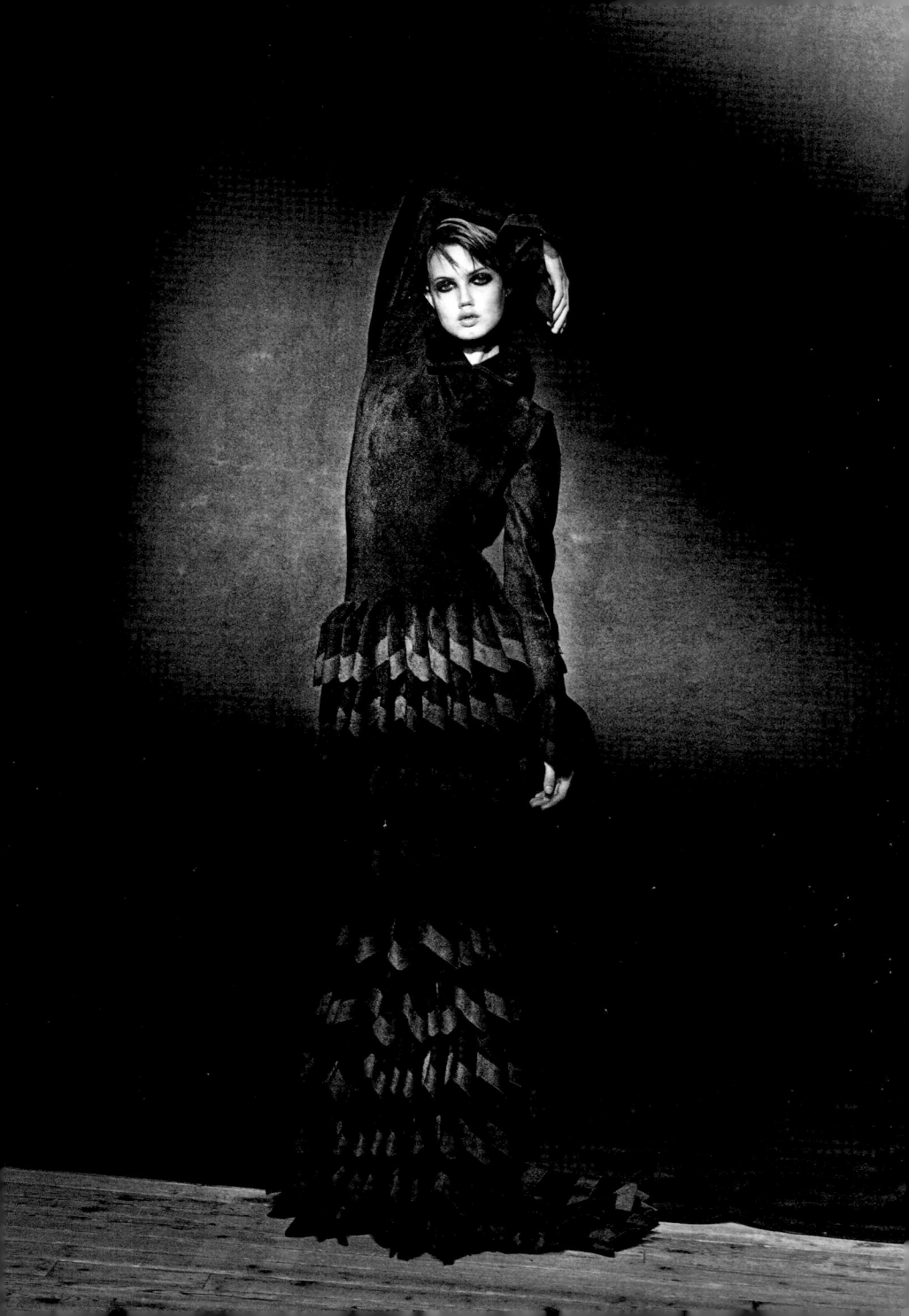

Lindsey Wixson, *Paris*, 2013. Dress, *Haute Couture Winter* 2012

Lindsey Wixson, *Paris*, 2013. Dress, *Haute Couture Winter* 2011

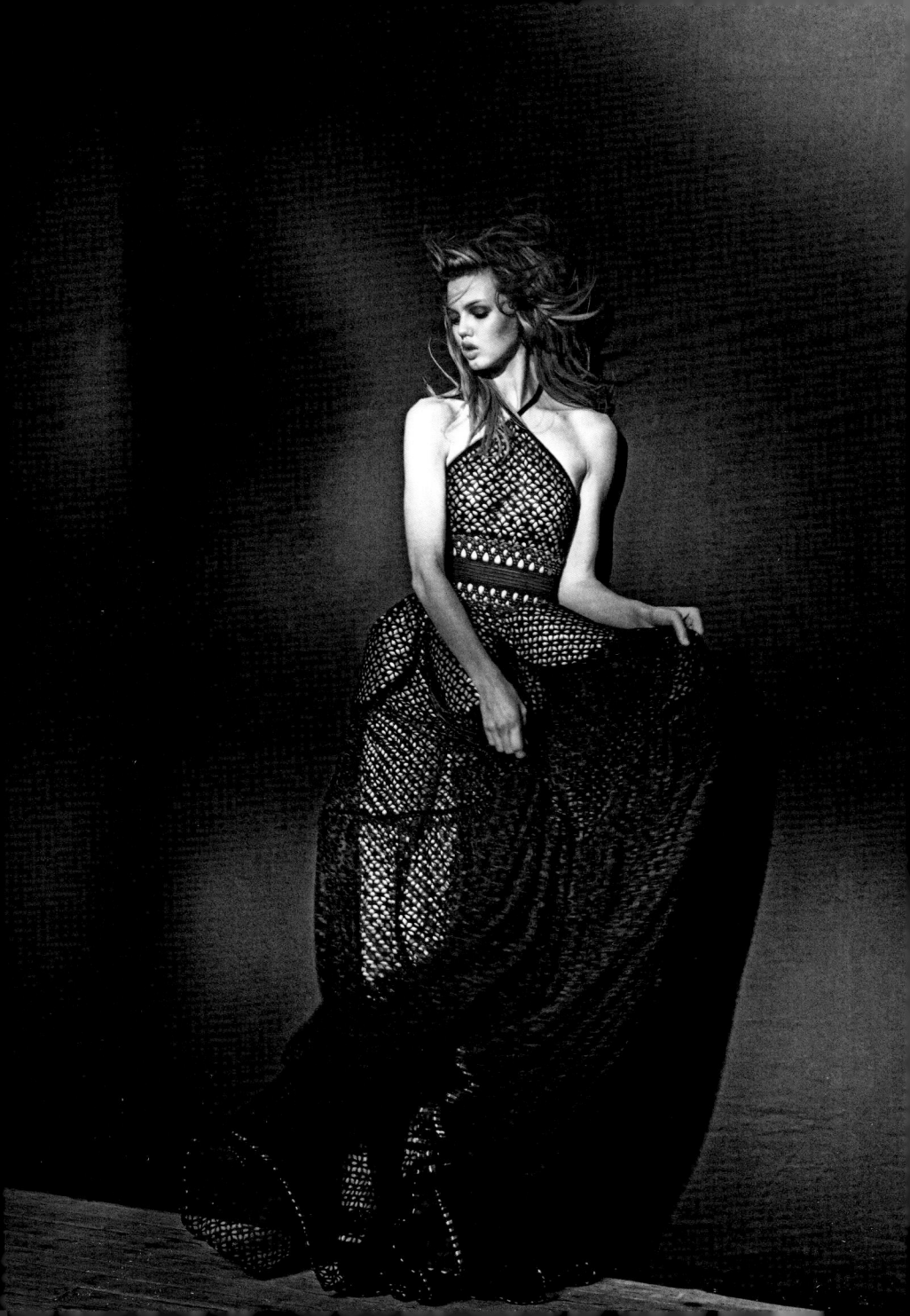

"A woman is like an actress:
She is always on stage.**"**
Azzedine Alaïa

Tina Turner, *Paris*, 1989. Dress, *Haute Couture* 1989

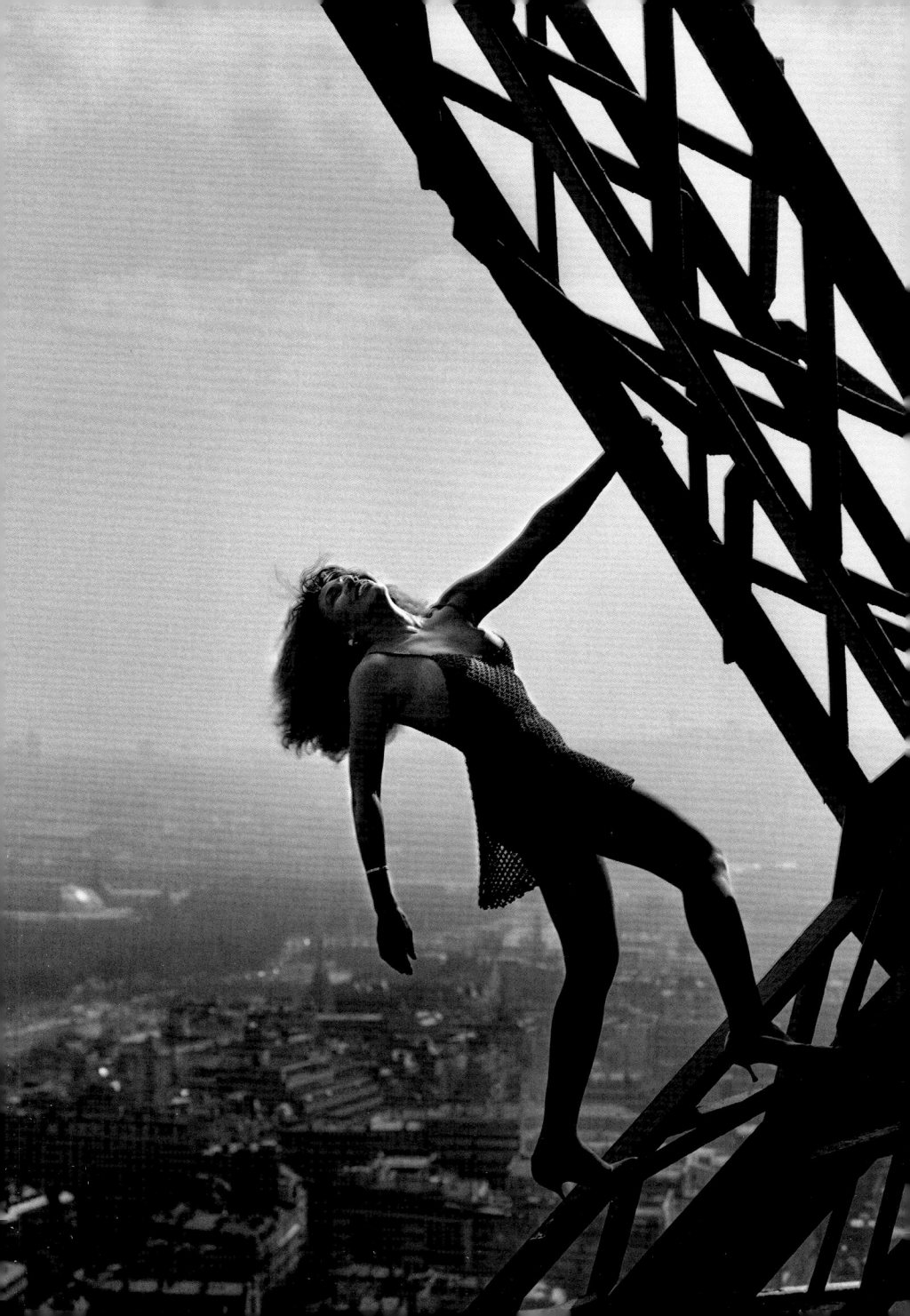

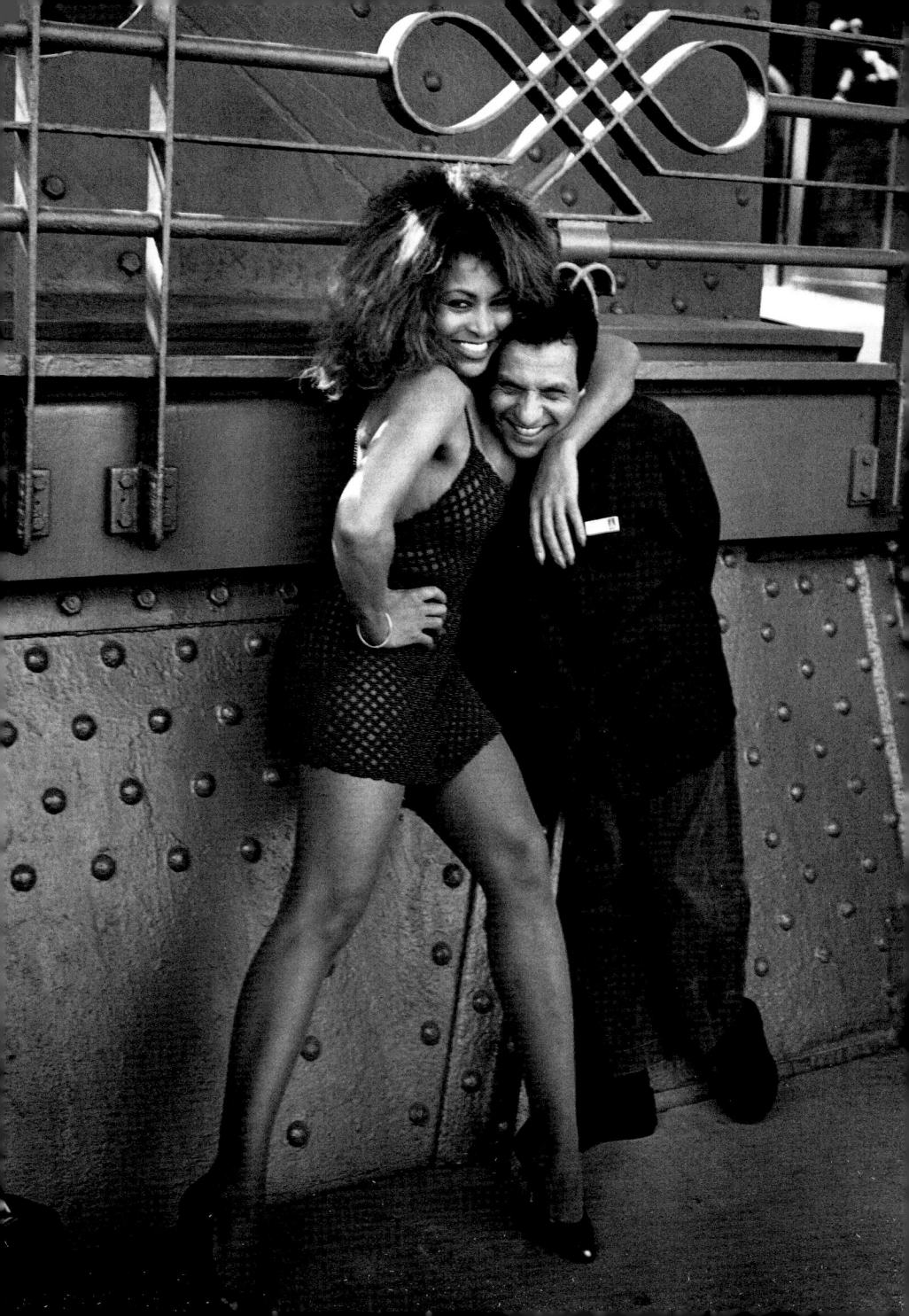

Tina Turner and Azzedine Alaïa, *Paris*, 1989. Dress, *Haute Couture* 1989
(Following spreads) Tina Turner, *Paris*, 1989. Dress, *Haute Couture* 1989

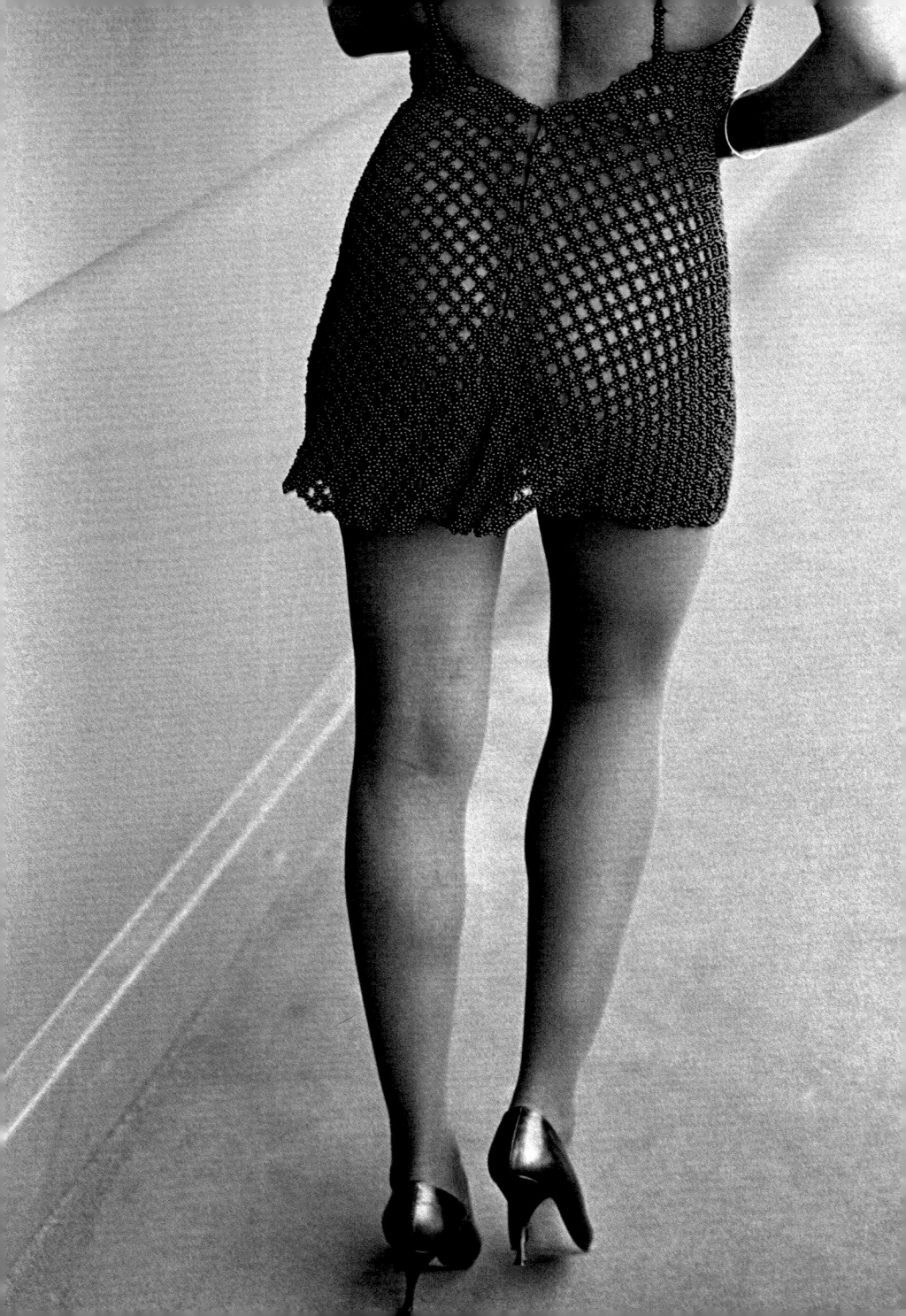

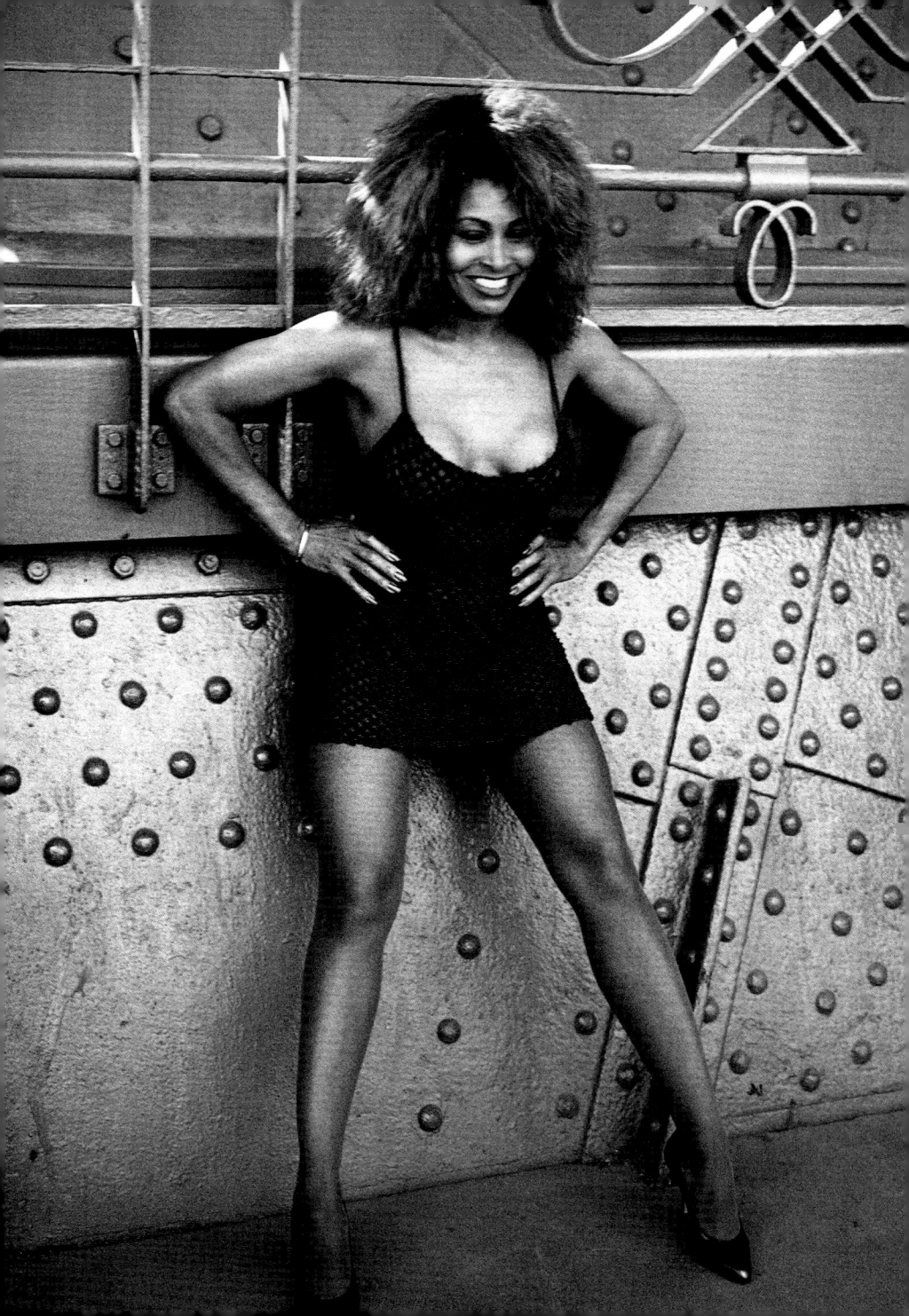

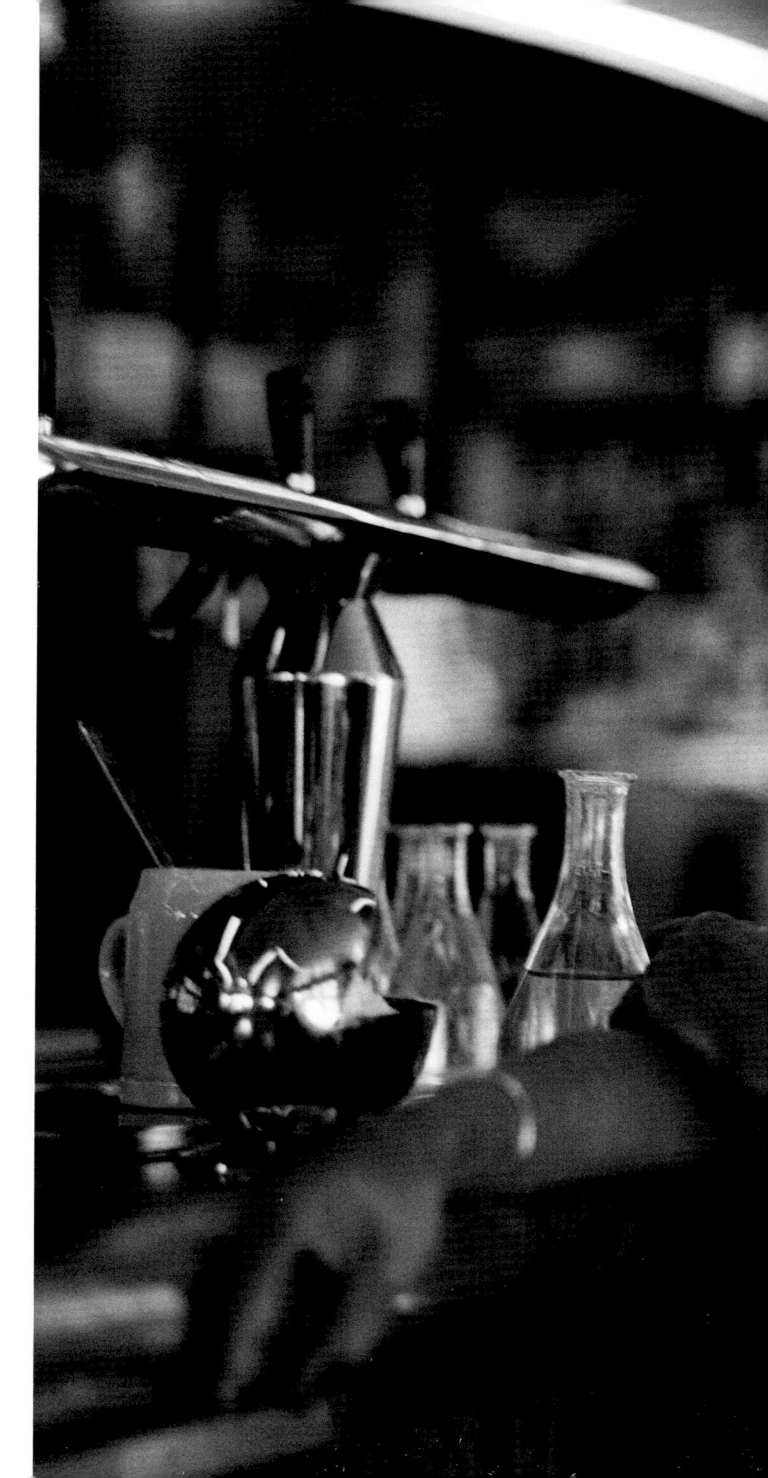

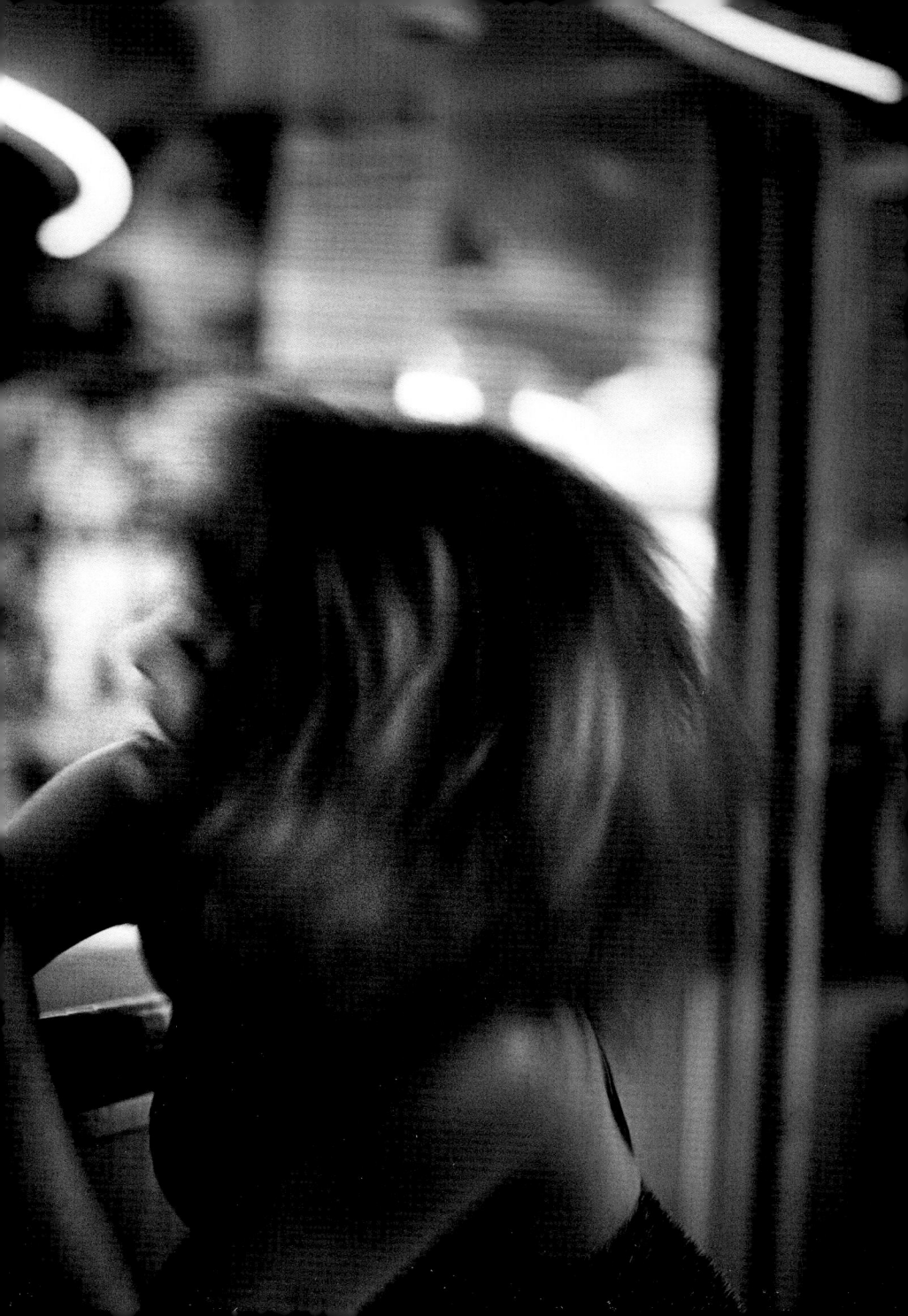

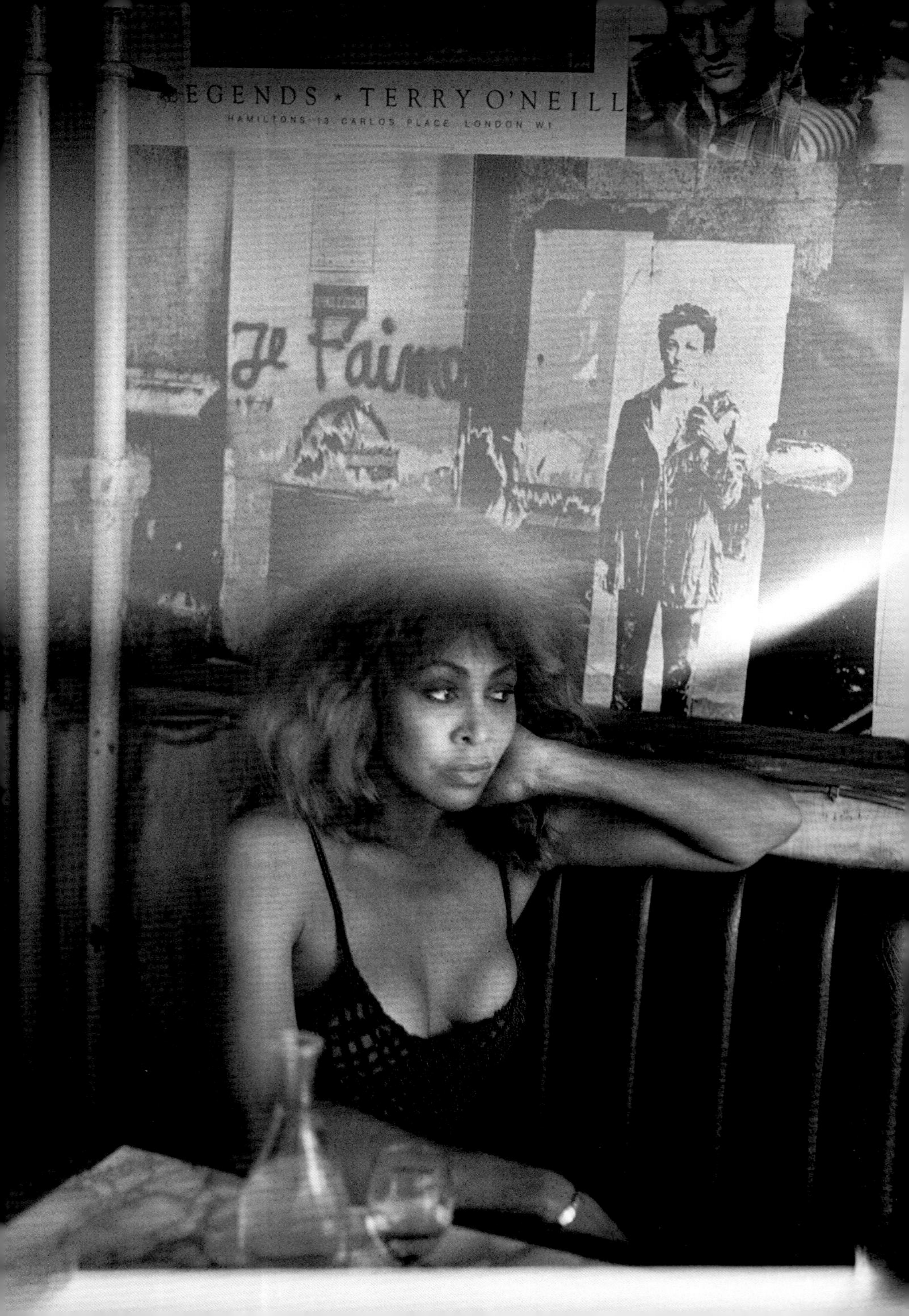
LEGENDS ★ TERRY O'NEILL
HAMILTONS 13 CARLOS PLACE LONDON W1.
Je t'aime

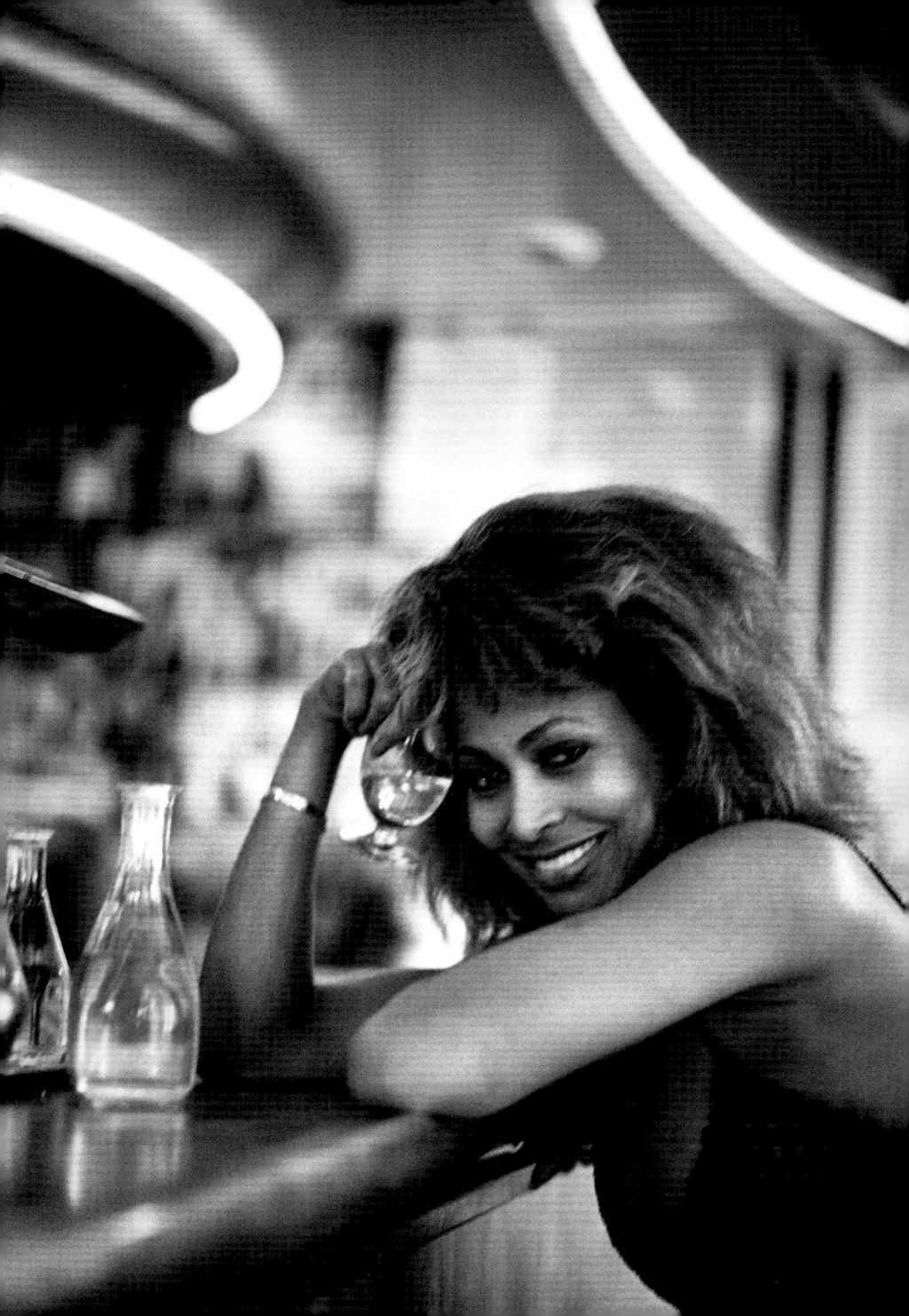

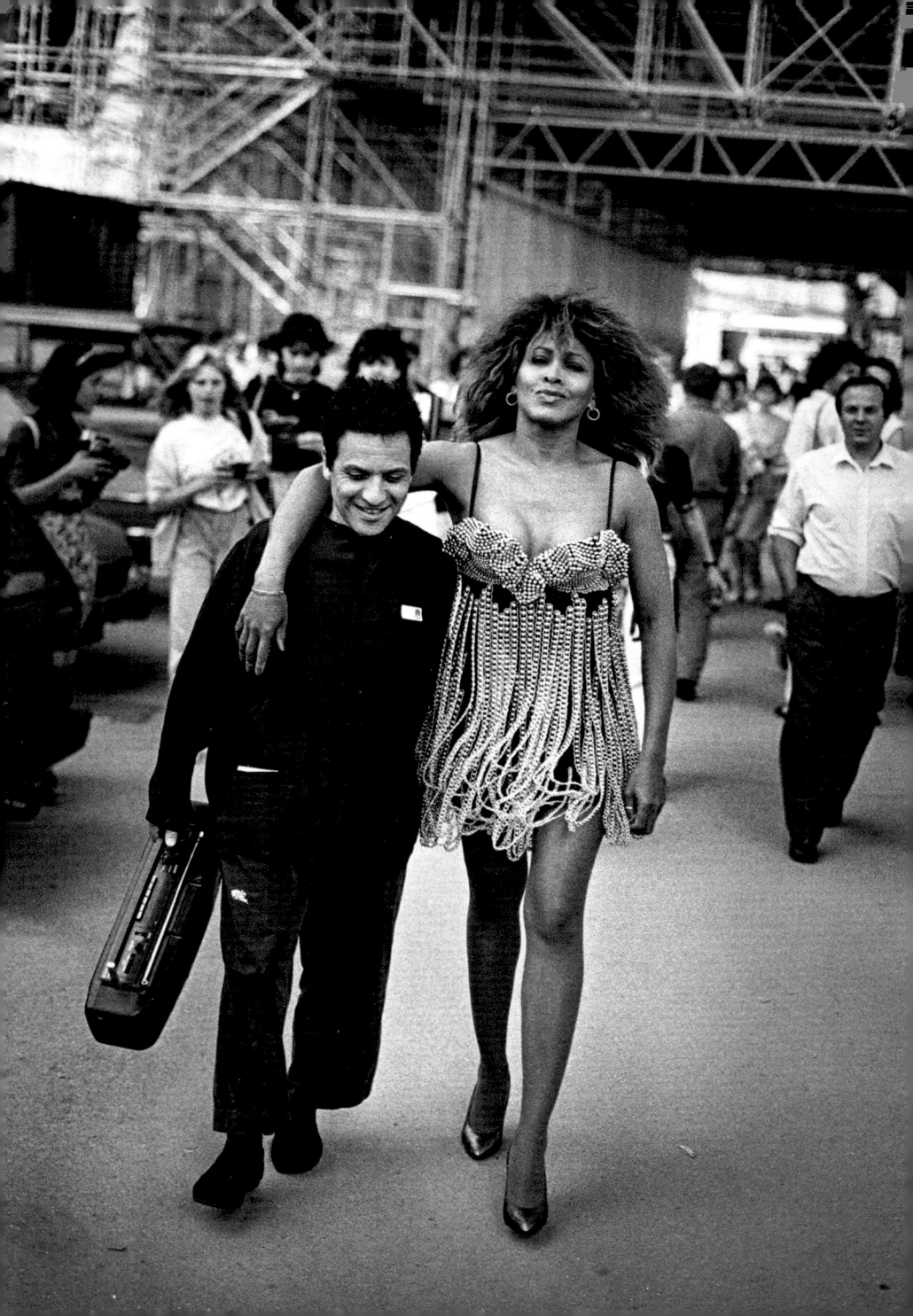

"For me every photograph
is a portrait; you are photographing
a relationship with the person you
are shooting; there is an exchange,
and that's what the picture is."
Peter Lindbergh

(Previous spread) Tina Turner, *Paris*, 1989. Dress, *Haute Couture* 1989
(Opposite) Tina Turner and Azzedine Alaïa, *Paris*, 1989. Dress, *Haute Couture* 1989
(Following spread) Tina Turner, *Paris*, 1989. Dress, *Haute Couture* 1989

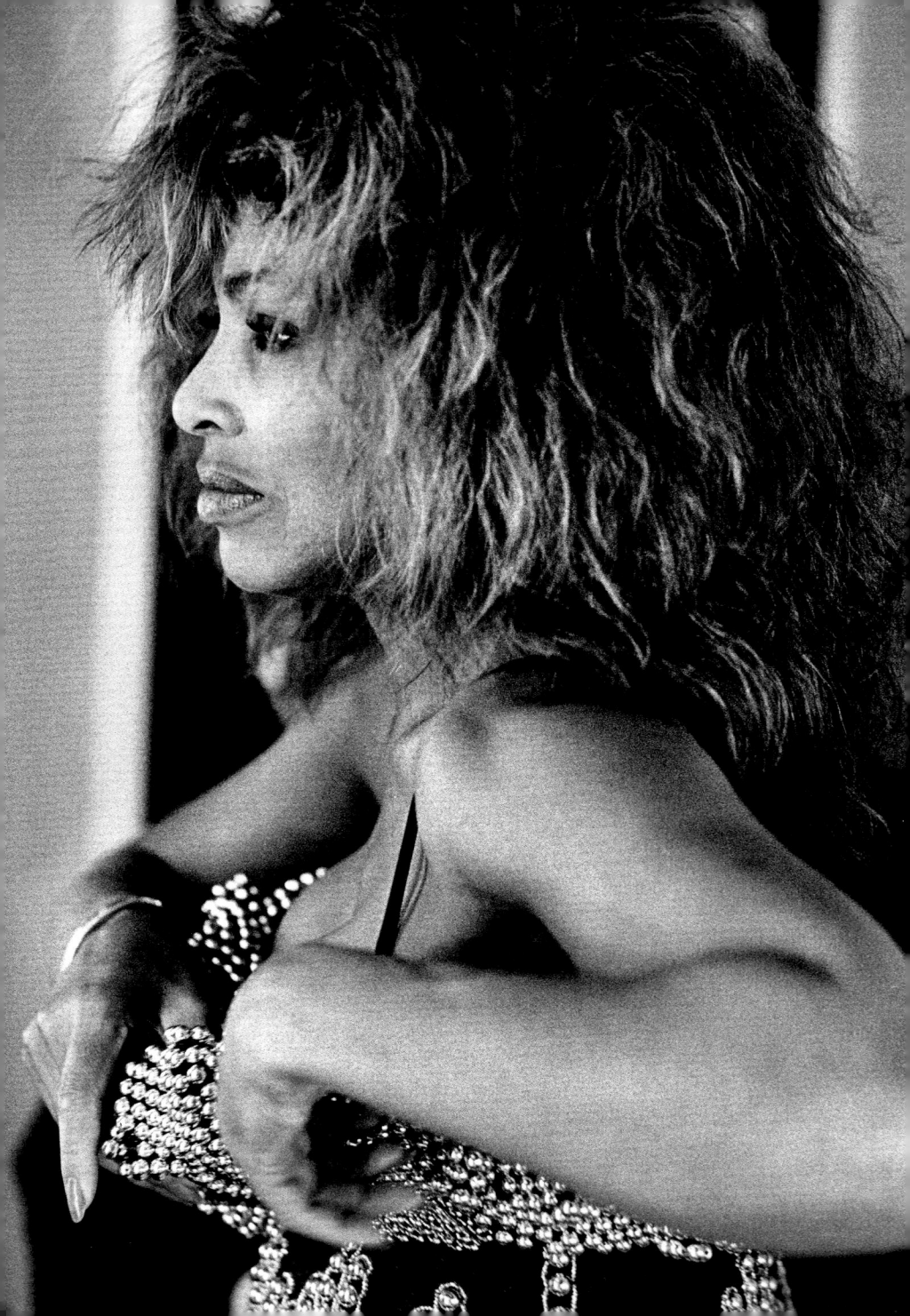

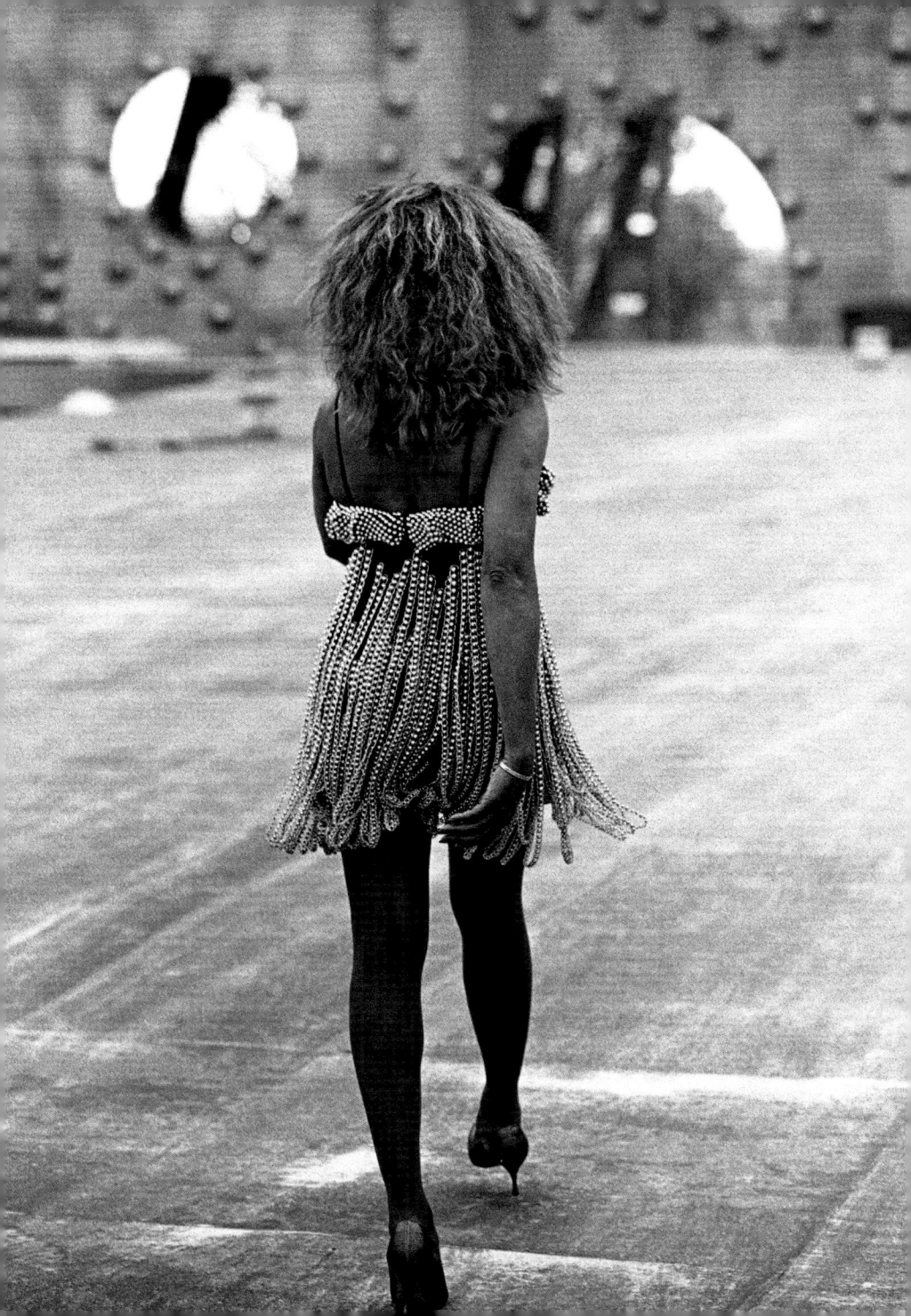

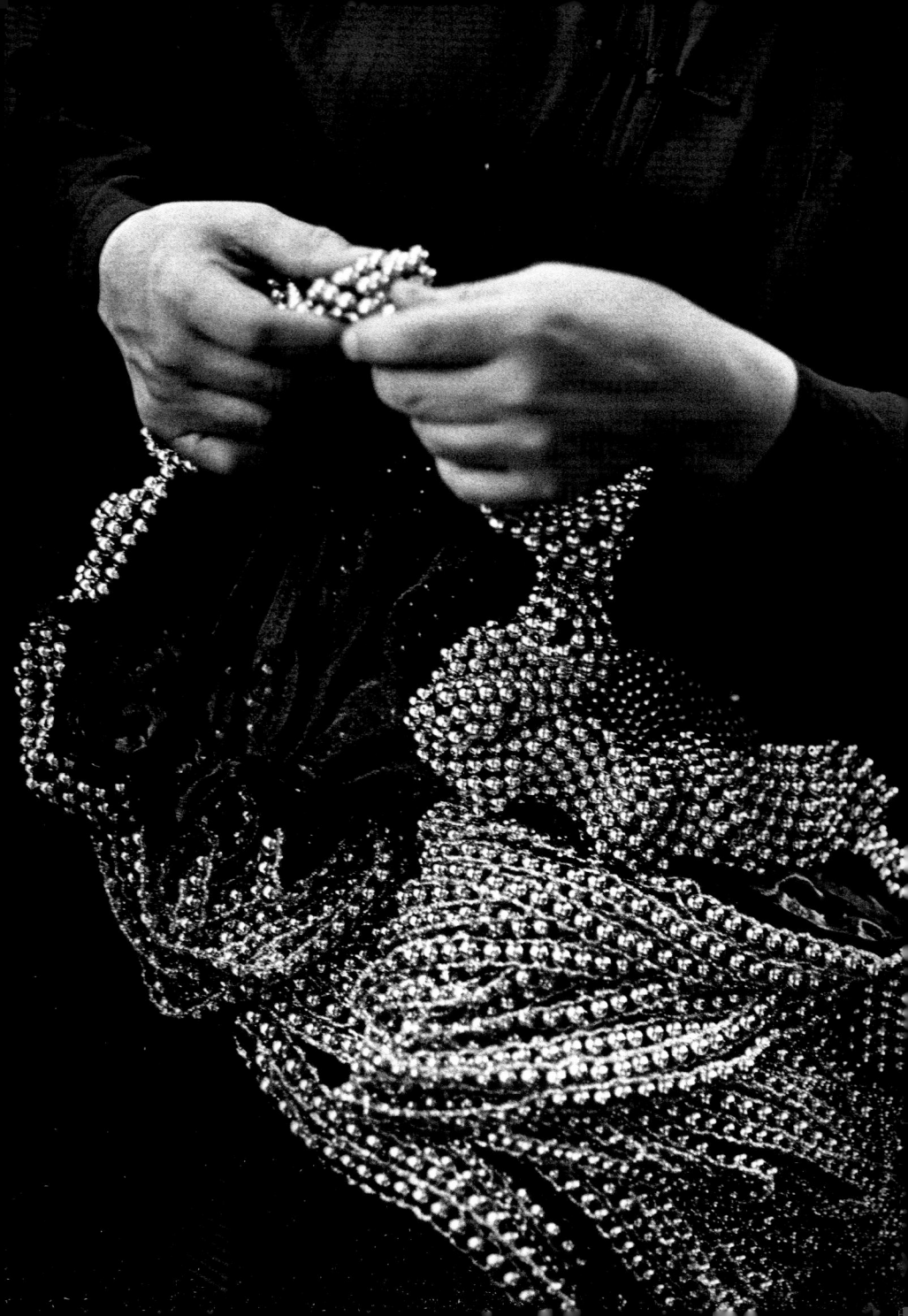

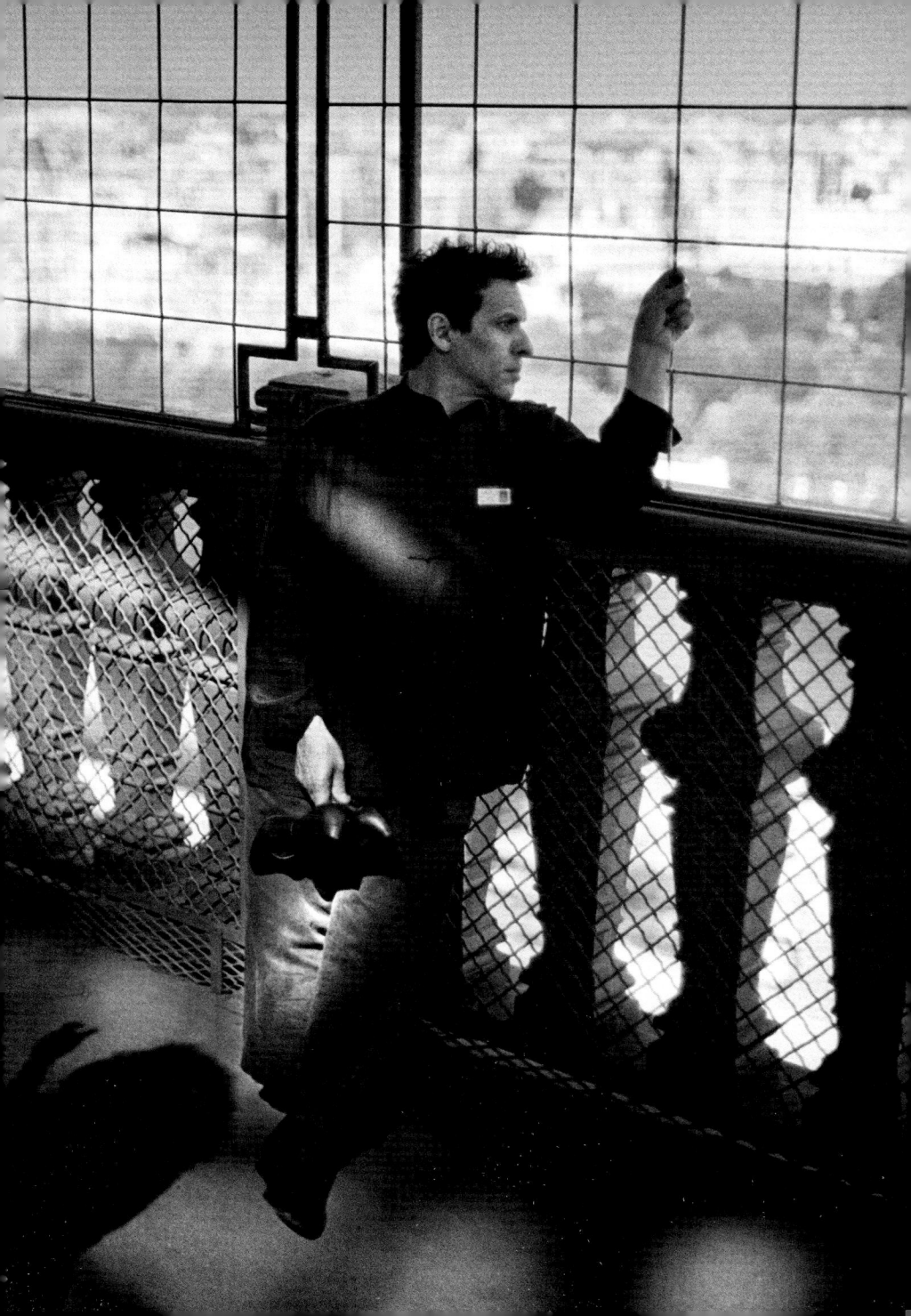

" Heartless retouching should not be chosen to represent women. When you subscribe to the idea that there cannot be beauty without truth, the answer is clear. How crazy and unreal is the idea of erasing all your experience from your face!"
Peter Lindbergh

(Previous spread) Azzedine Alaïa, *Paris*, 1989. Dress, *Haute Couture* 1989
(Opposite) Tina Turner, *Paris*, 1989. Dress, *Summer* 1988
(Following spread) Tina Turner, *Paris*, 1989. Shirt, *Winter* 1989

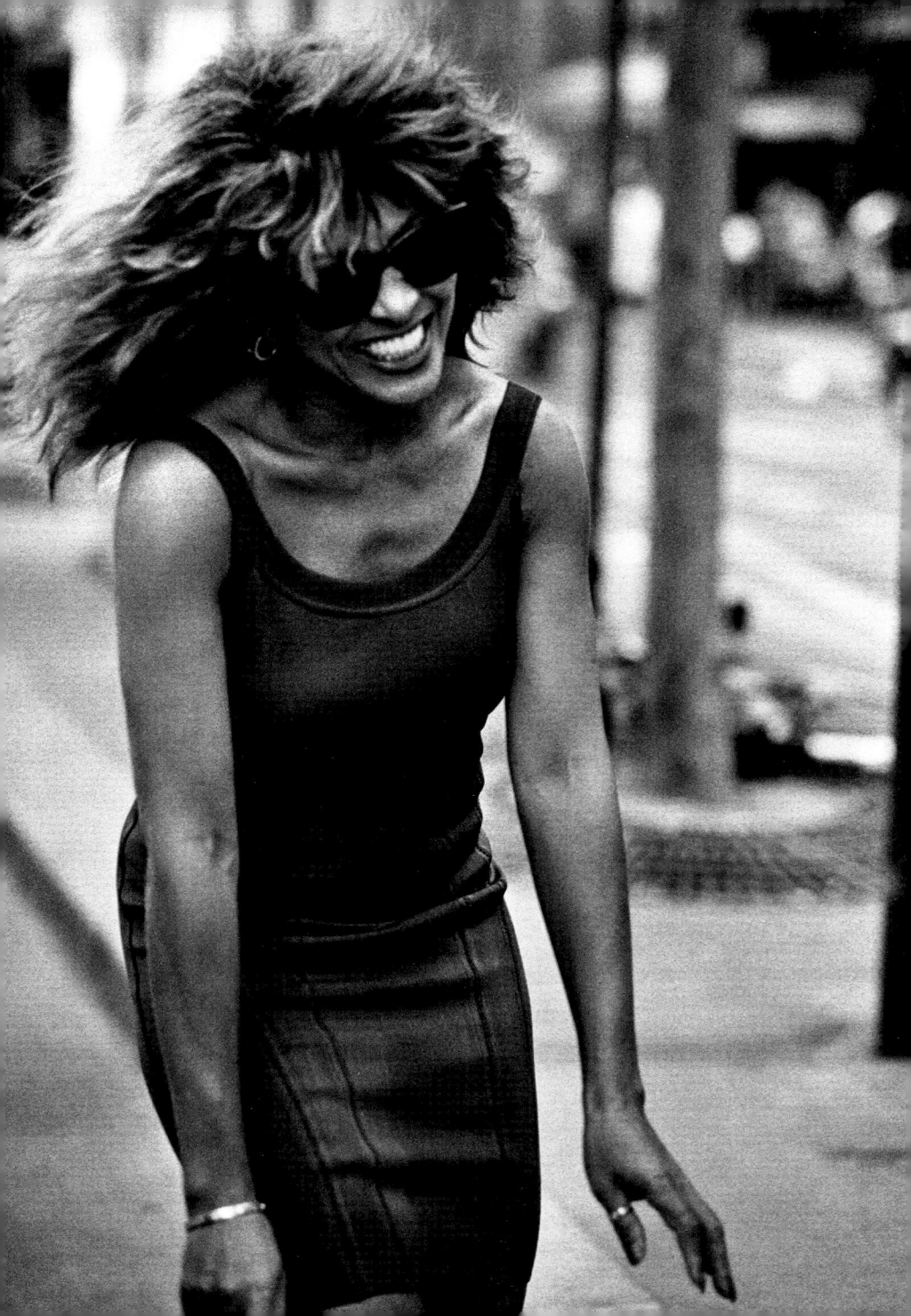

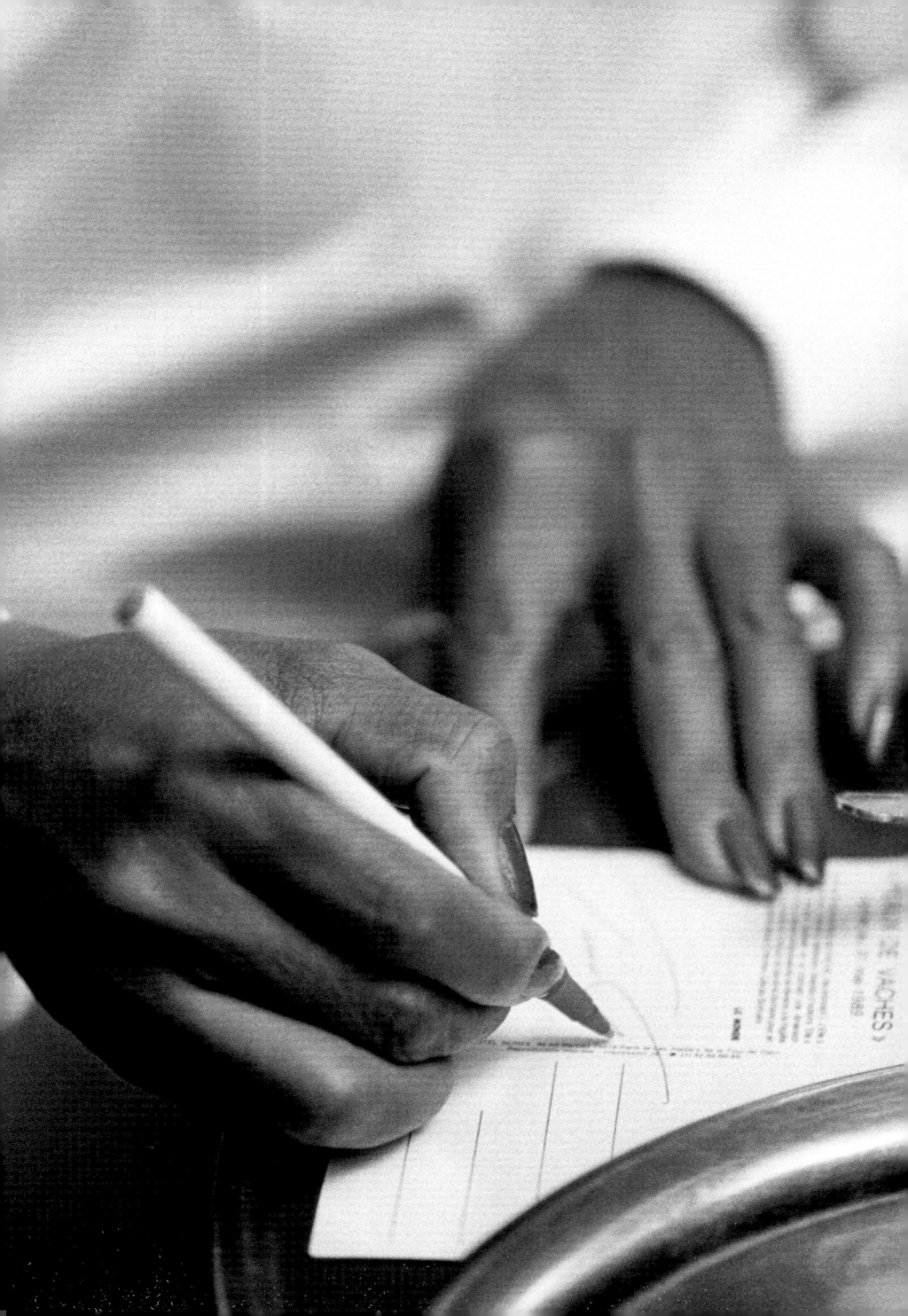

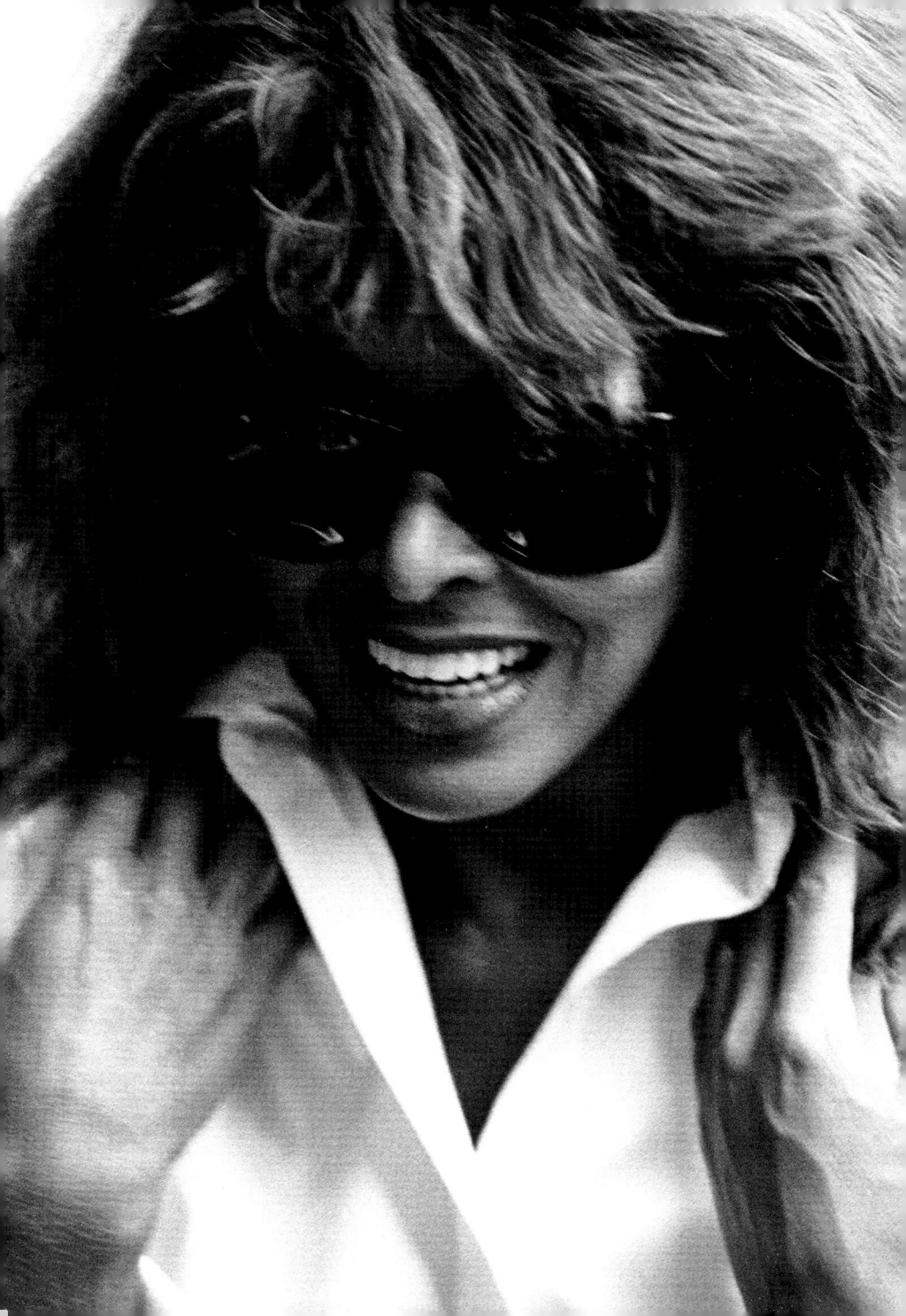

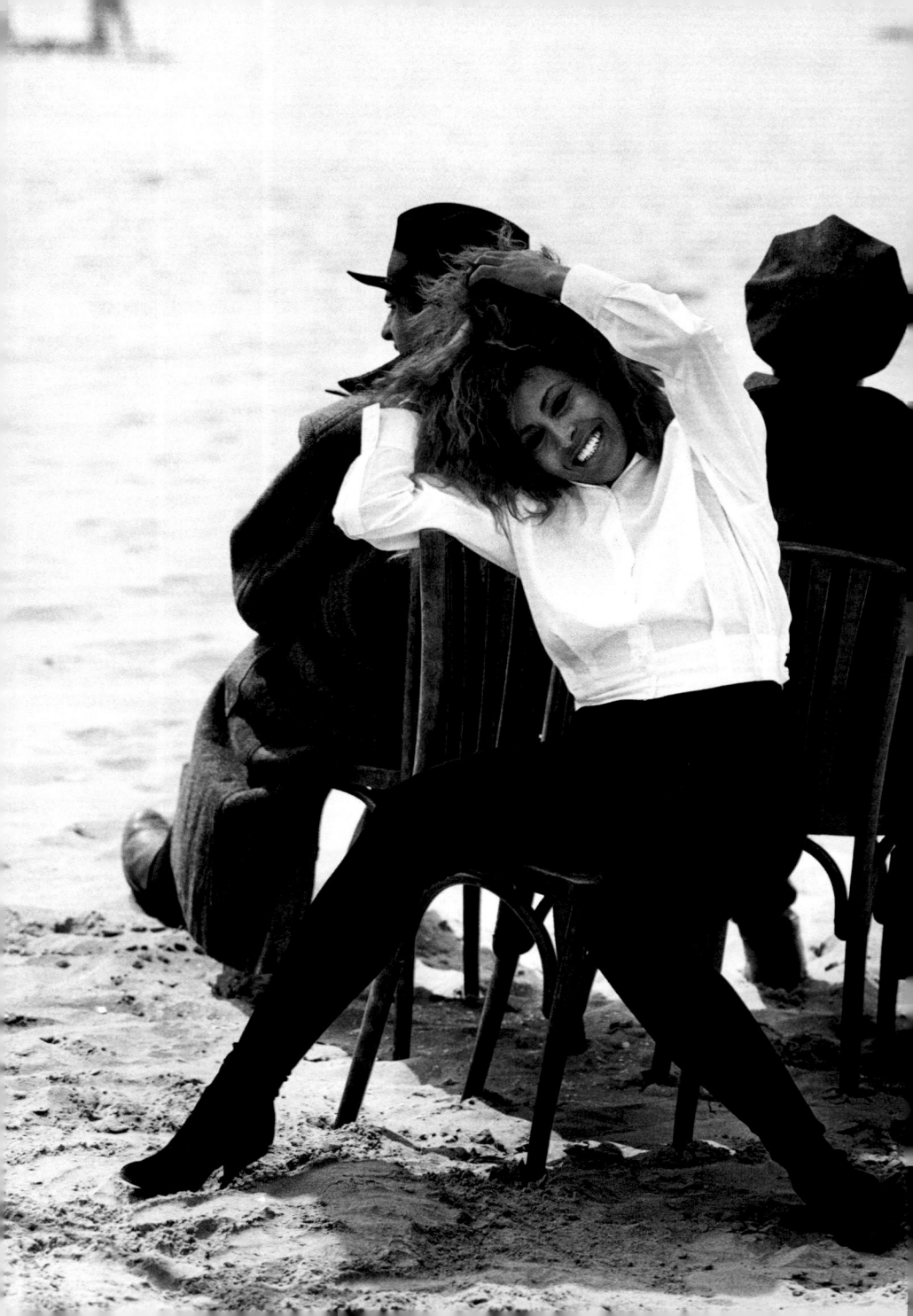

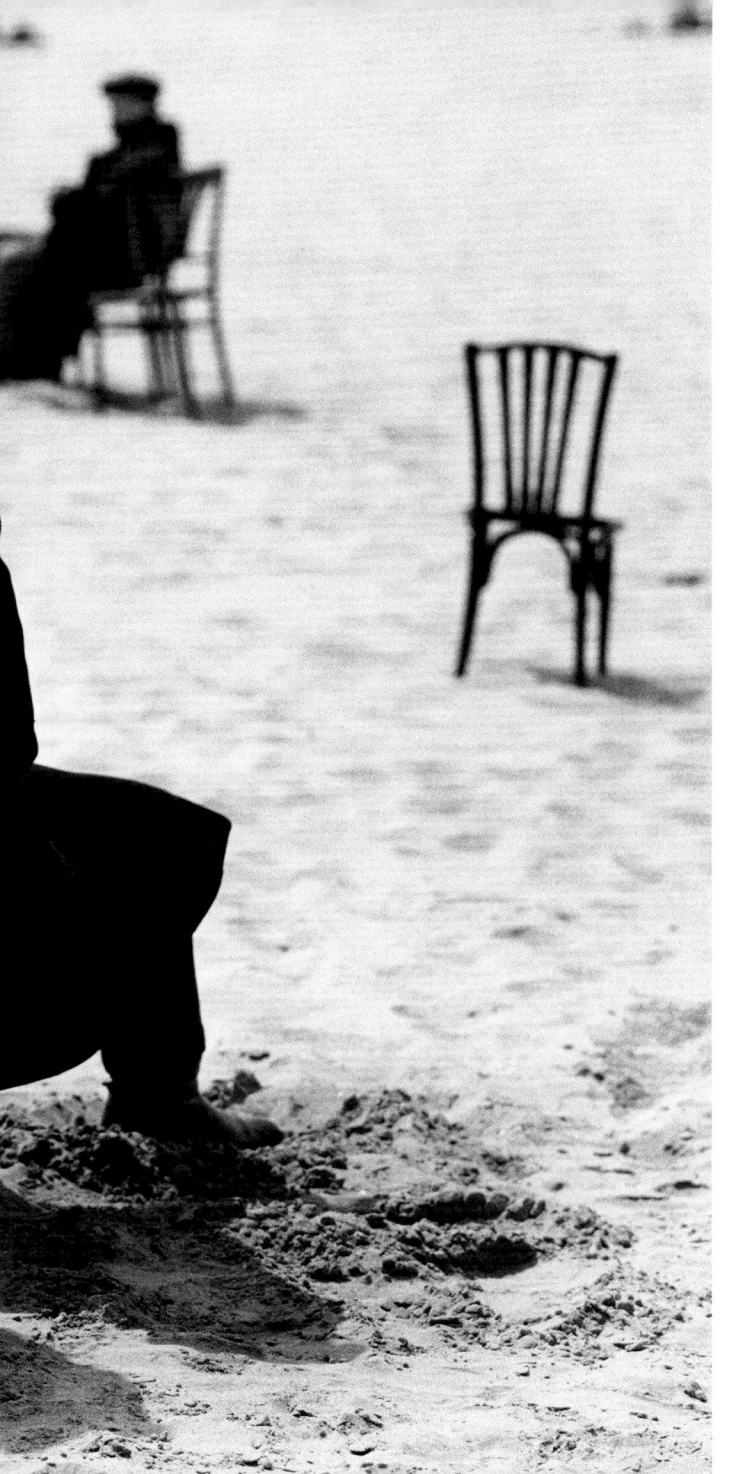

(Previous spread) Tina Turner, *Deauville*, 1989. Shirt and leggings, *Winter* 1989
(Opposite) Tina Turner, *Deauville*, 1989. Dress, *Haute Couture Winter* 1989
(Following spread) Tina Turner, *Deauville*, 1989. Coat, *Winter* 1989

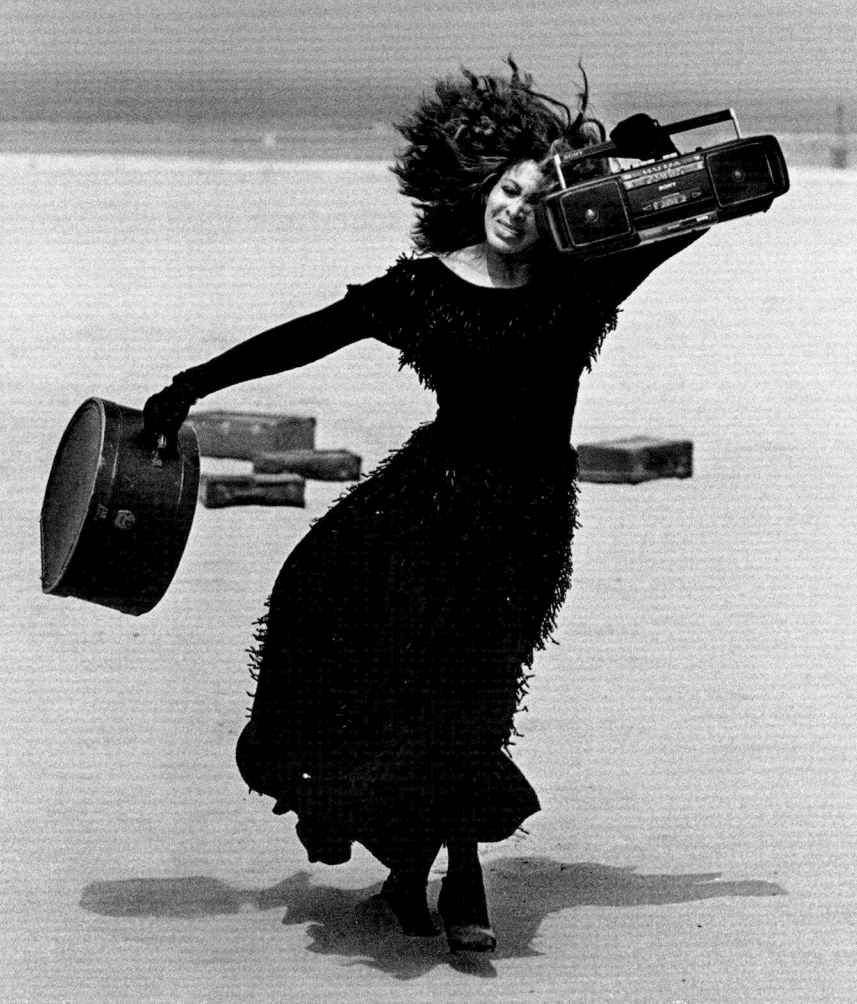

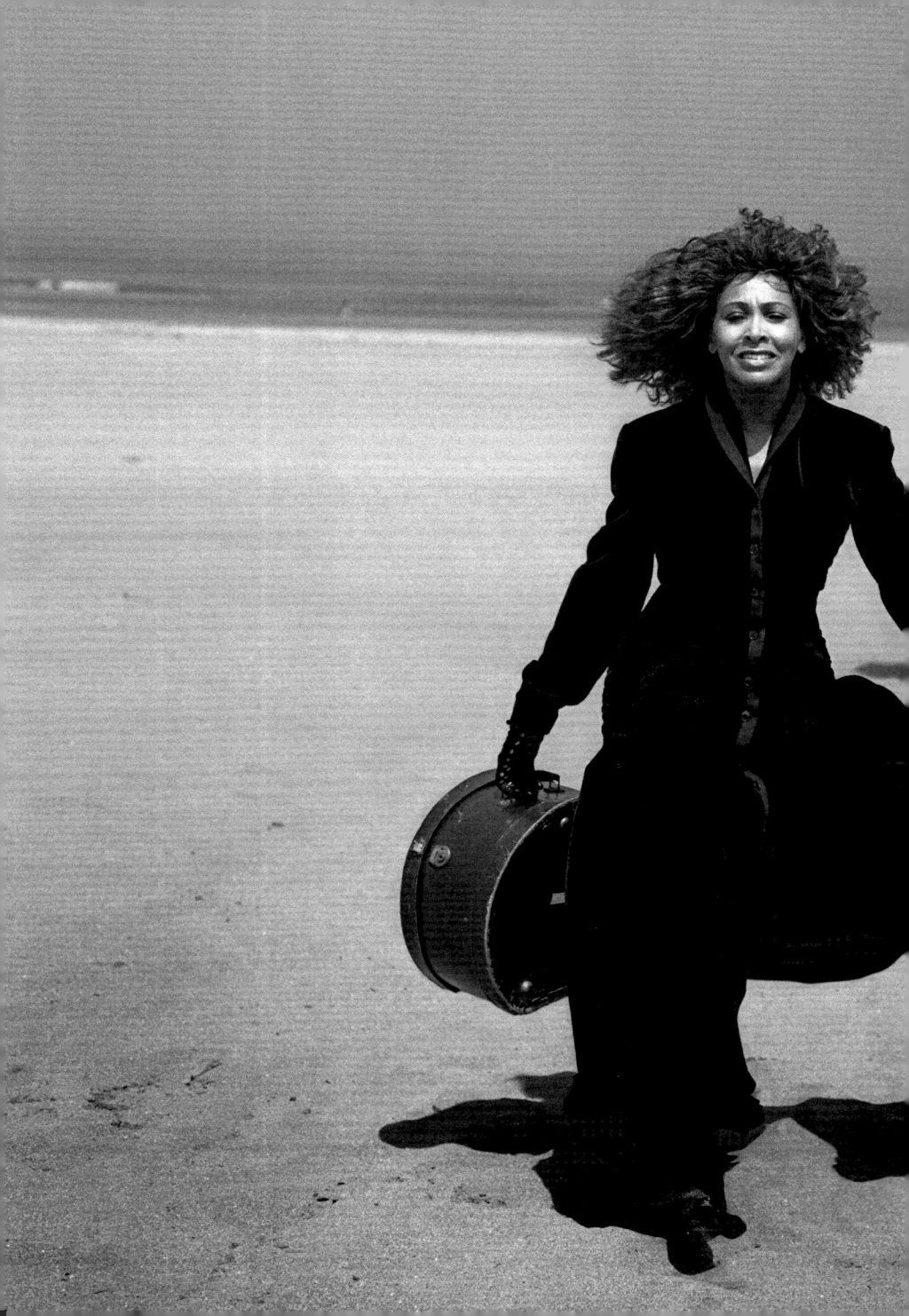

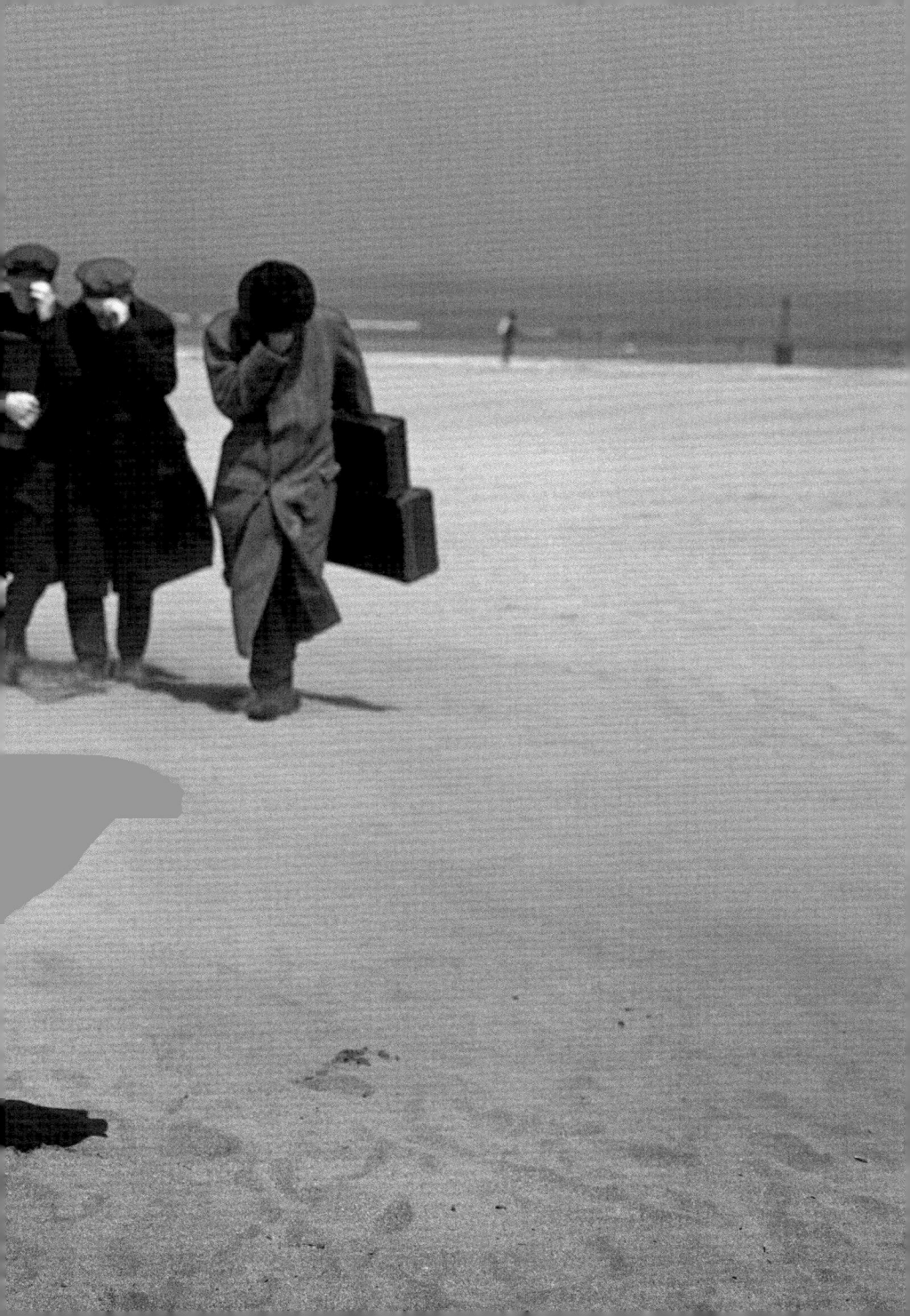

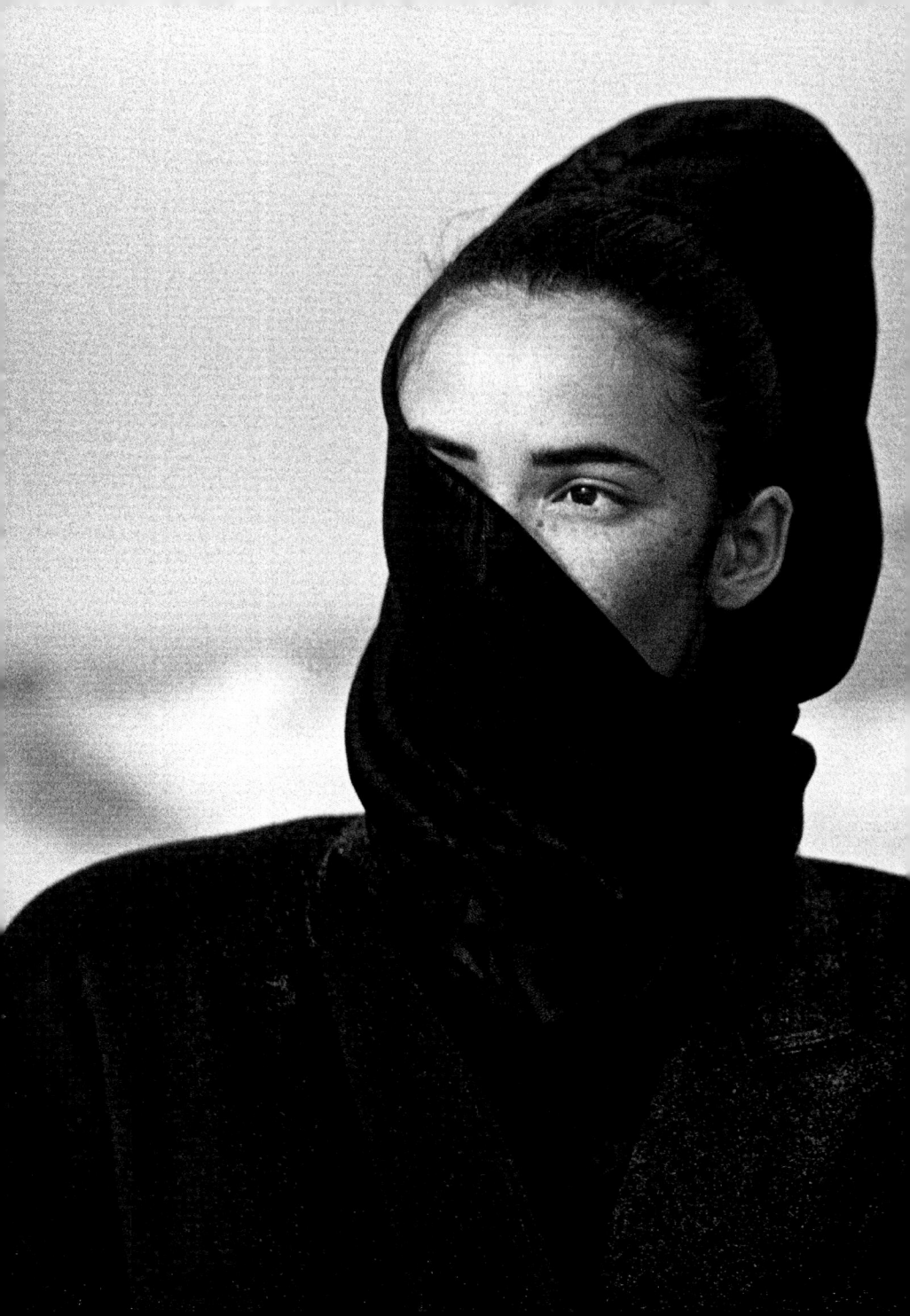

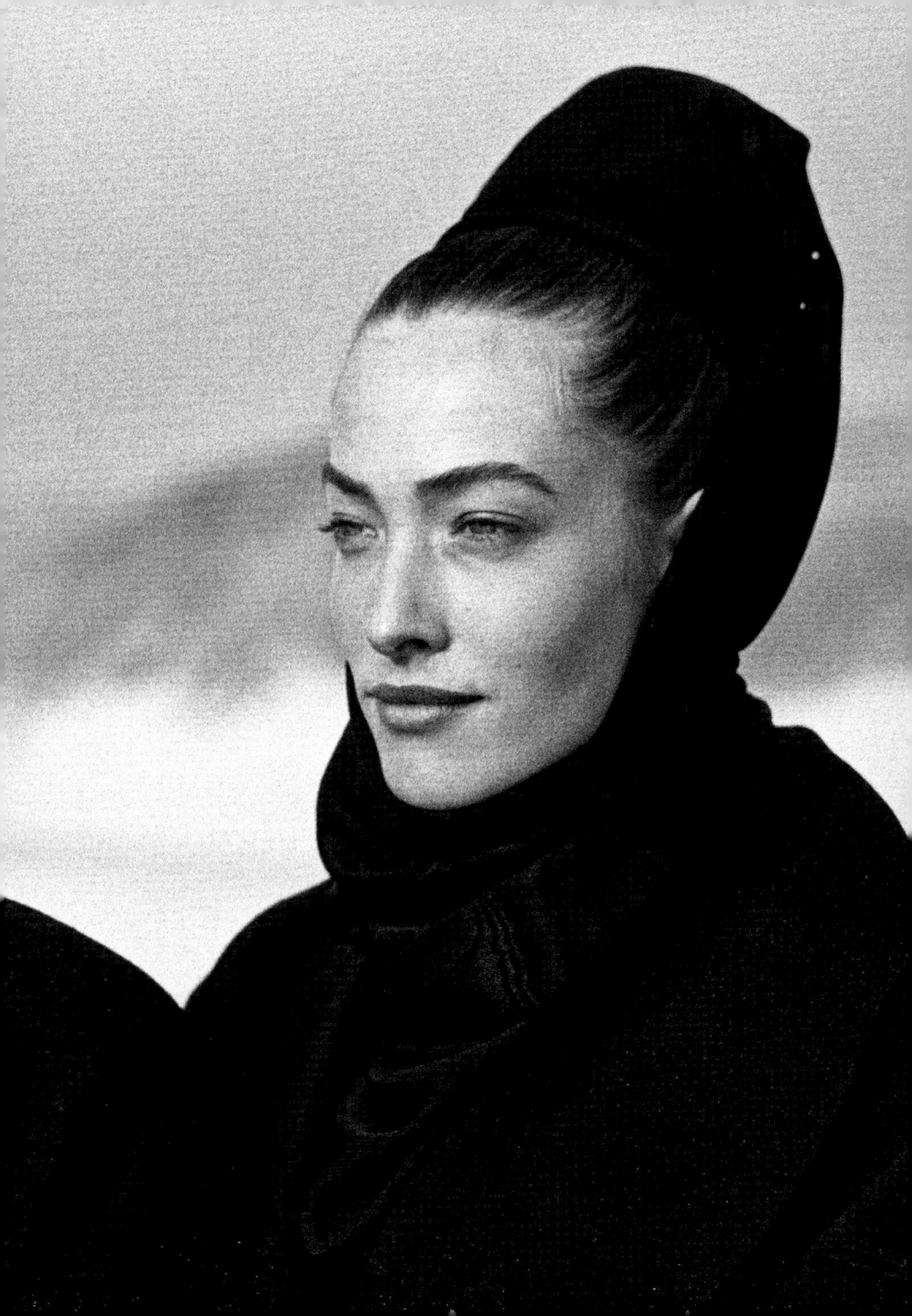

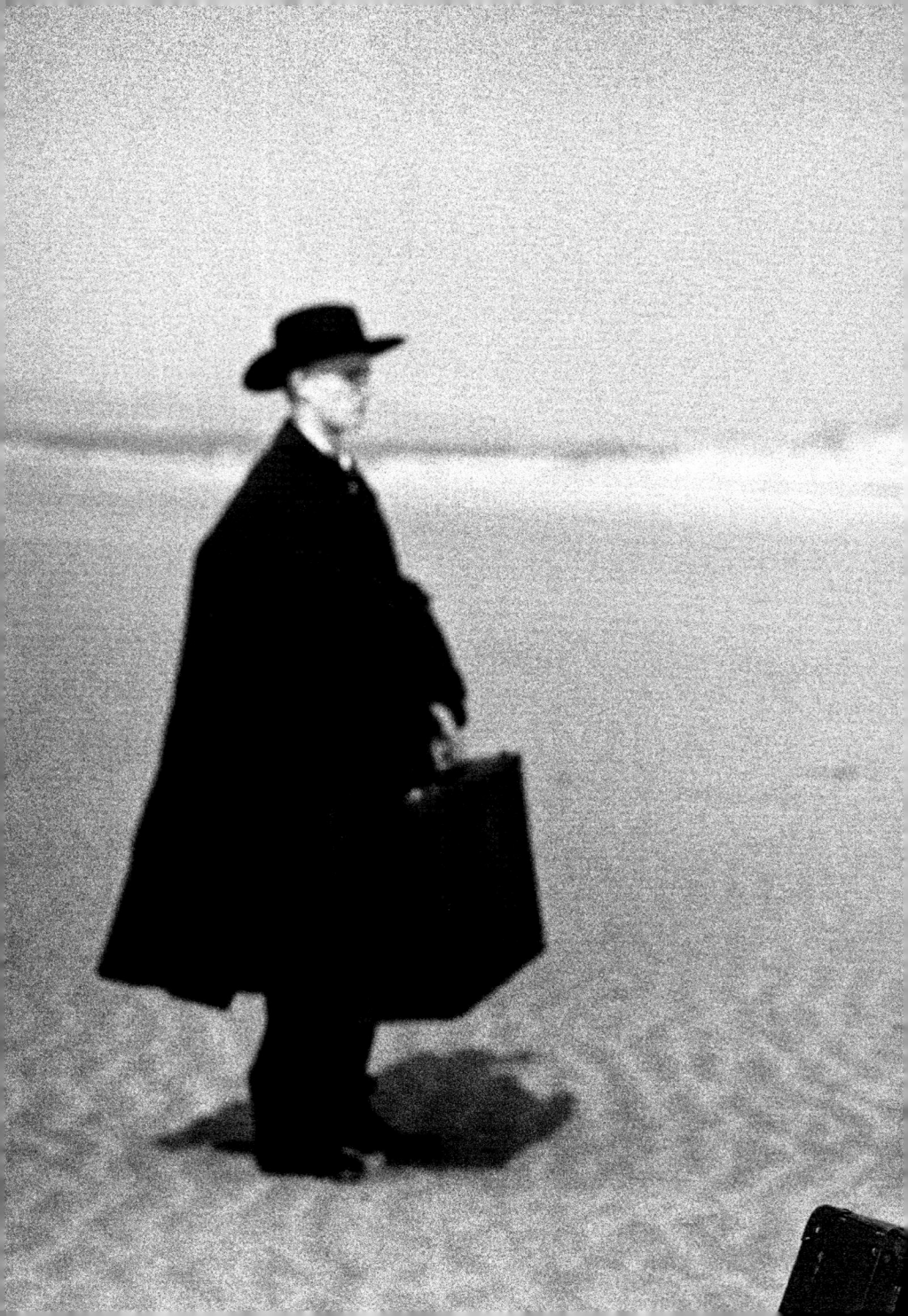

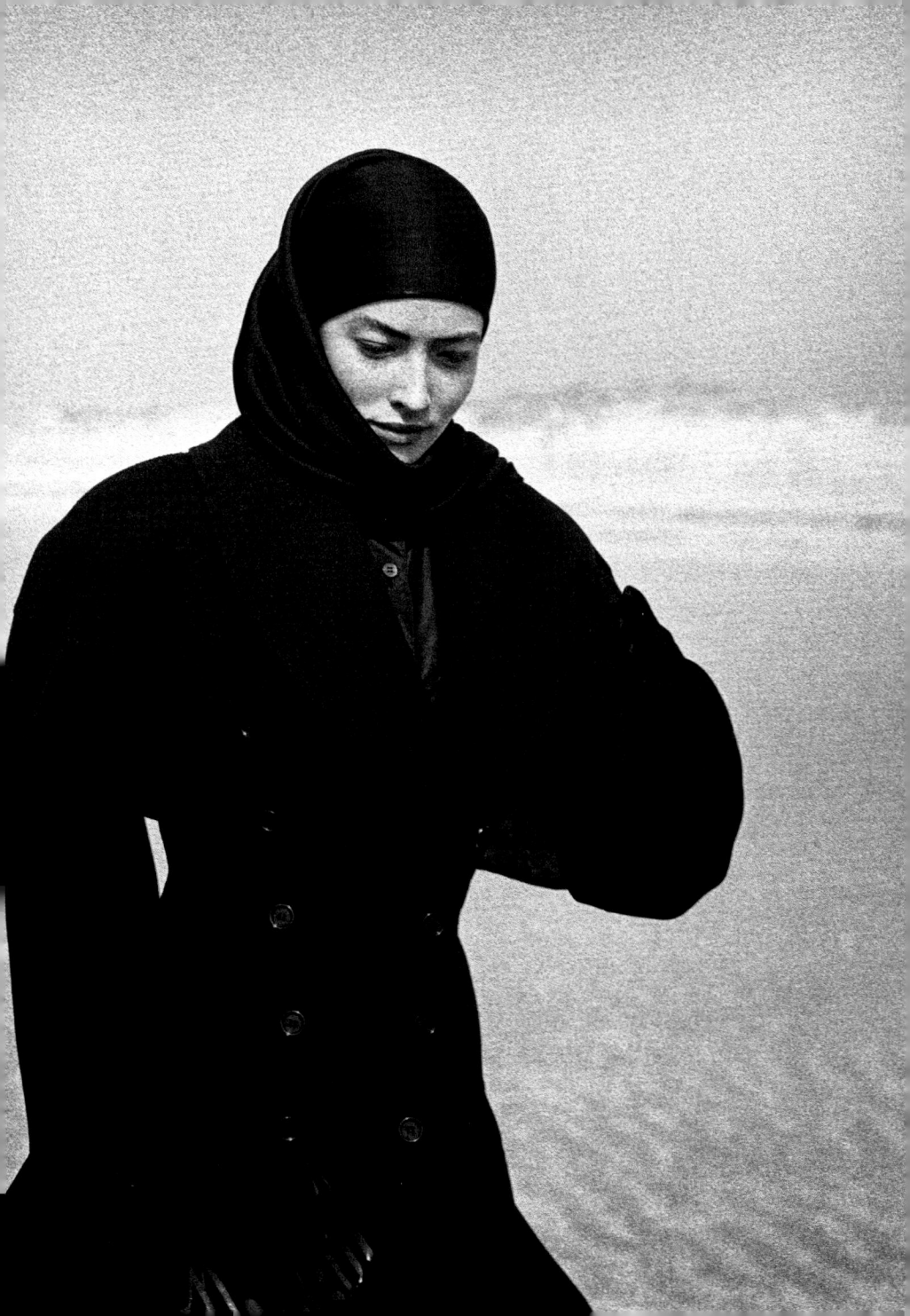

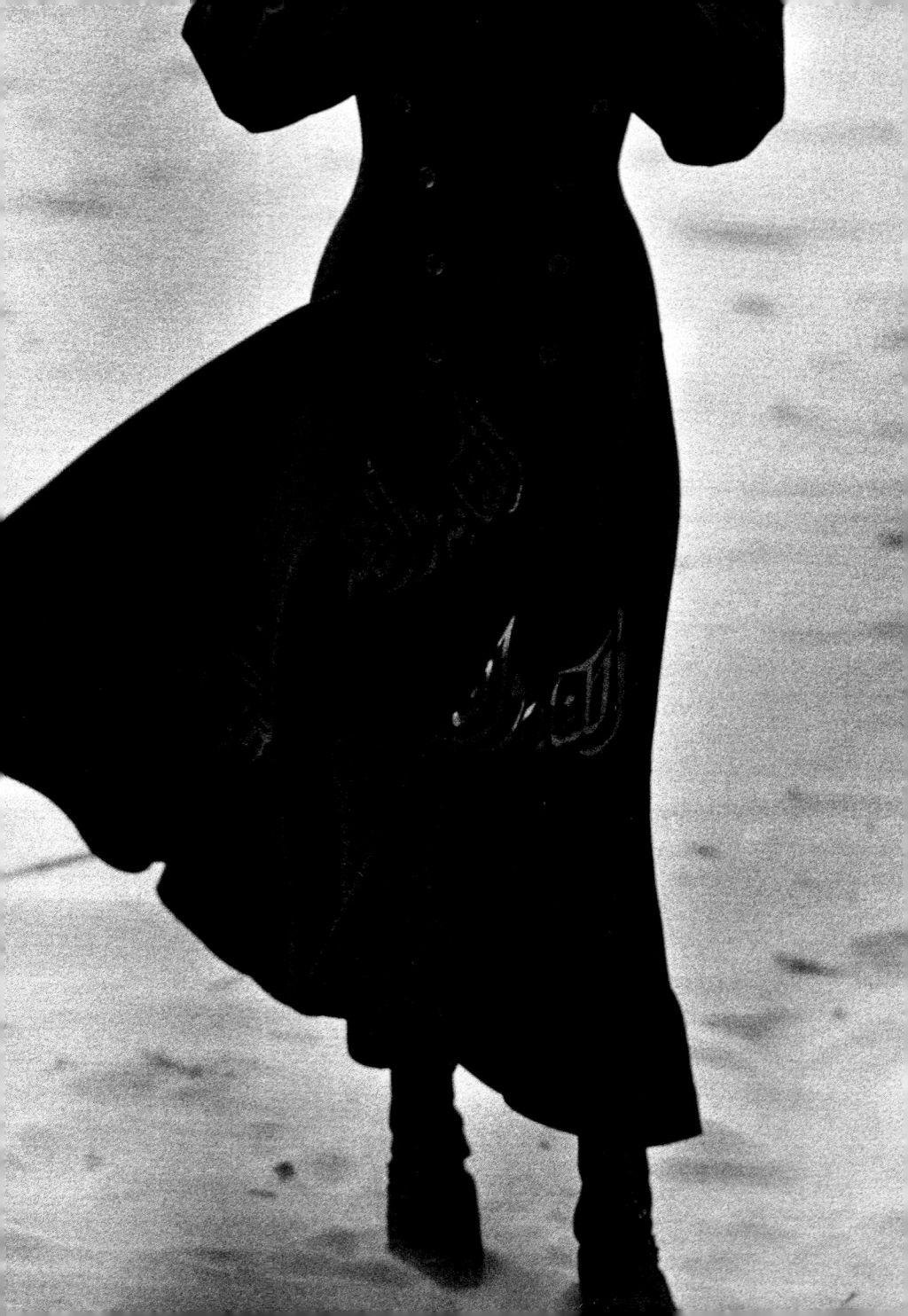

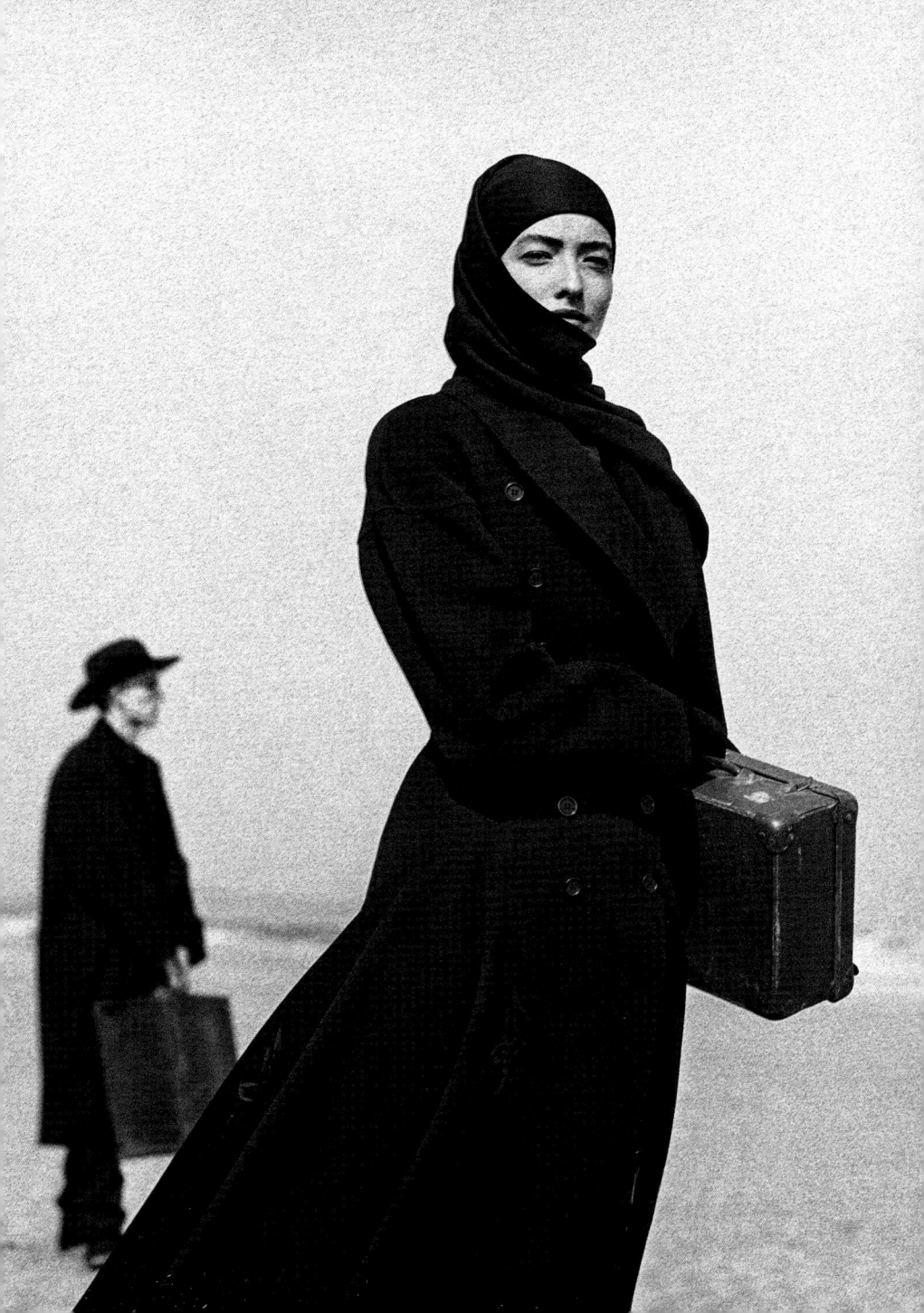

(Previous spreads) Tatjana Patitz and Linda Spierings, *Le Touquet*, 1986
Coats and hooded dresses, *Winter* 1986
(Opposite) Tatjana Patitz, *Le Touquet*, 1986
Coat and hooded dress, *Winter* 1986
(Following spread) Tatjana Patitz, *Le Touquet*, 1986
Coat and hooded dress, *Haute Couture* 1986

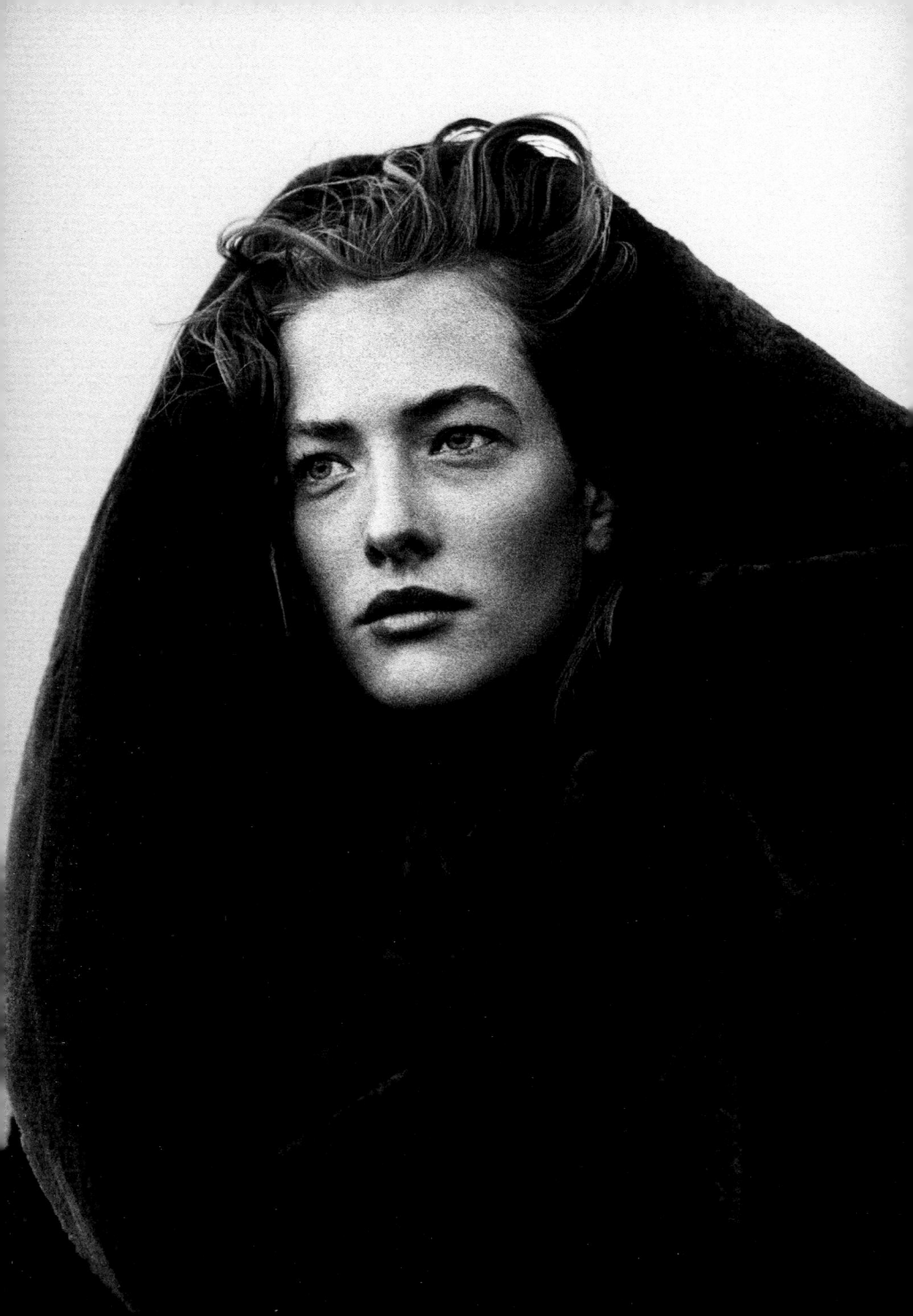

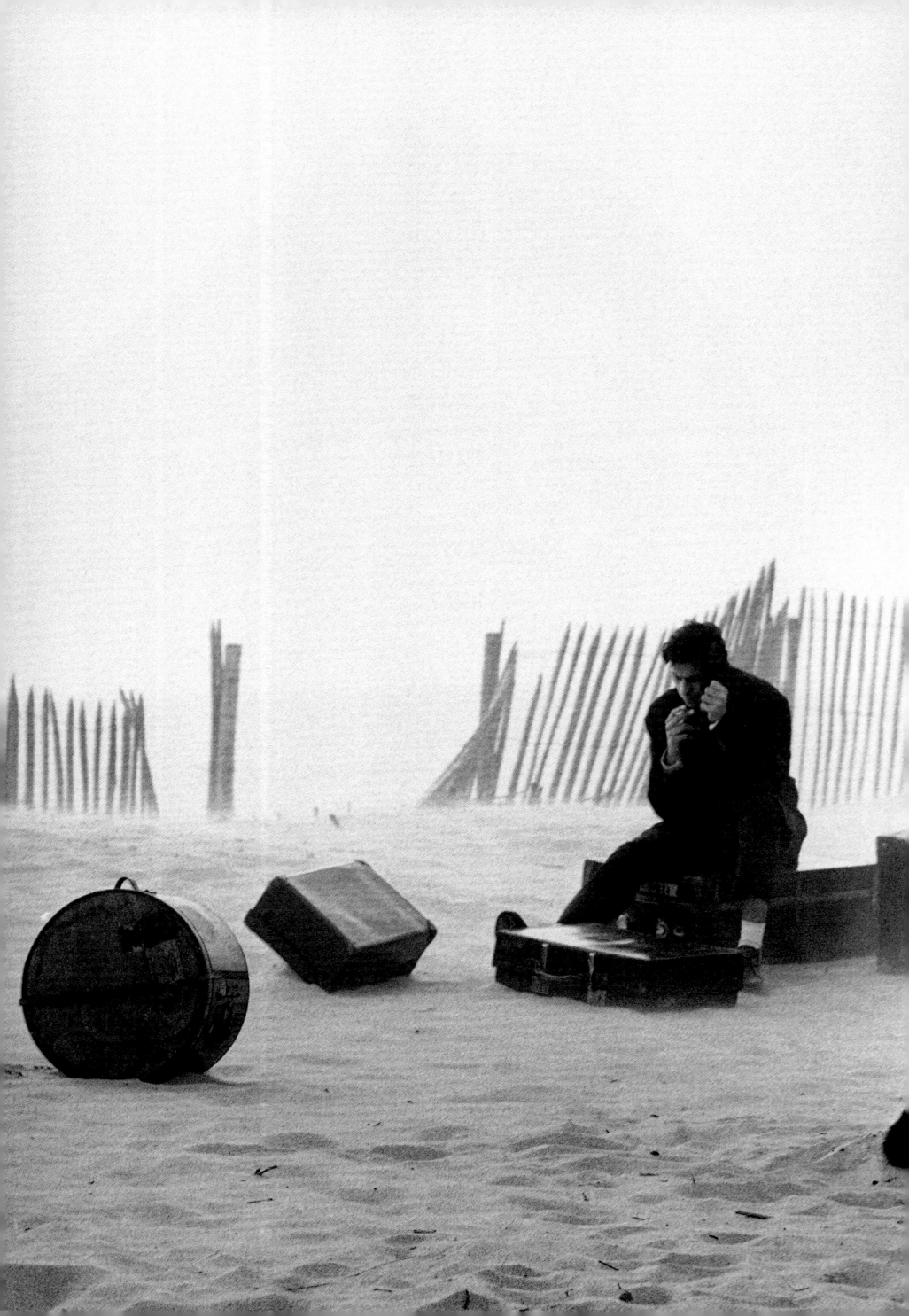

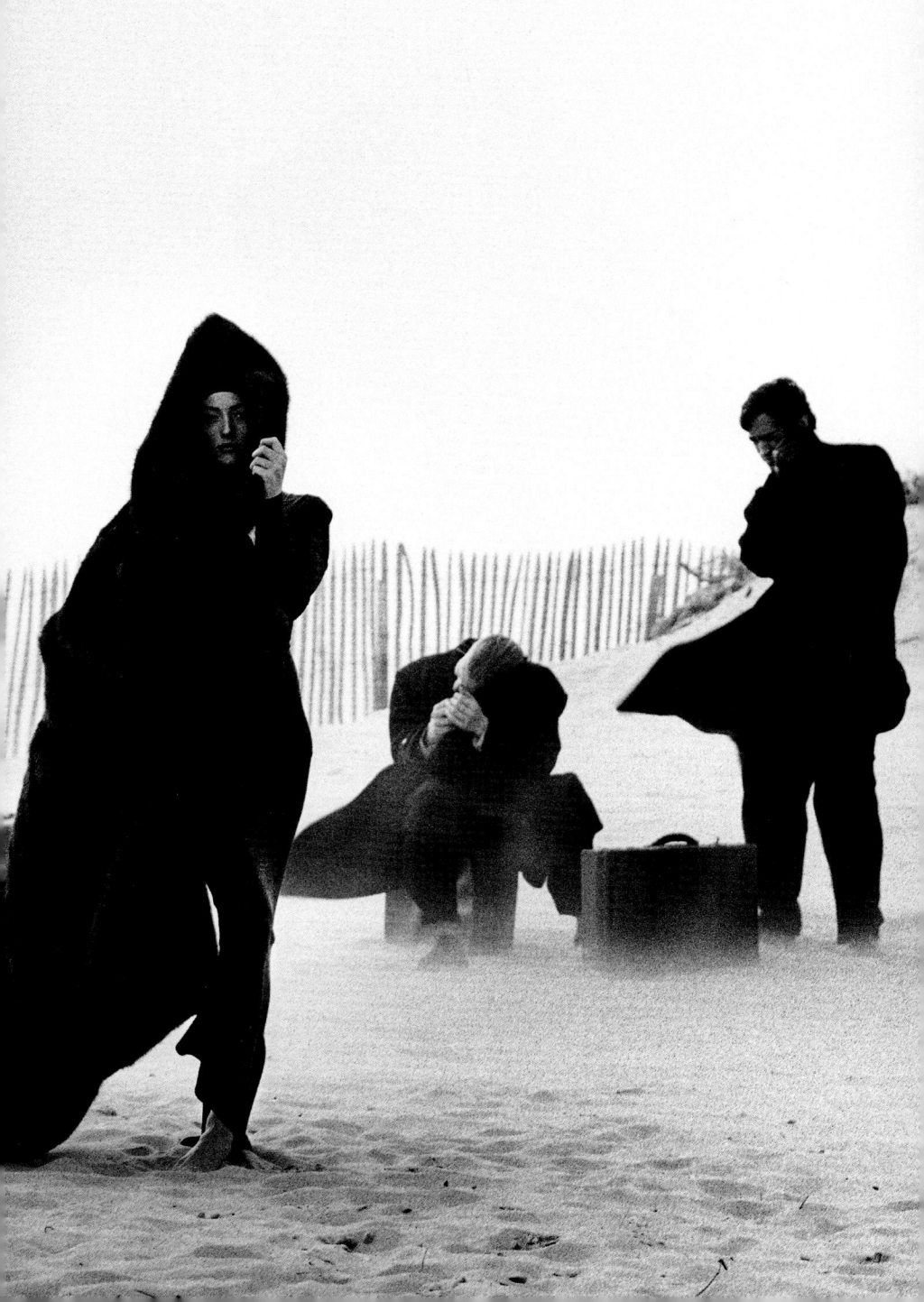

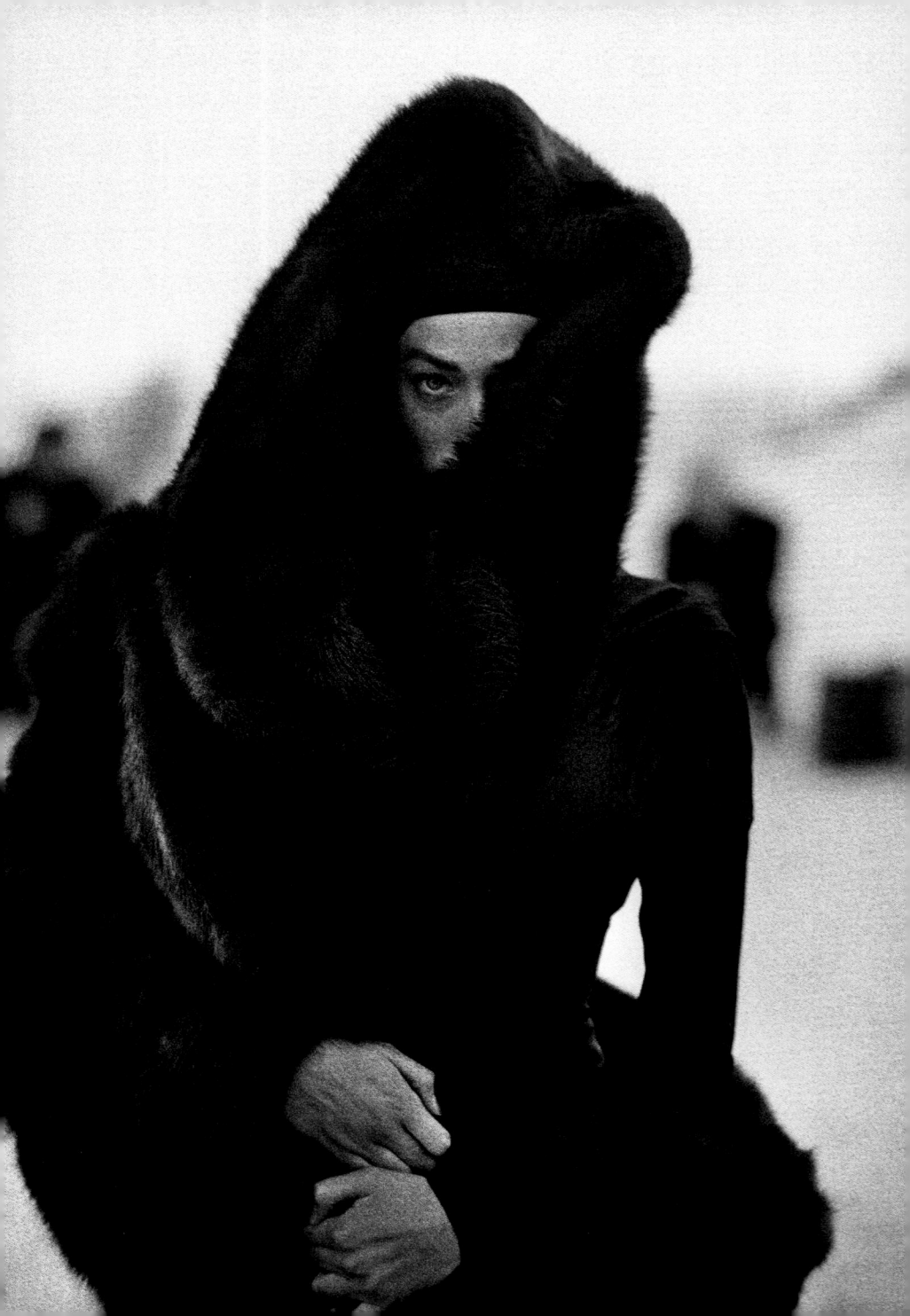

Tatjana Patitz, *Le Touquet*, 1986. Coat and hooded dress, *Haute Couture* 1986
(Following spread) Linda Spierings, *Le Touquet*, 1986. Dress, *Winter* 1986

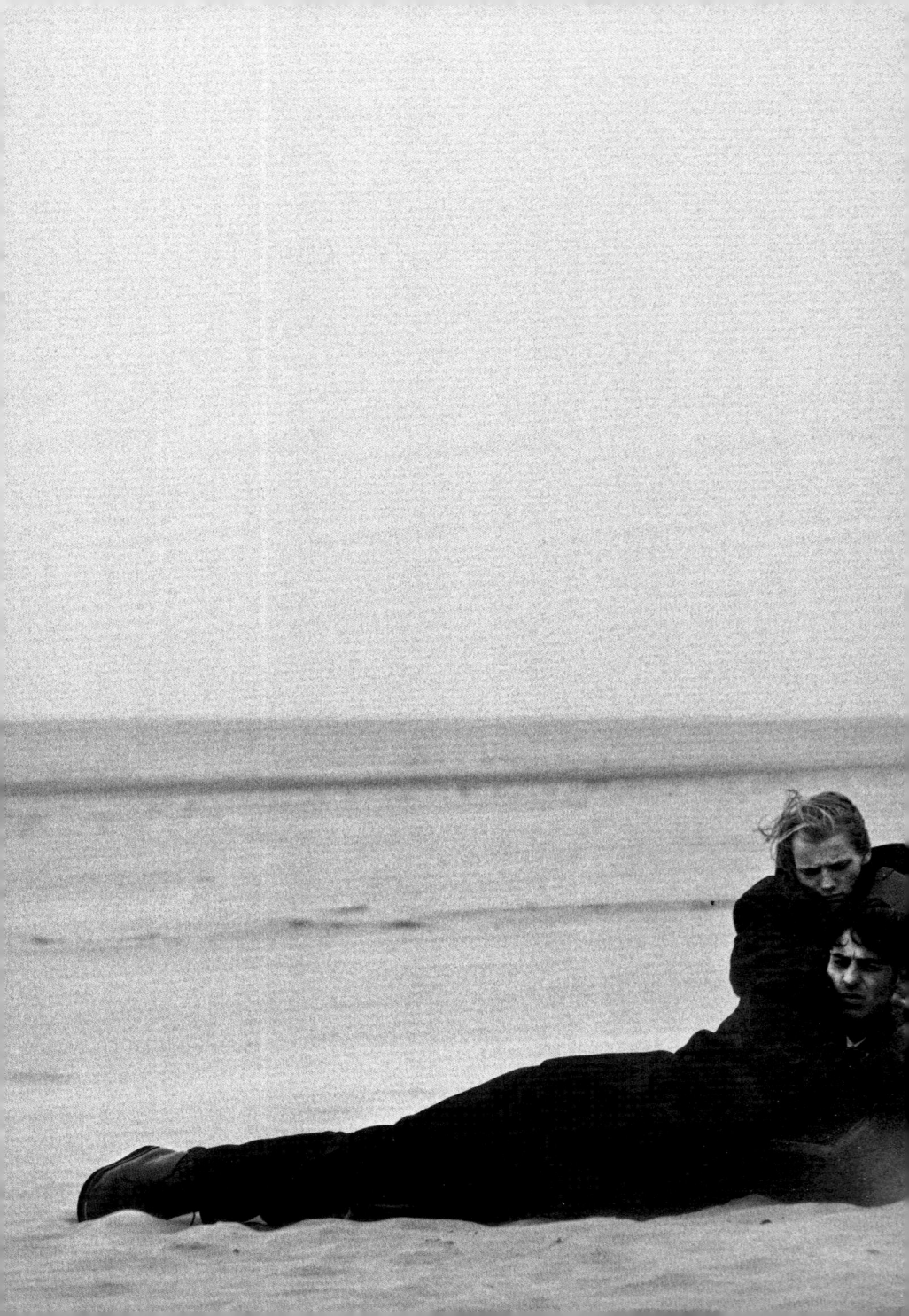

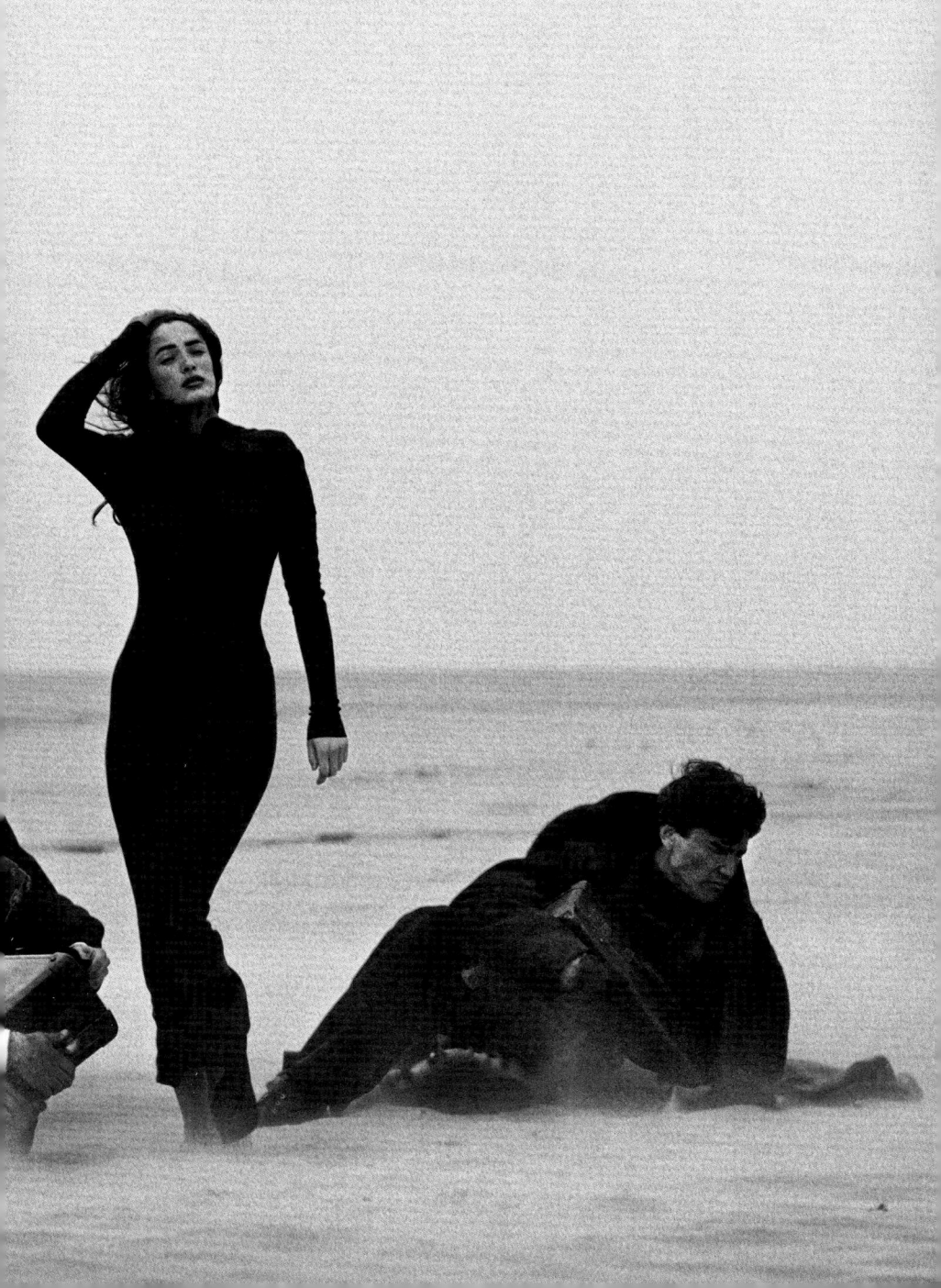

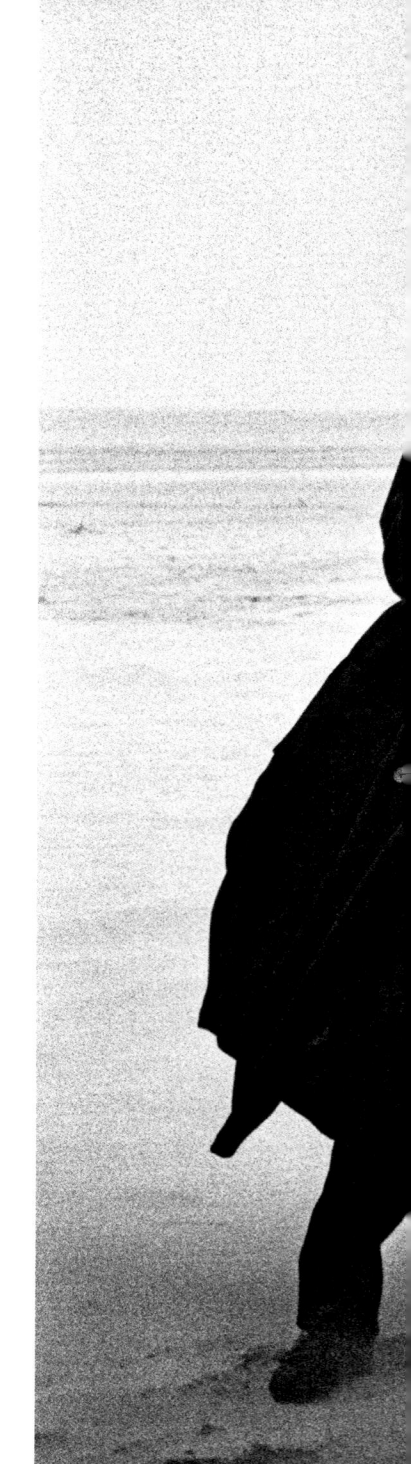

Linda Spierings, *Le Touquet*, 1986
Hooded dress, *Haute Couture* 1986
(Following spread) Linda Spierings, *Le Touquet*, 1986
Dress, *Winter* 1986

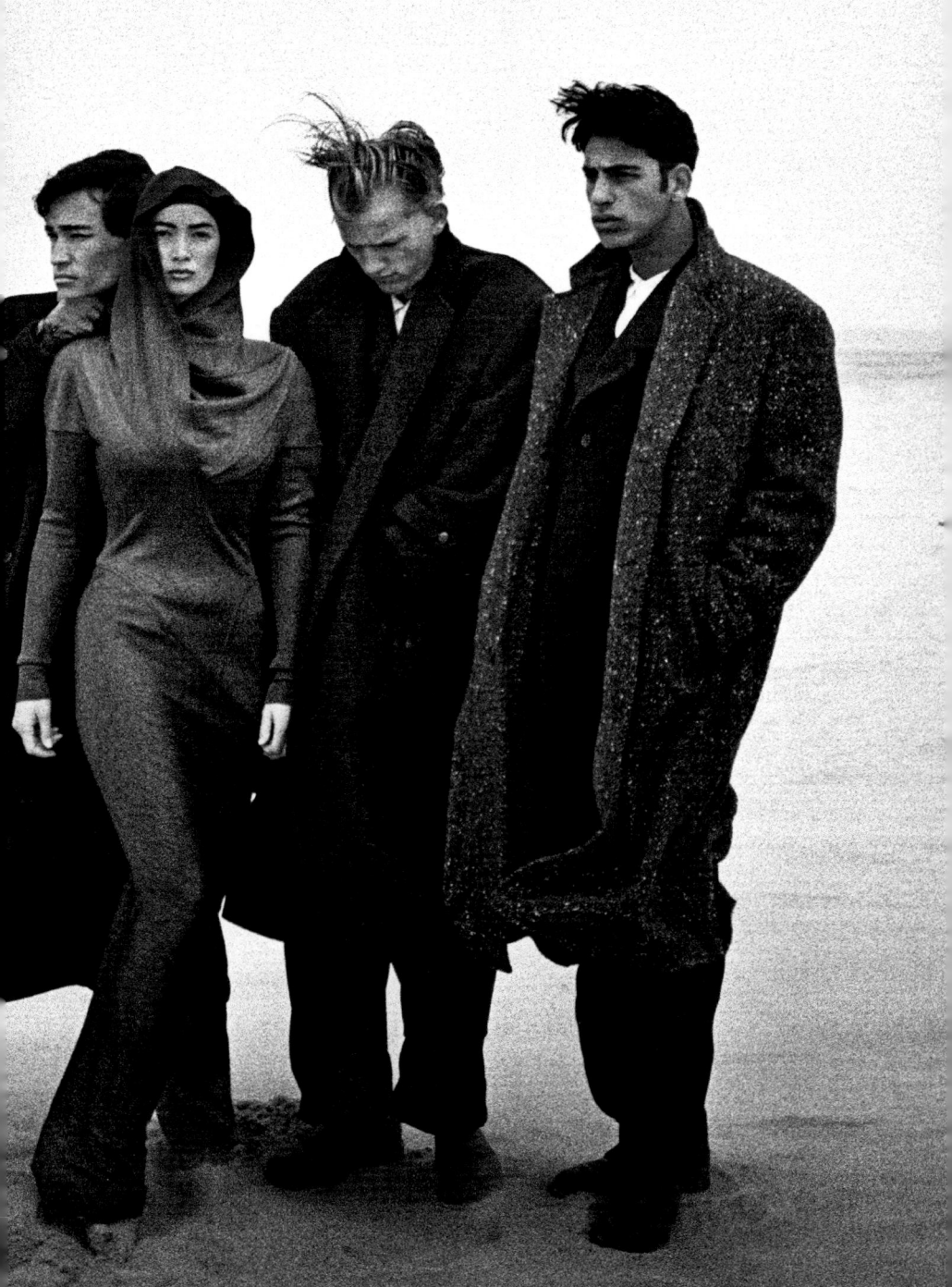

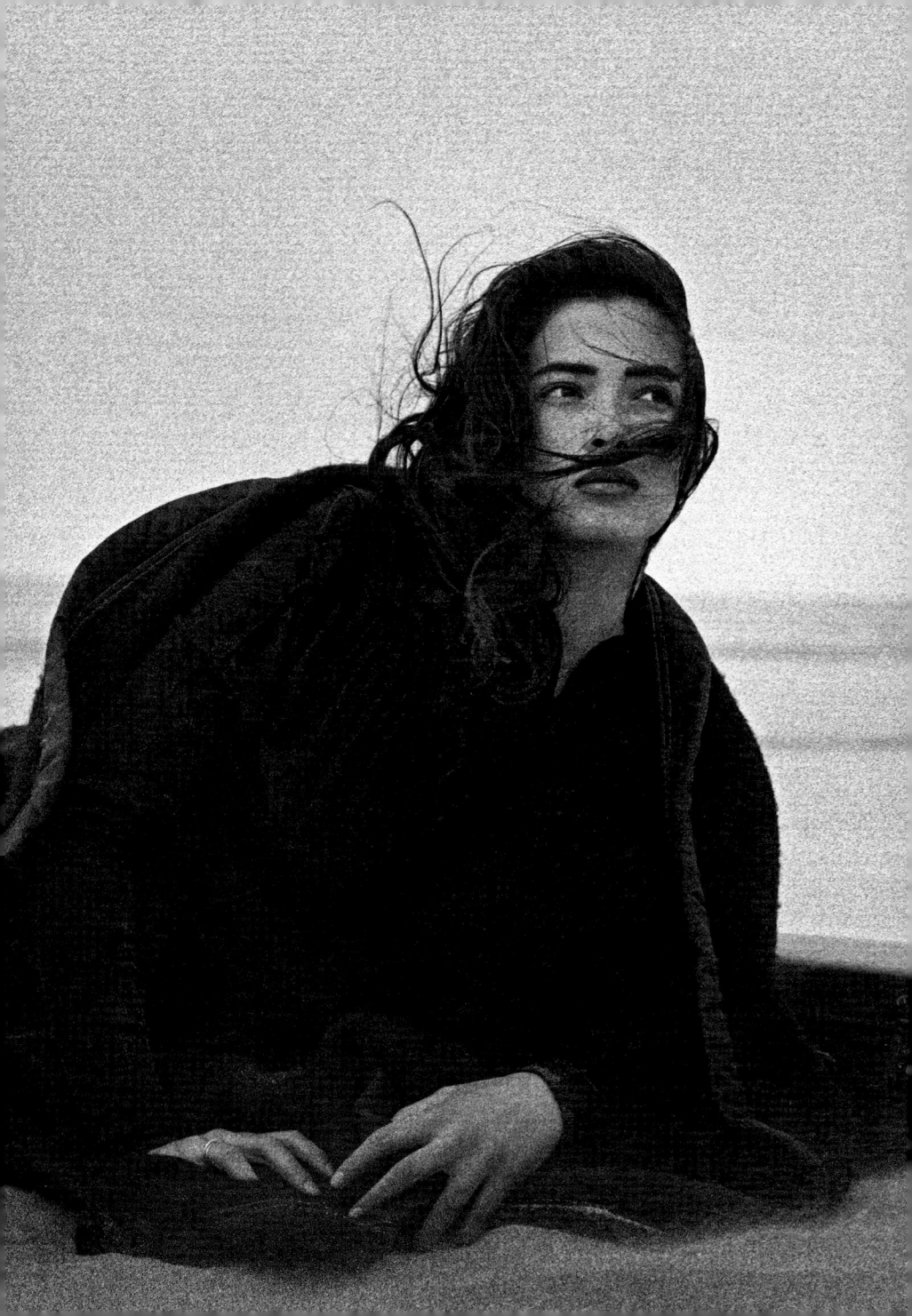

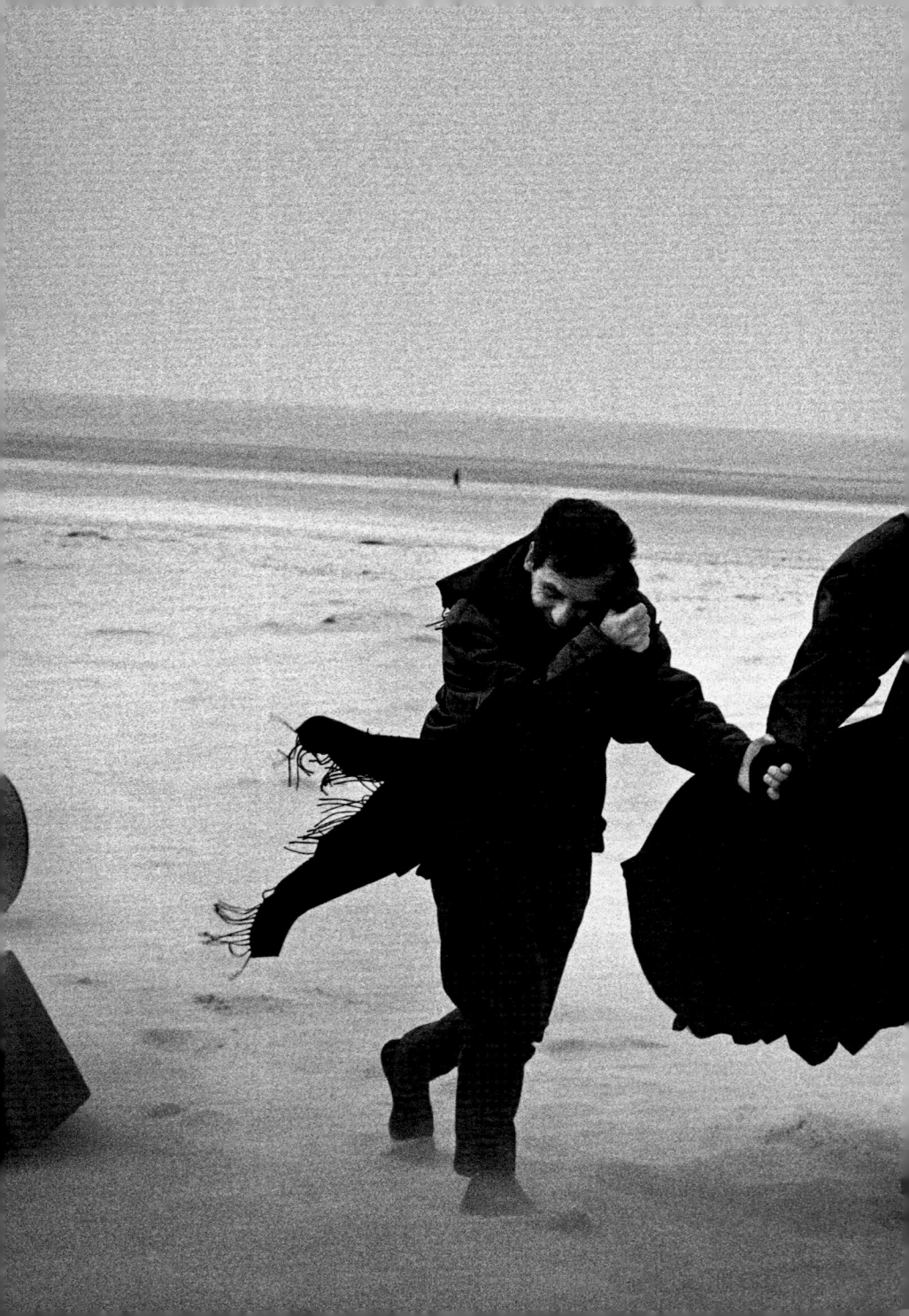

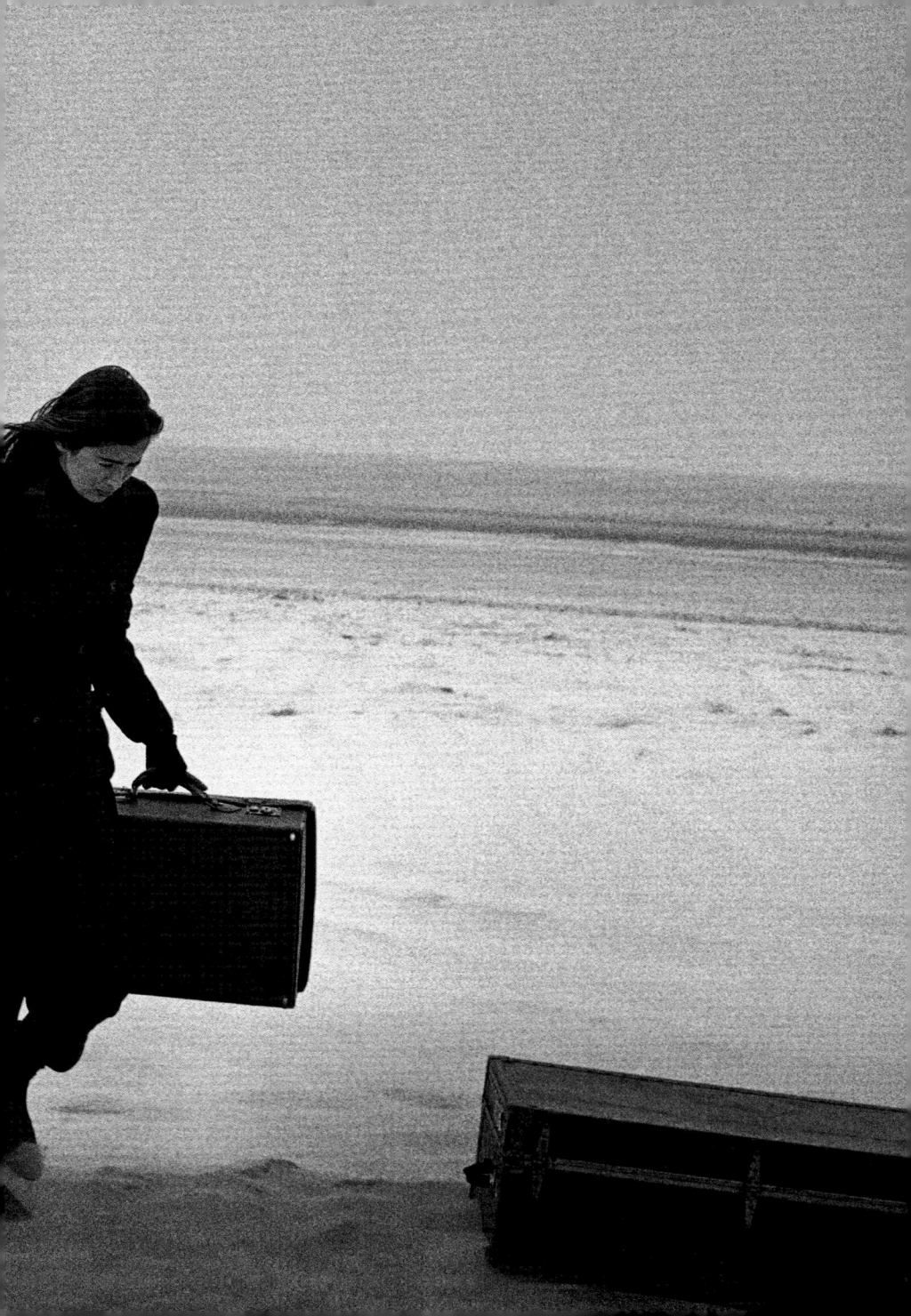

(Previous spread) Azzedine Alaïa and Linda Spierings,
Le Touquet, 1986. Coat, *Winter* 1986
(Opposite) Marie-Sophie Wilson, *Paris*, 1988. Jacket and skirt, *Winter* 1986
(Following spread) Marie-Sophie Wilson, *Paris*, 1988
Jacket, *Winter* 1986. Jacket and skirt, *Winter* 1987

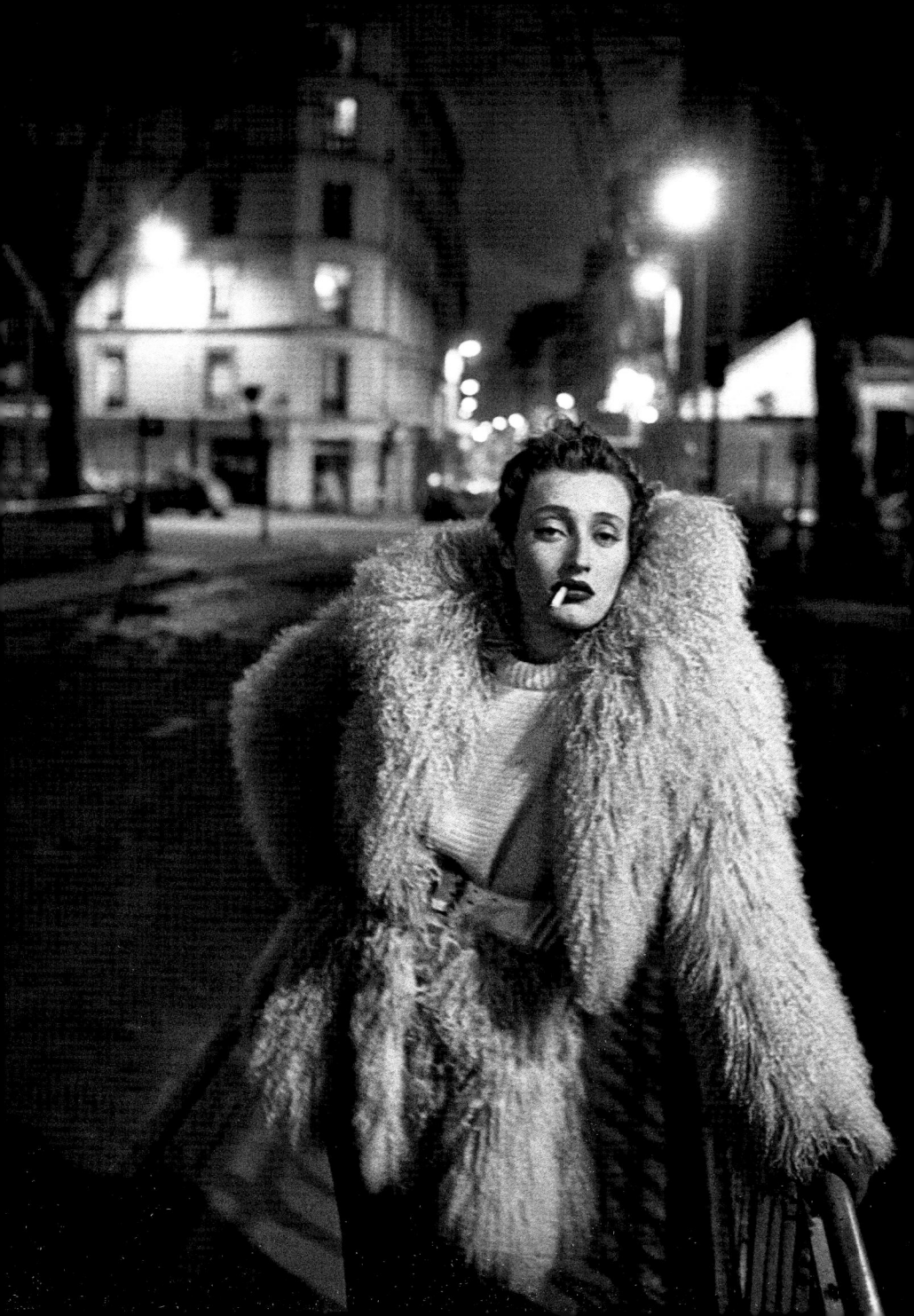

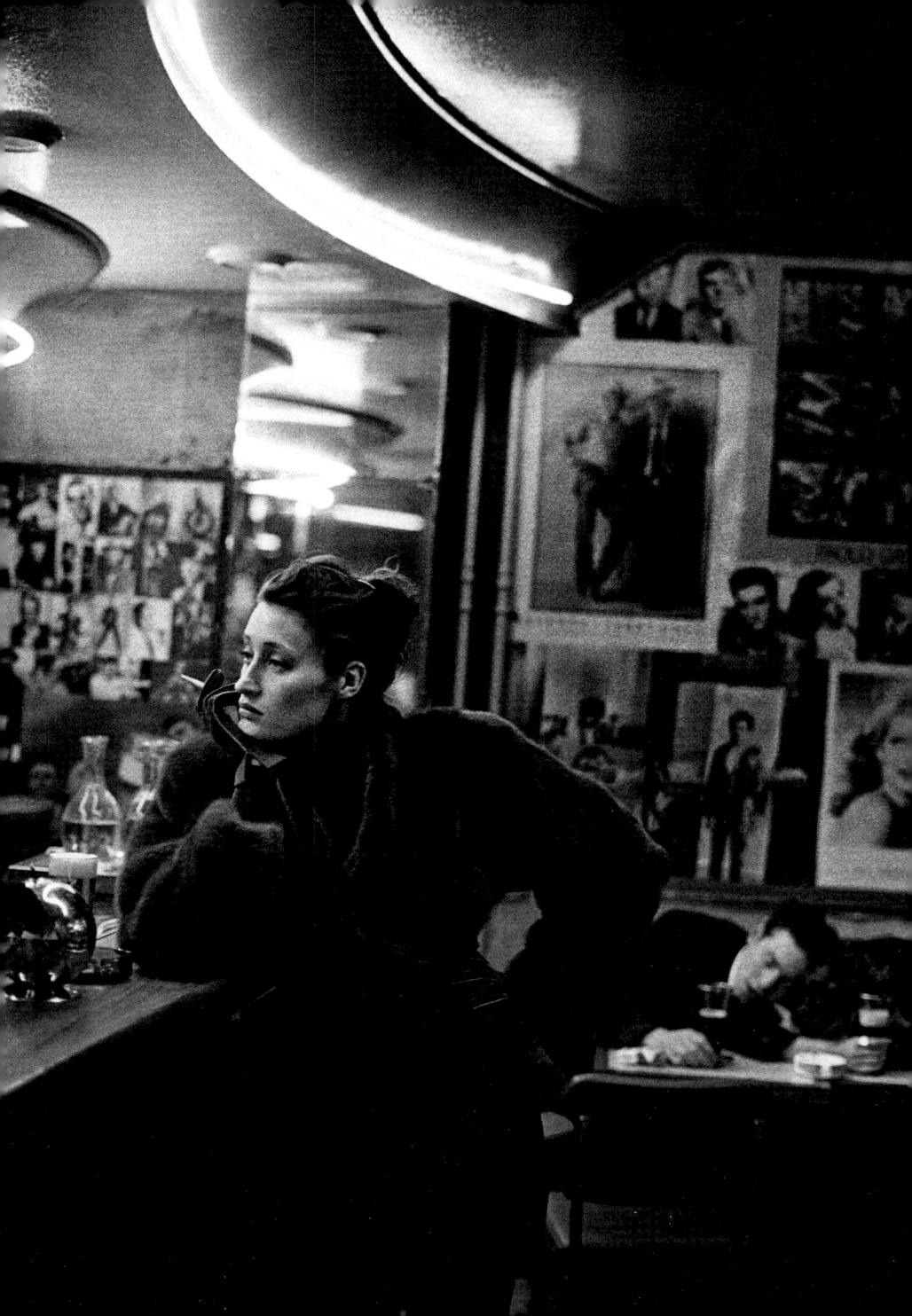

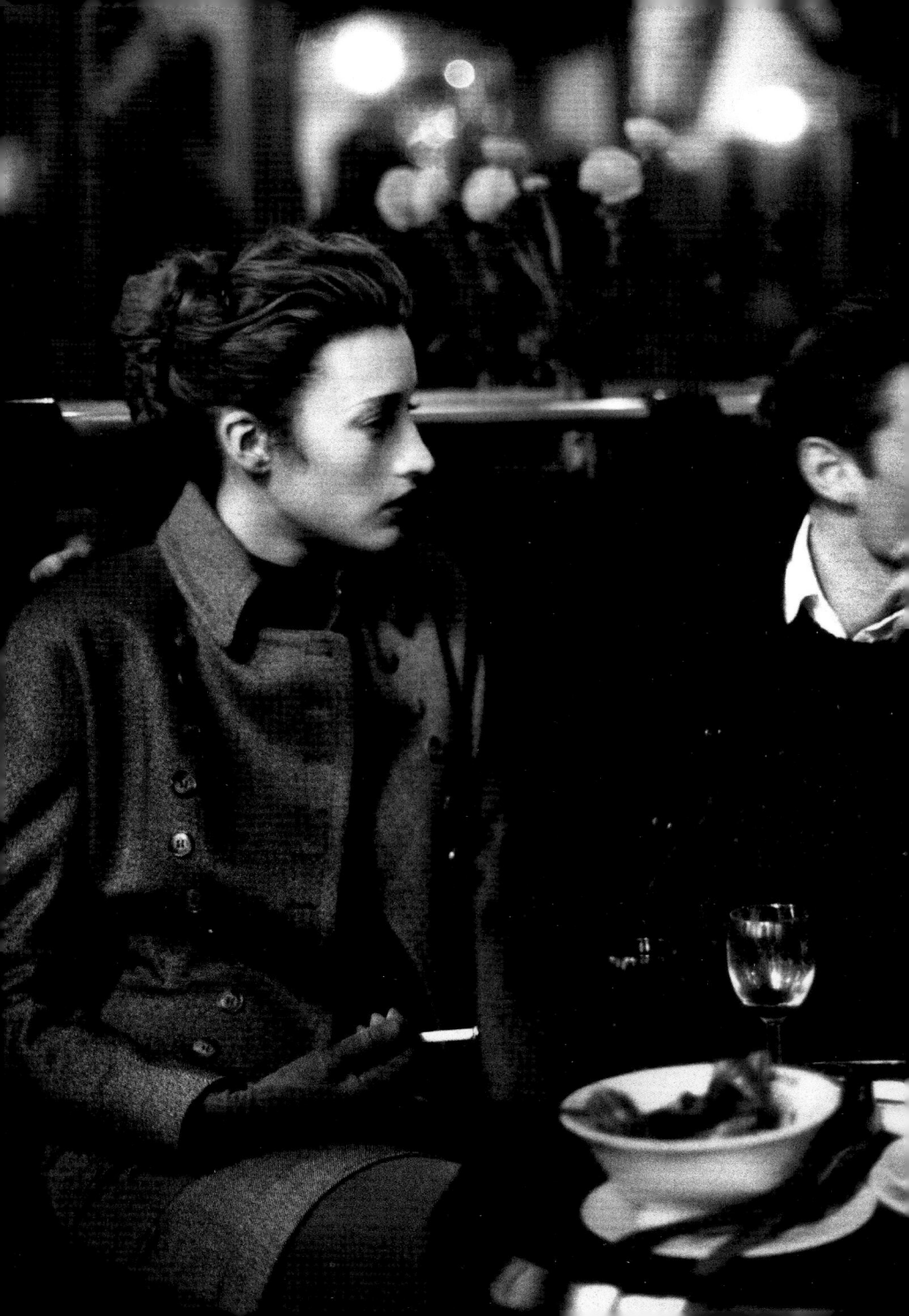

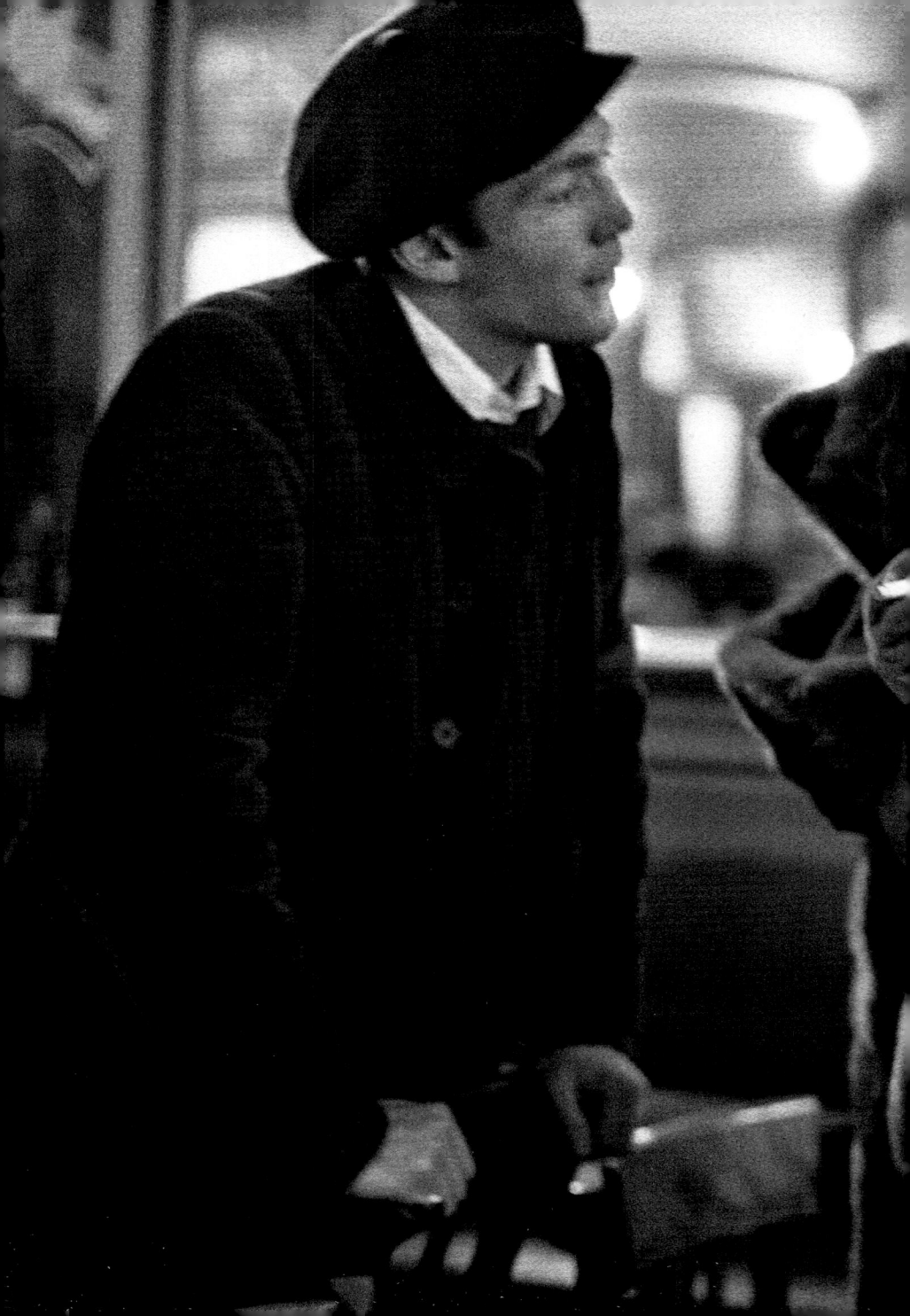

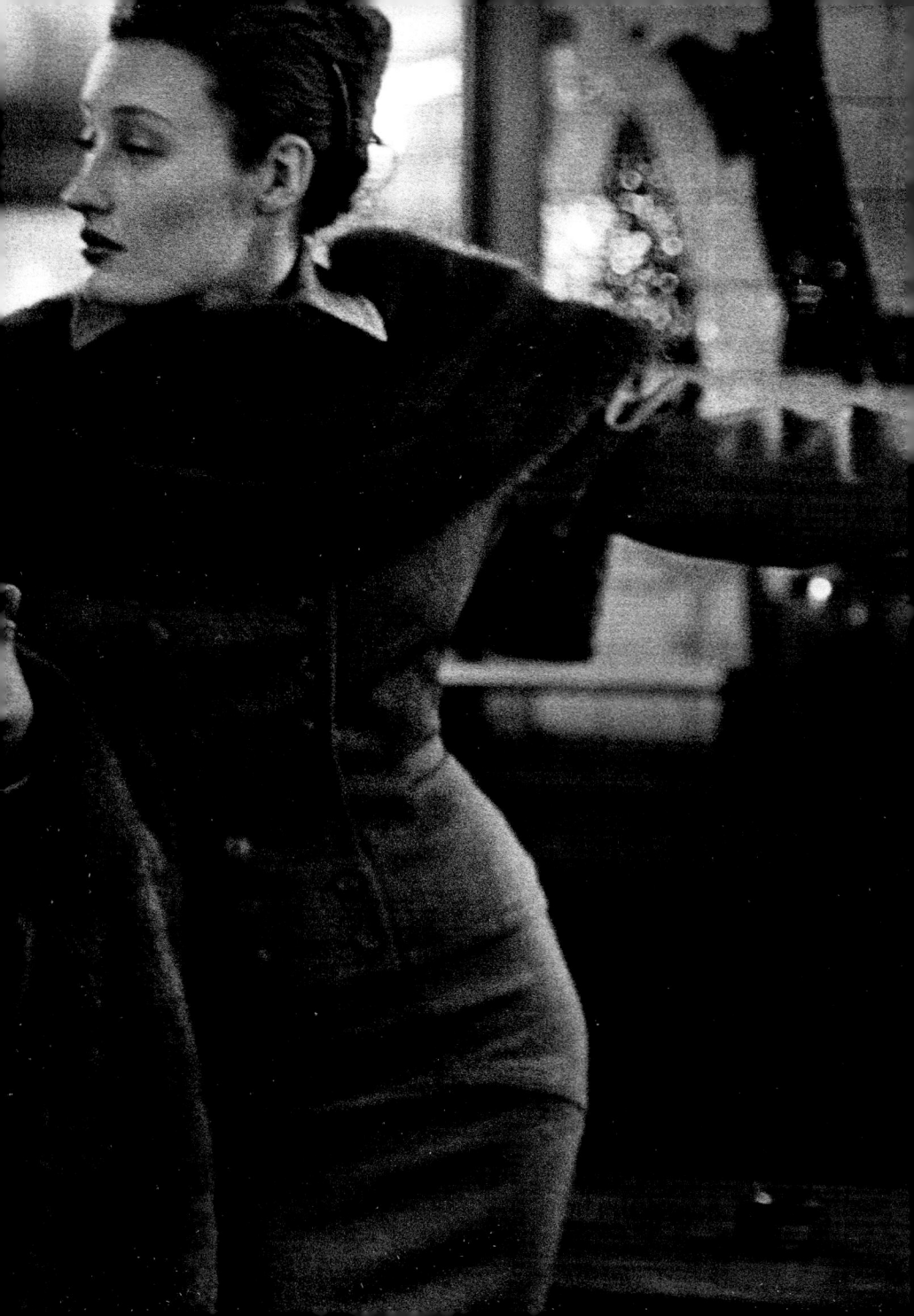

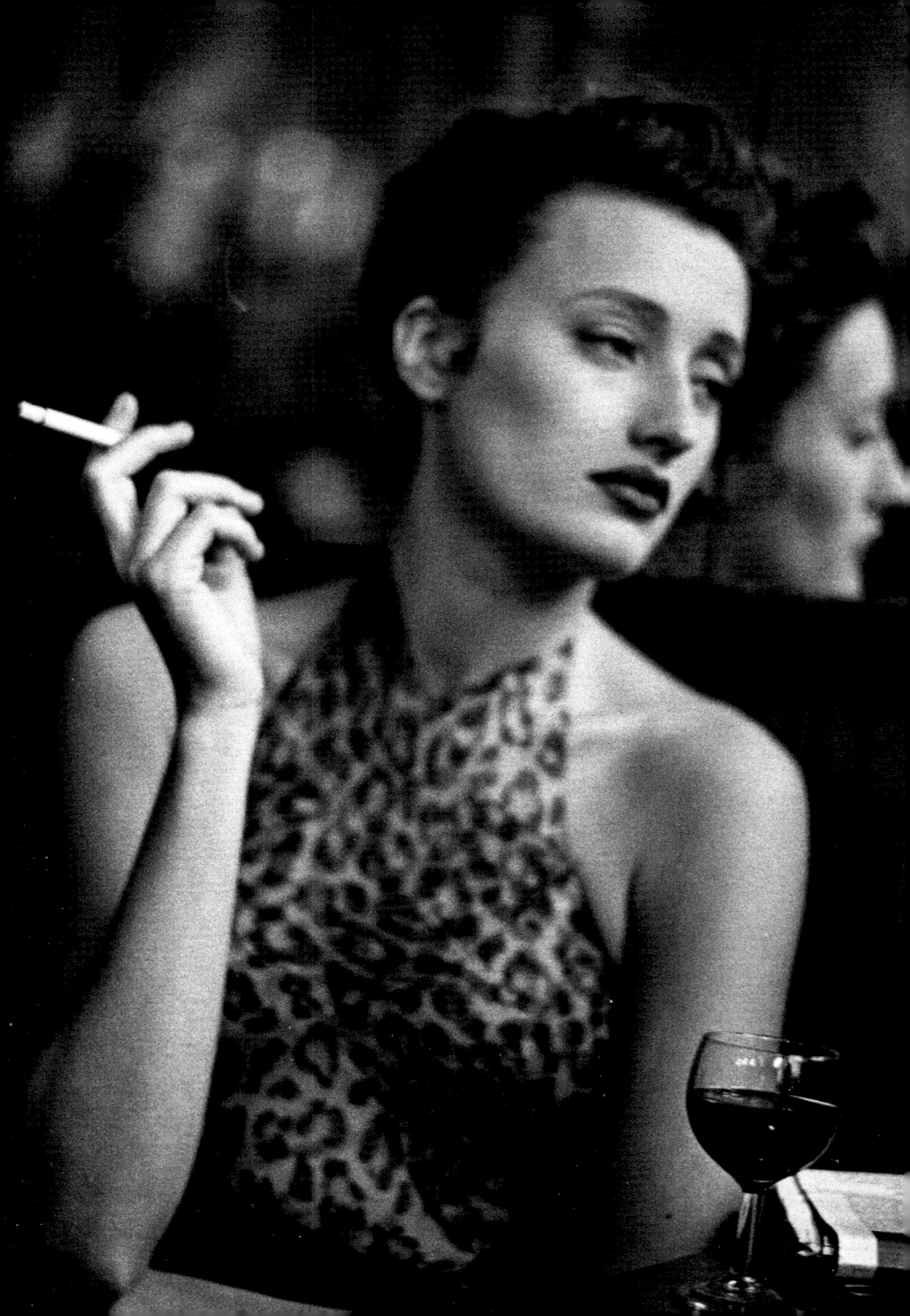

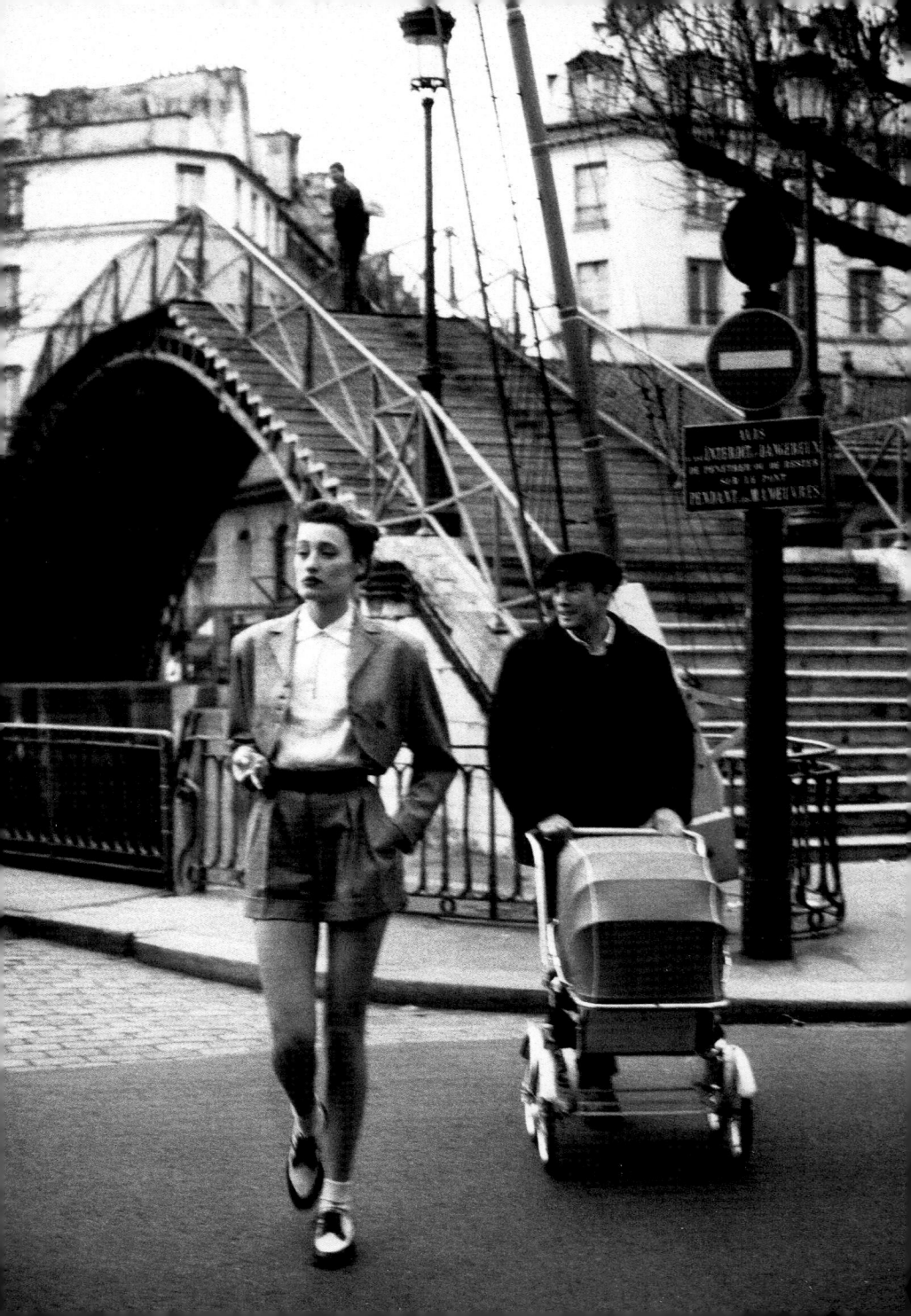

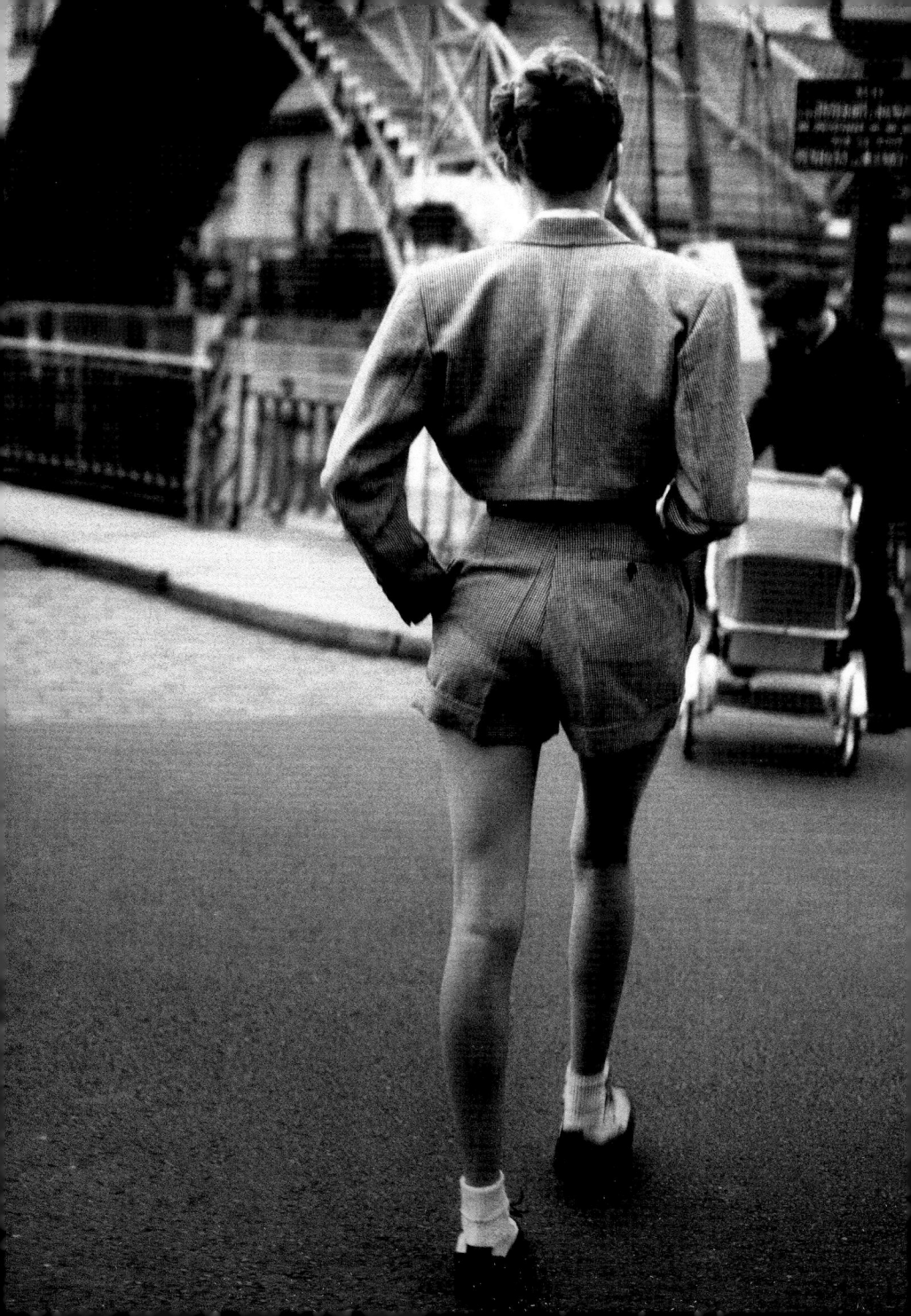

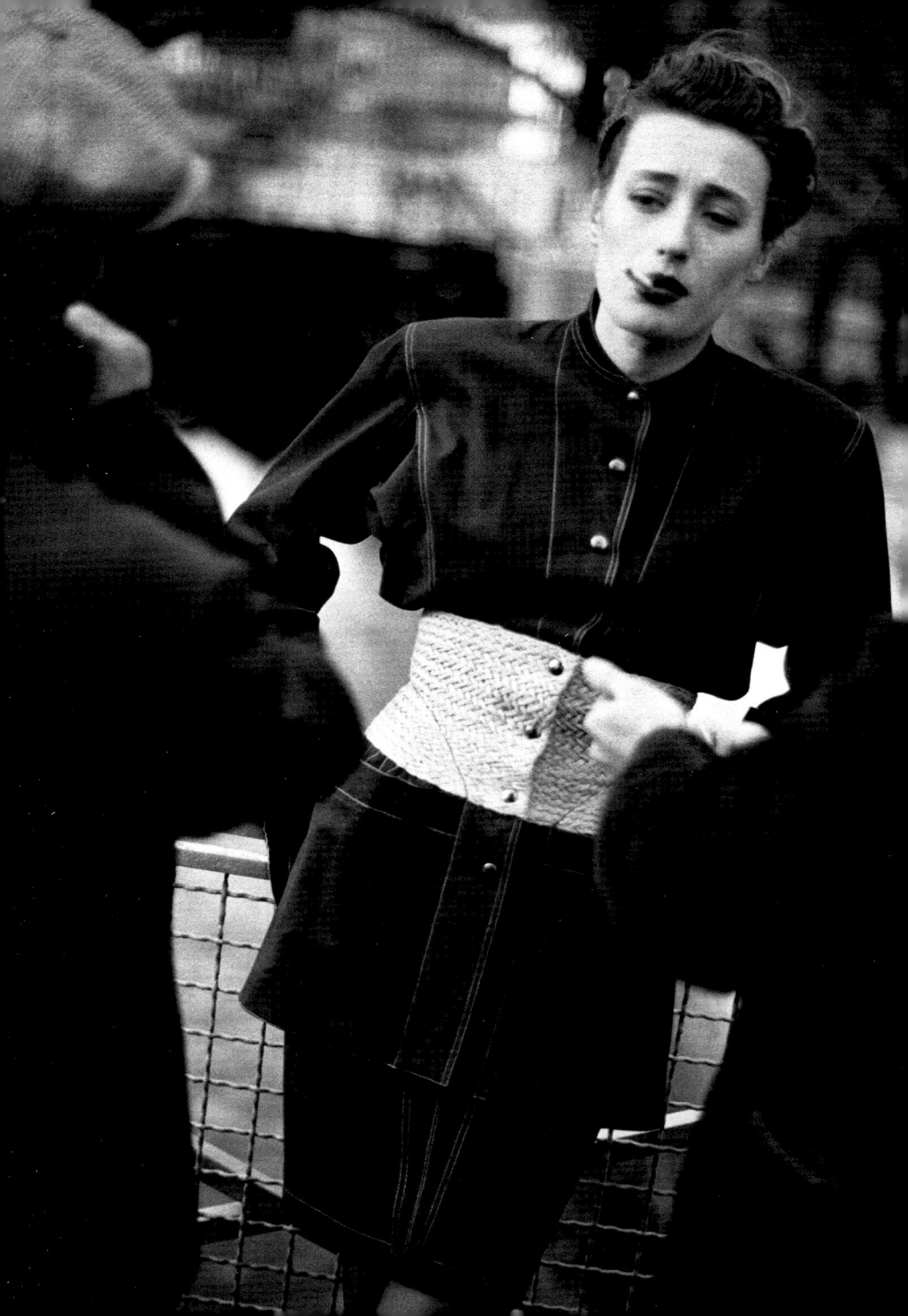

(Previous spread) Marie-Sophie Wilson, *Paris*, 1988
Jacket and shorts, *Summer* 1988
(Opposite) Marie-Sophie Wilson, *Paris*, 1988
Jacket and skirt, *Haute Couture Summer* 1983

Marie-Sophie Wilson, *Paris*, 1988. Ensemble, *Summer* 1988
(Following spread) Marie-Sophie Wilson, *Paris*, 1988. Dress and shirt, *Summer* 1988

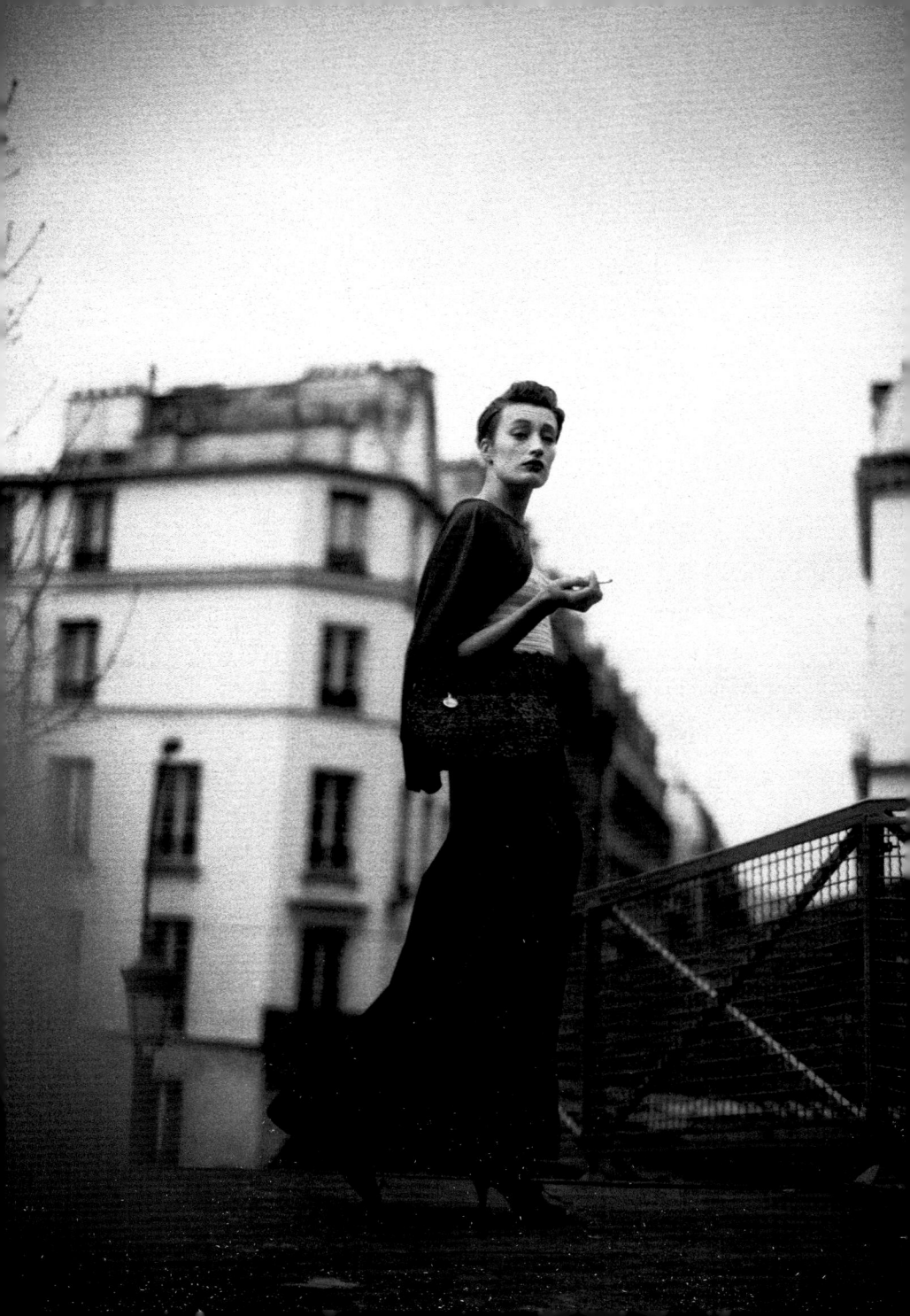

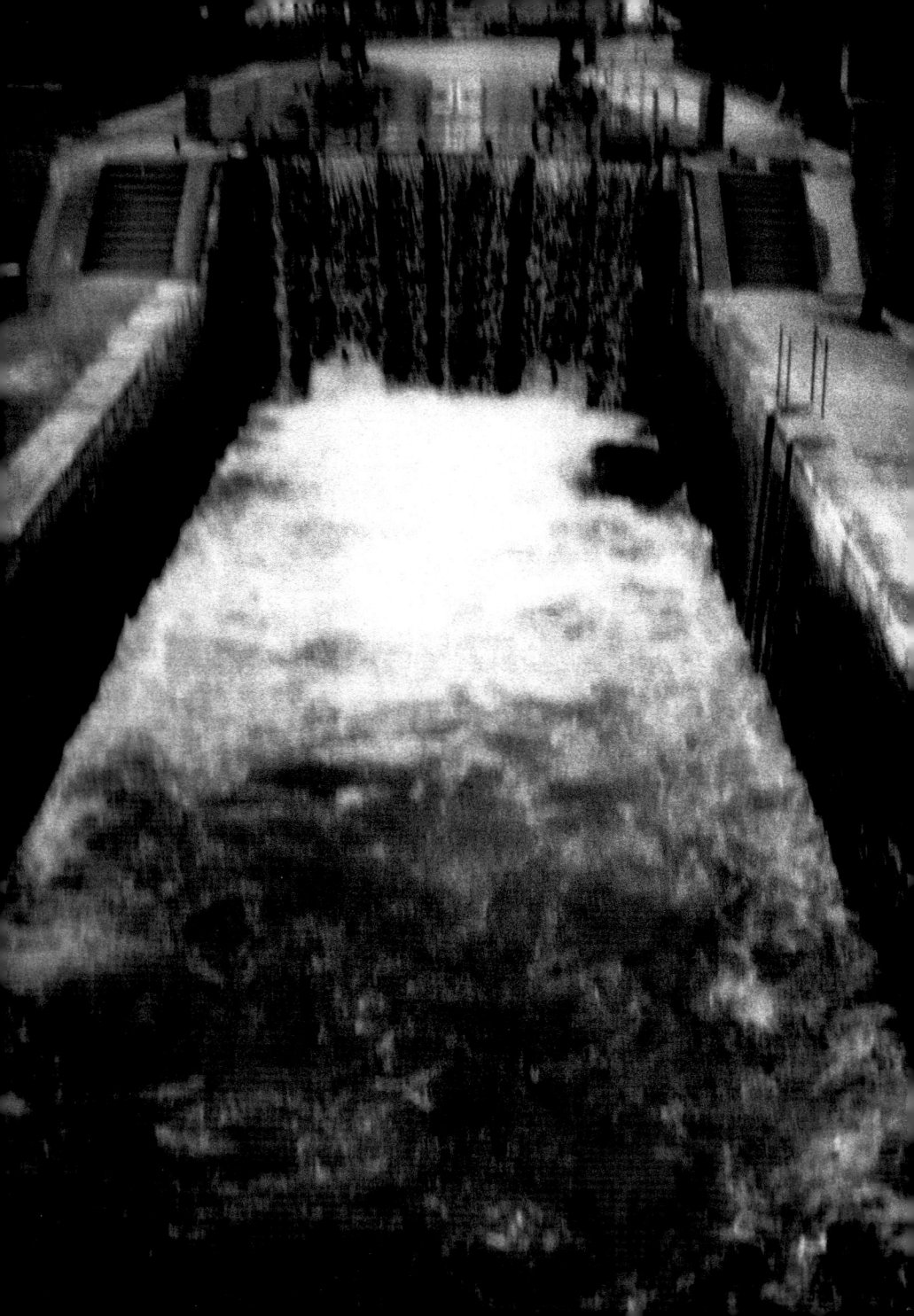

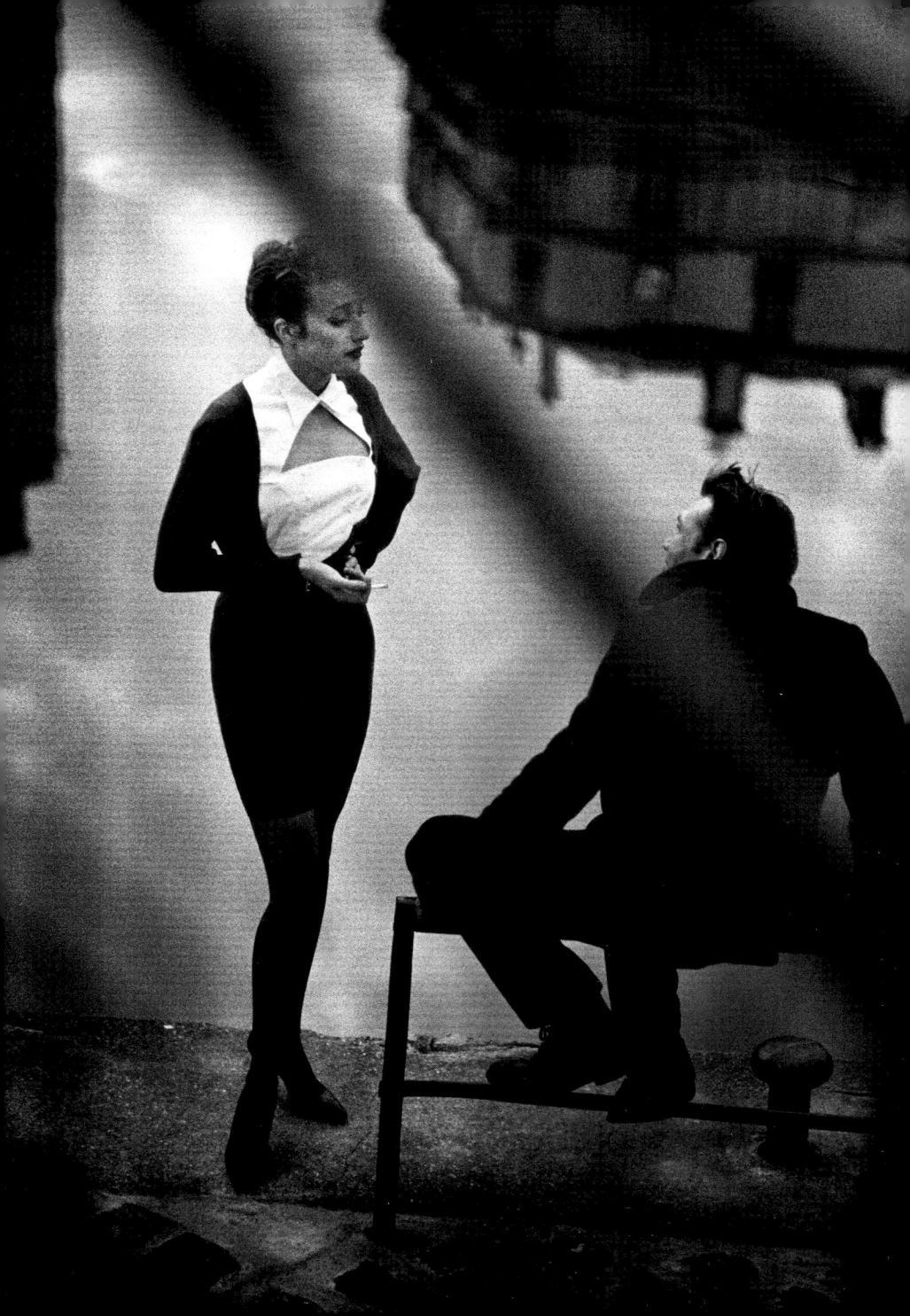

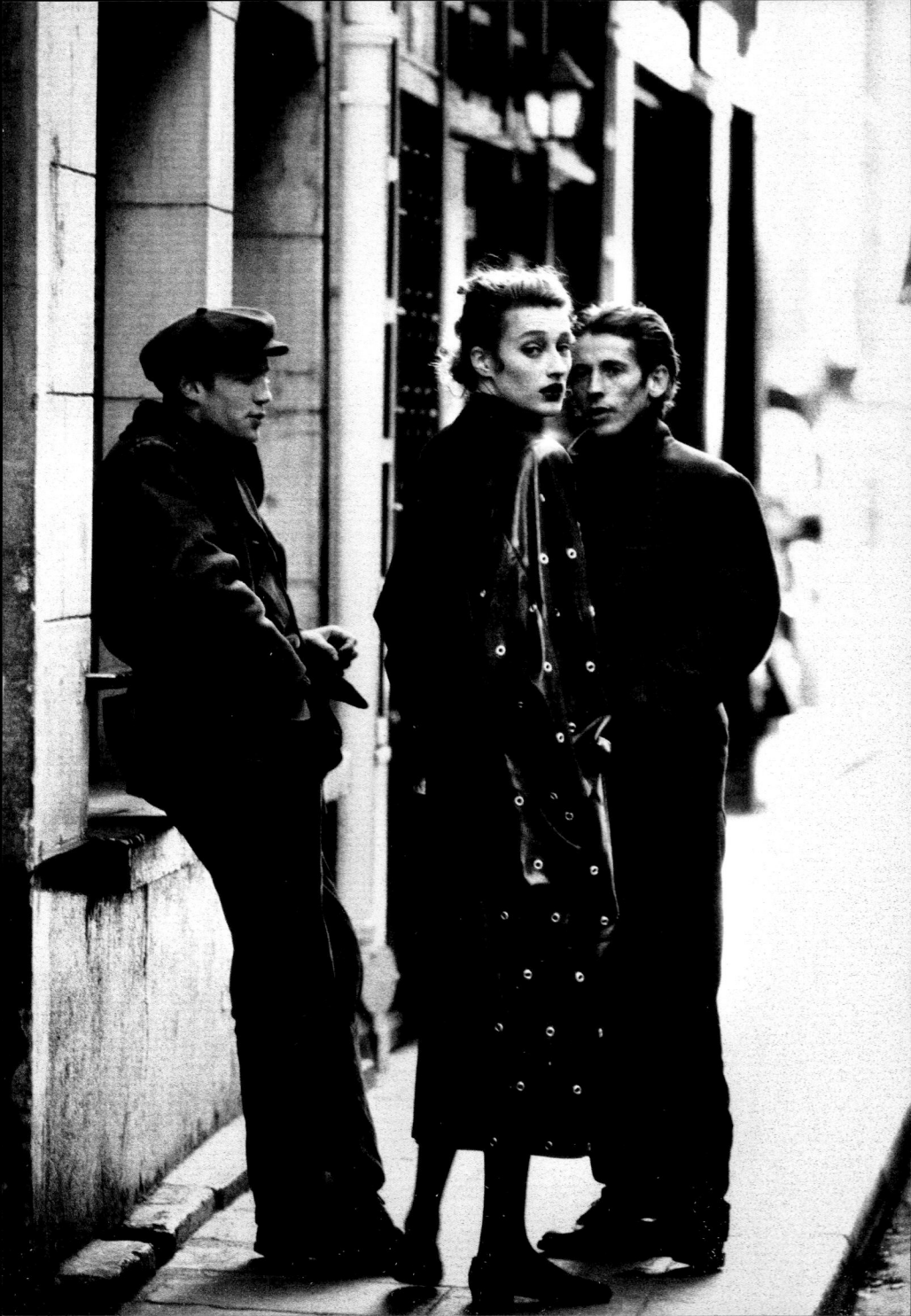

Marie-Sophie Wilson, *Paris*, 1988. Coat, *Haute Couture* 1981
(Following spread) Marie-Sophie Wilson, *Paris*, 1988. Coat, *Haute Couture* 1985

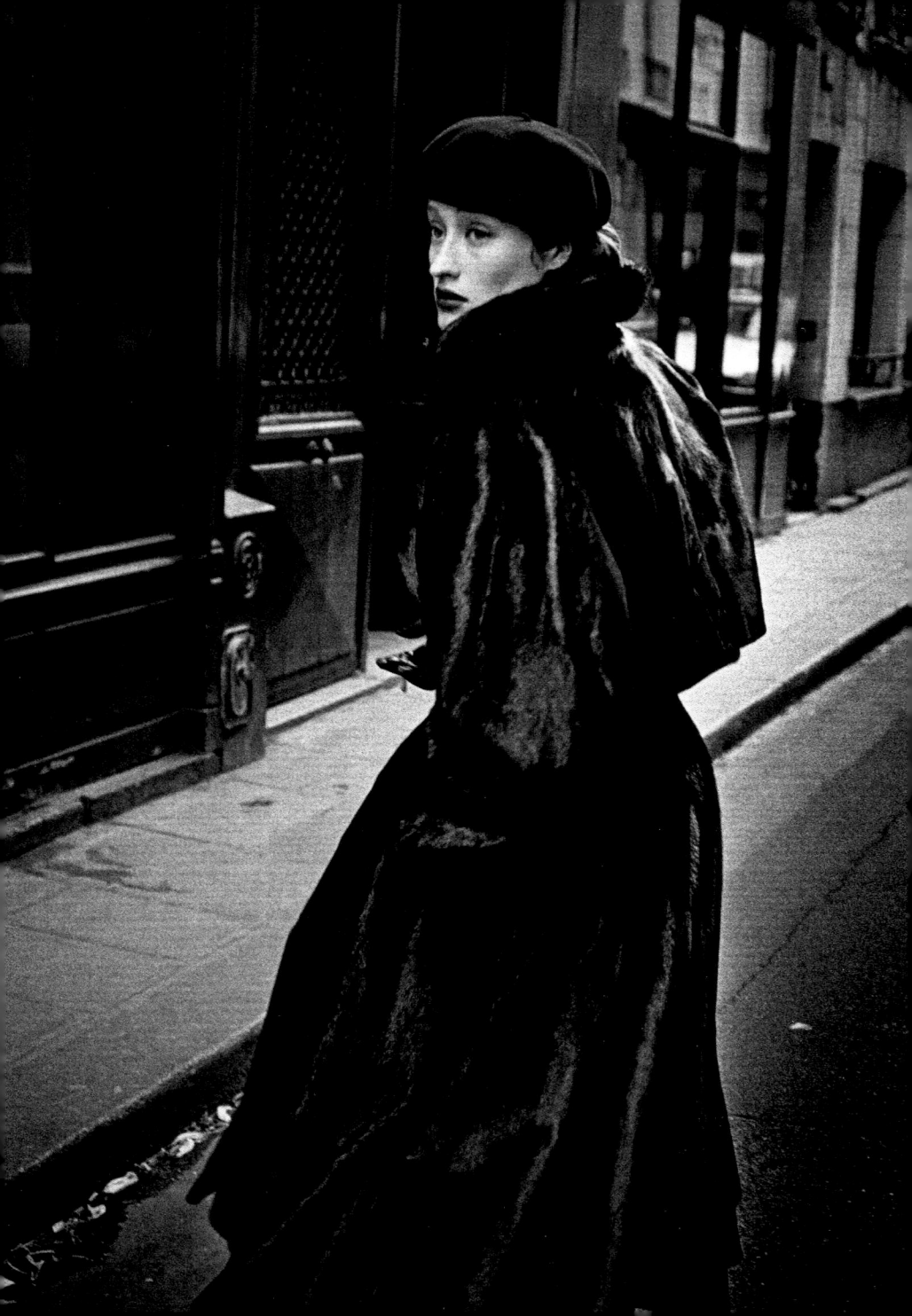

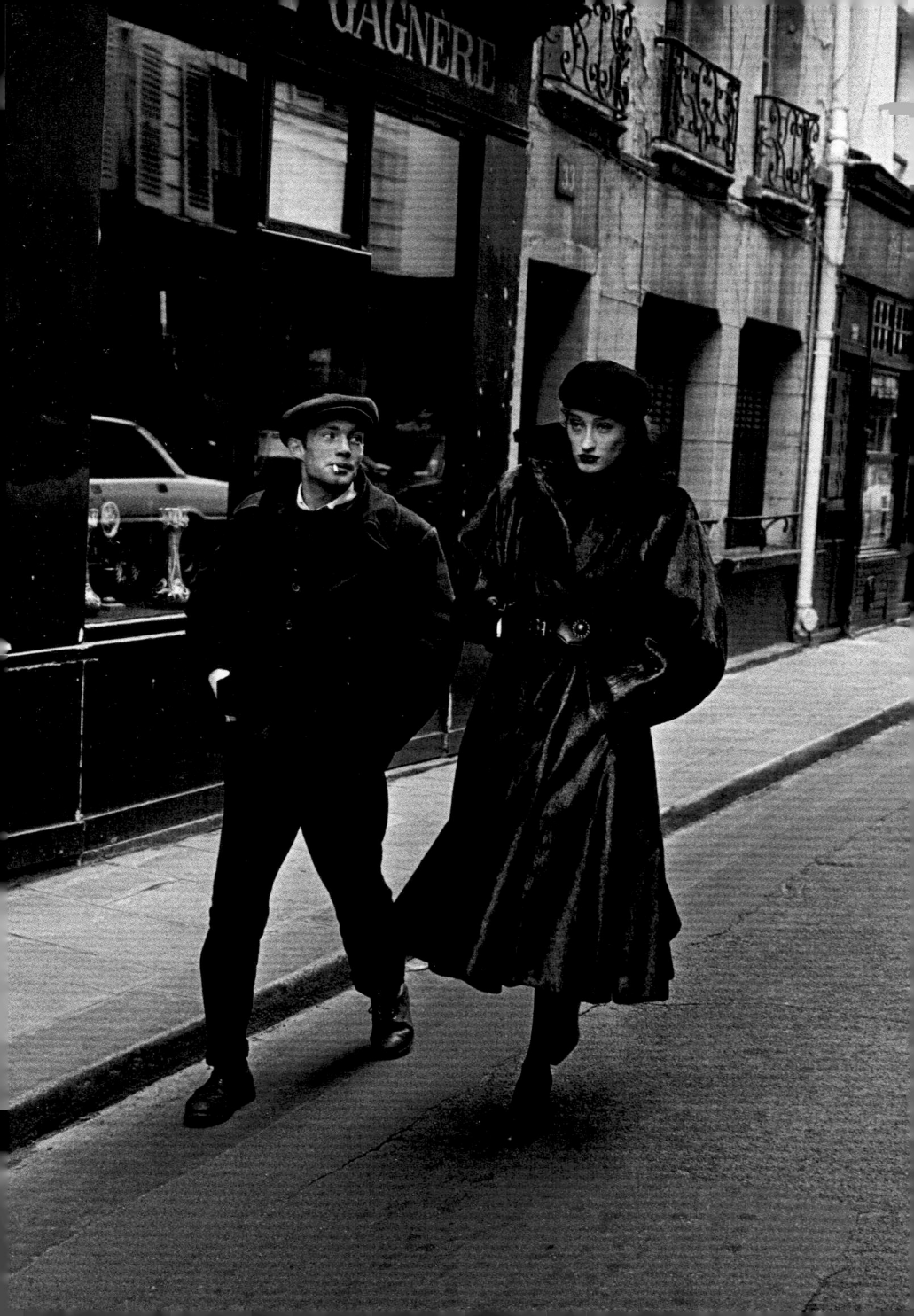

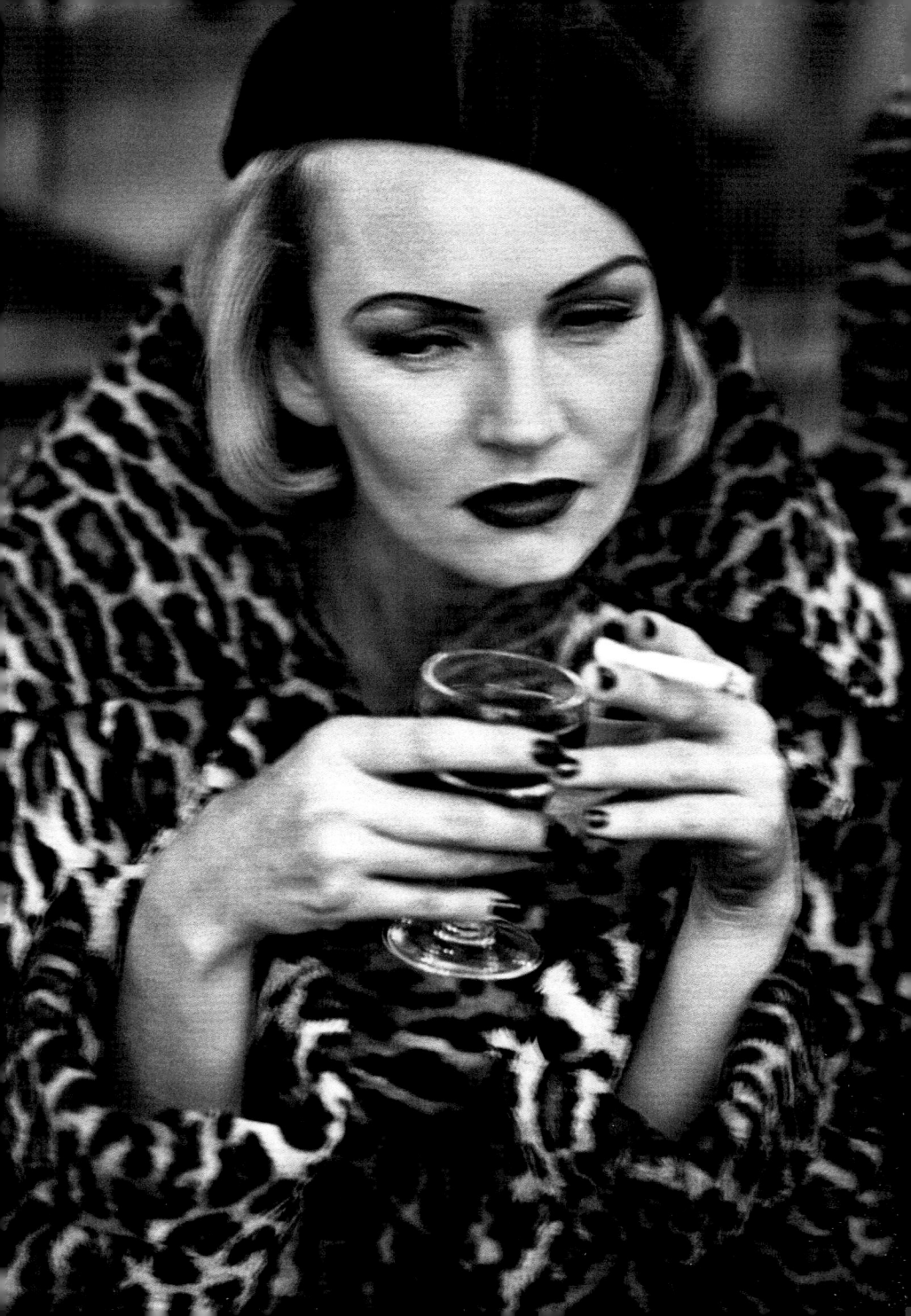

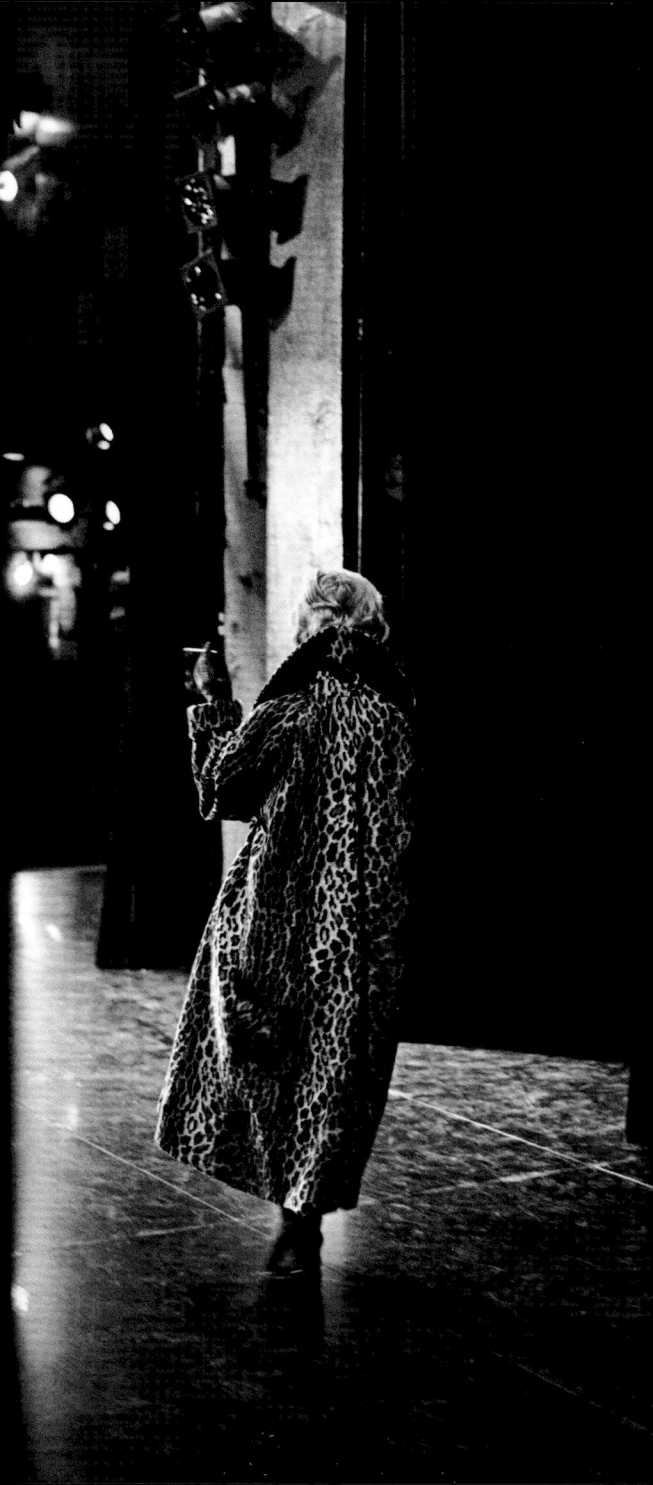

"Never think that you did anything great. As soon as you do, everything great disappears."
Peter Lindbergh

"Every day when I wake up
I wonder what I'm
going to learn today.**"**
Azzedine Alaïa

(Previous spread) Pia Frithiof, *L'Olympia, Paris*, 1991. Coat, *Winter* 1991
(Following spread) Azzedine Alaïa, Maria Johnson, and Peter Lindbergh, *Paris*, 1984

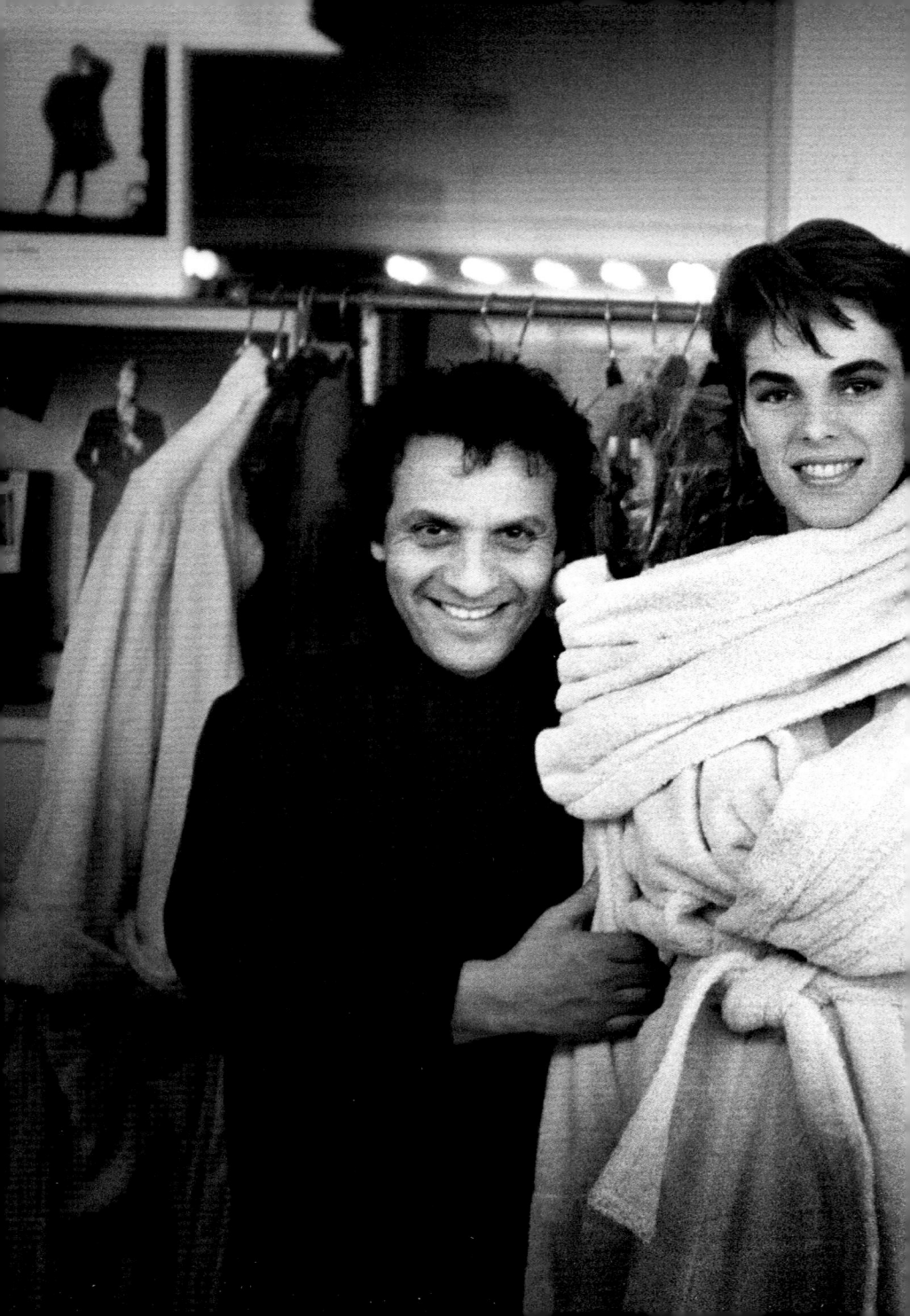

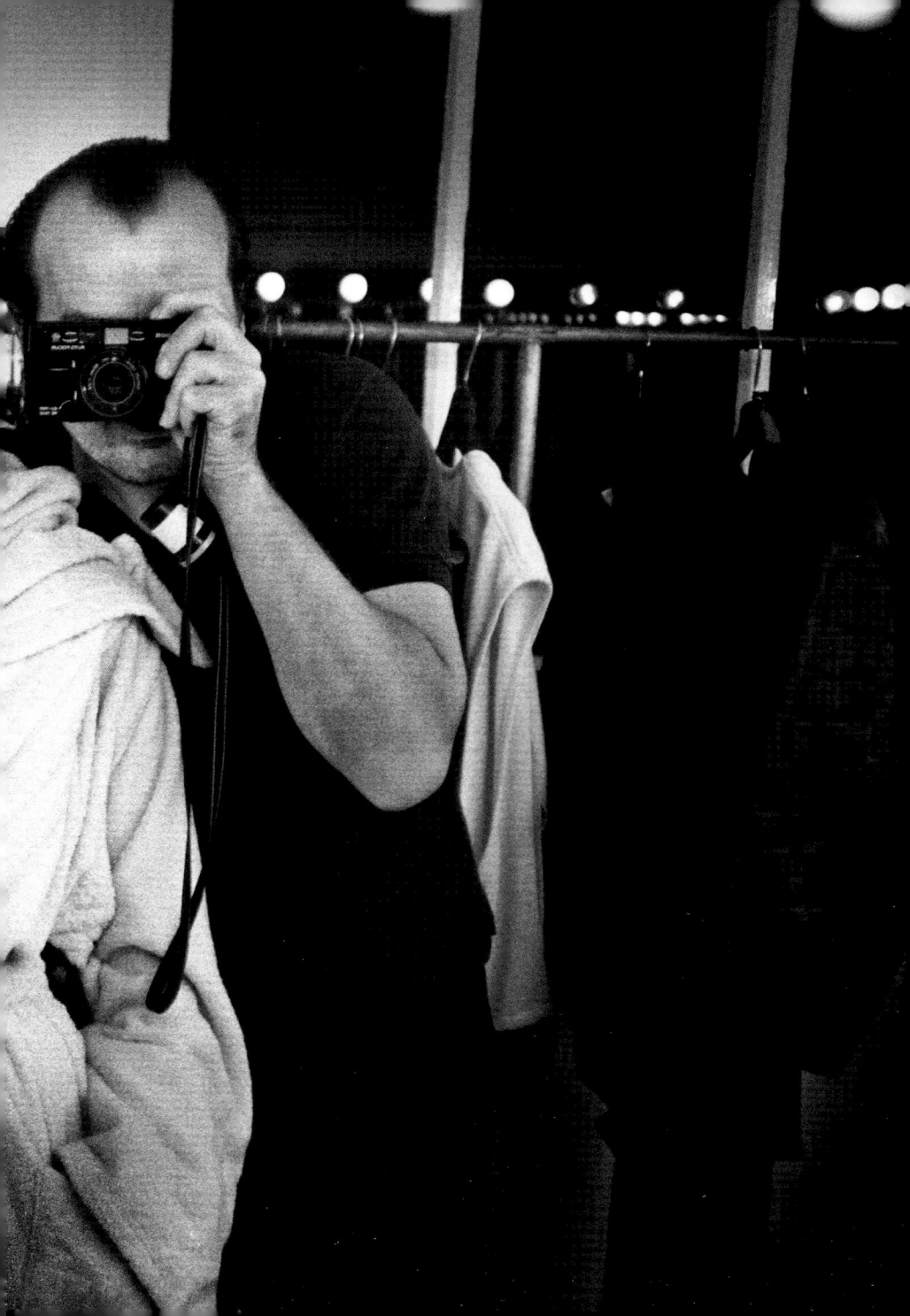

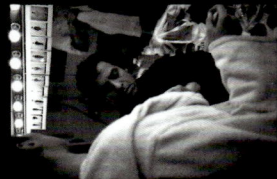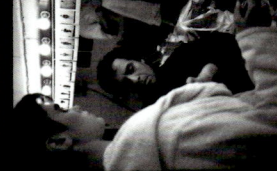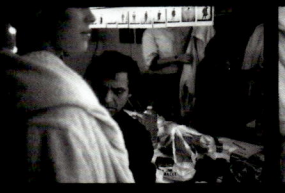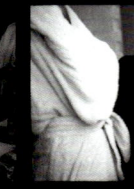

→2A →3 →3A →4 →4A →5 →5A

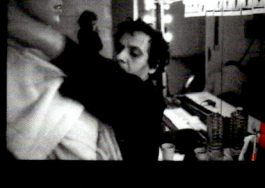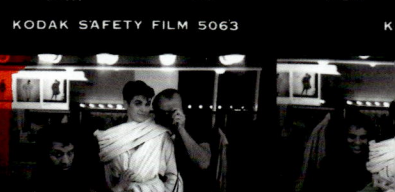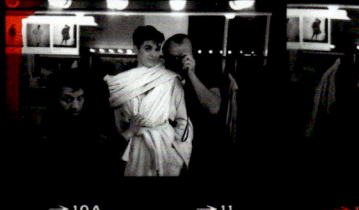

→8A →9 →9A →10 →10A →11 →11A

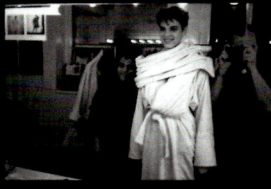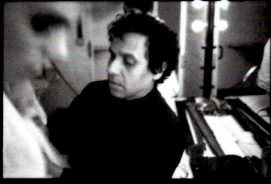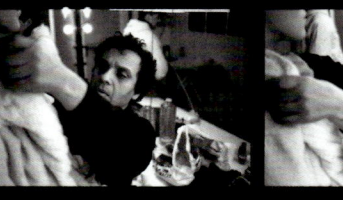

→14A →15 →15A →16 →16A →17 →17A

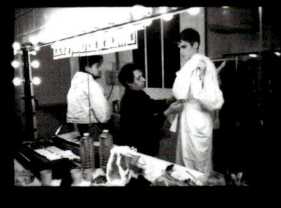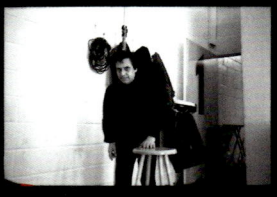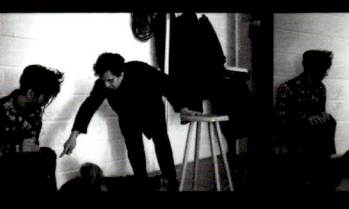

8 0 9 1 3 →21A →22 →22A →23 →23A

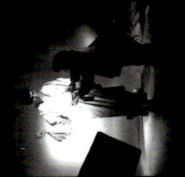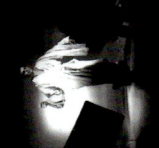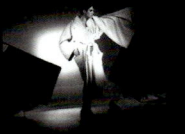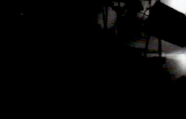

→26A →27 →27A →28 →28A →29 →29A

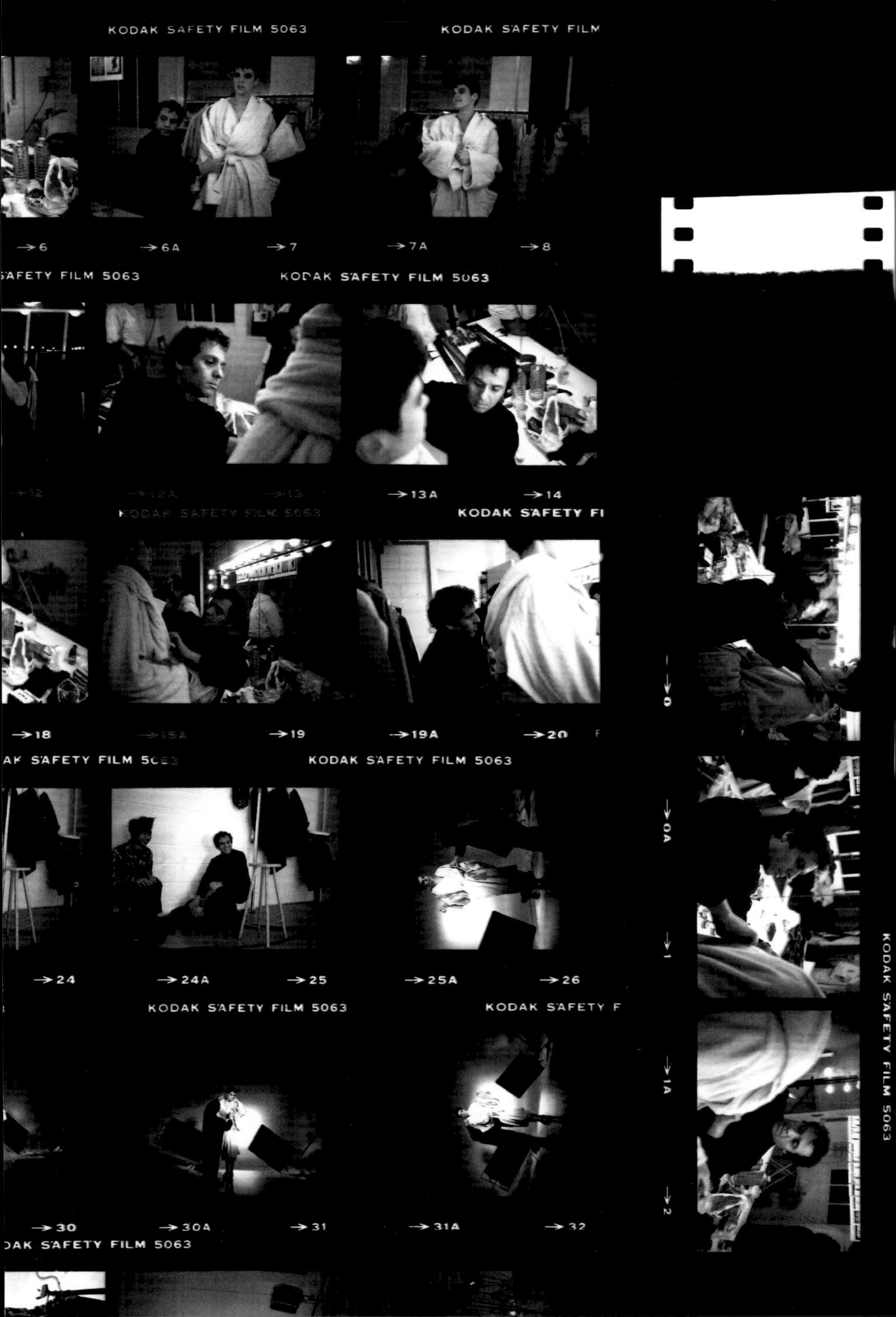
KODAK SAFETY FILM 5063
KODAK SAFETY FILM
→6
→6A
→7
→7A
→8
SAFETY FILM 5063
KODAK SAFETY FILM 5063
→13A
→14
KODAK SAFETY FI
→18
→19
→19A
→20
AK SAFETY FILM 50
KODAK SAFETY FILM 5063
→24
→24A
→25
→25A
→26
KODAK SAFETY FILM 5063
KODAK SAFETY F
→30
→30A
→31
→31A
→32
DAK SAFETY FILM 5063
KODAK SAFETY FILM 5063

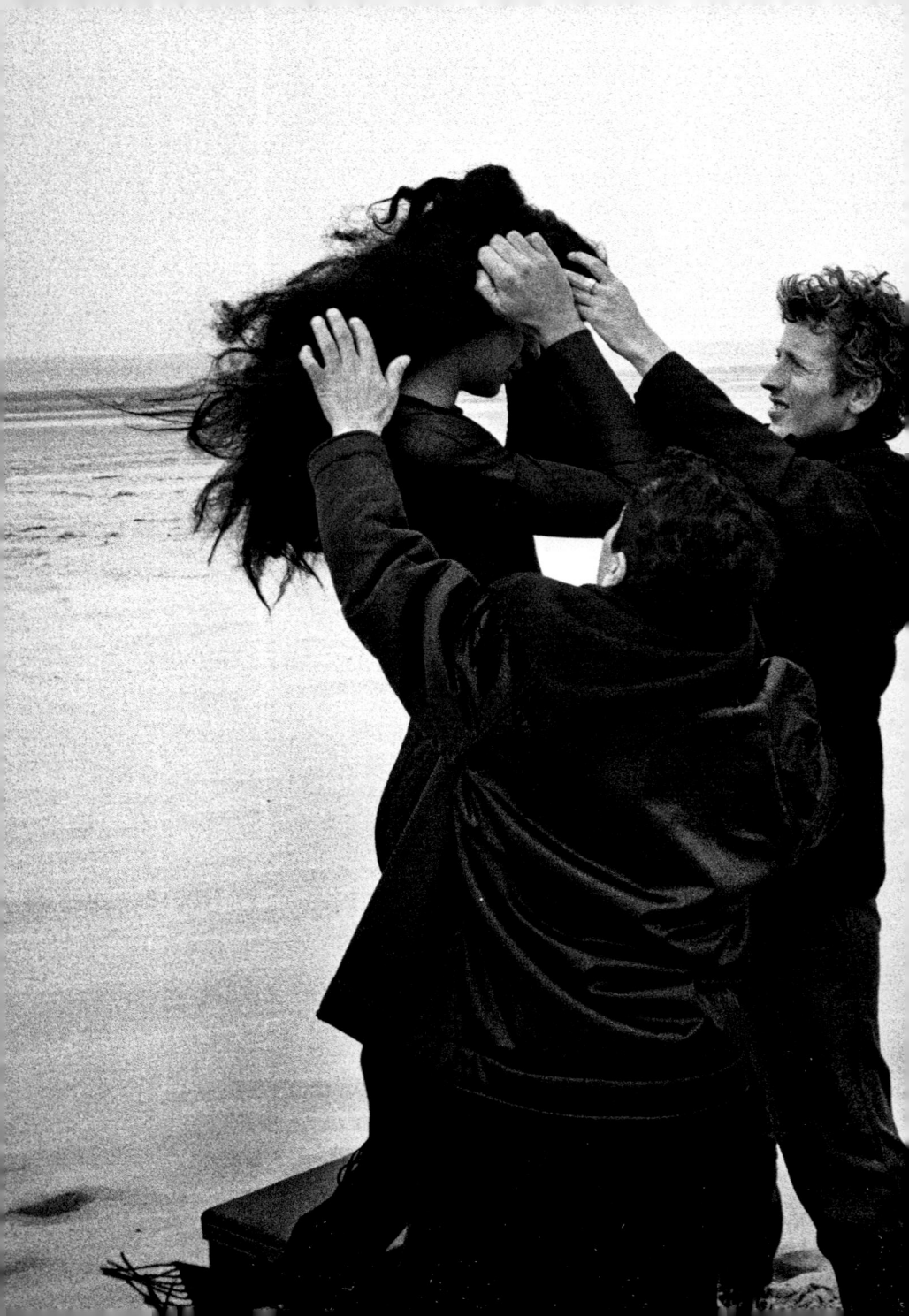

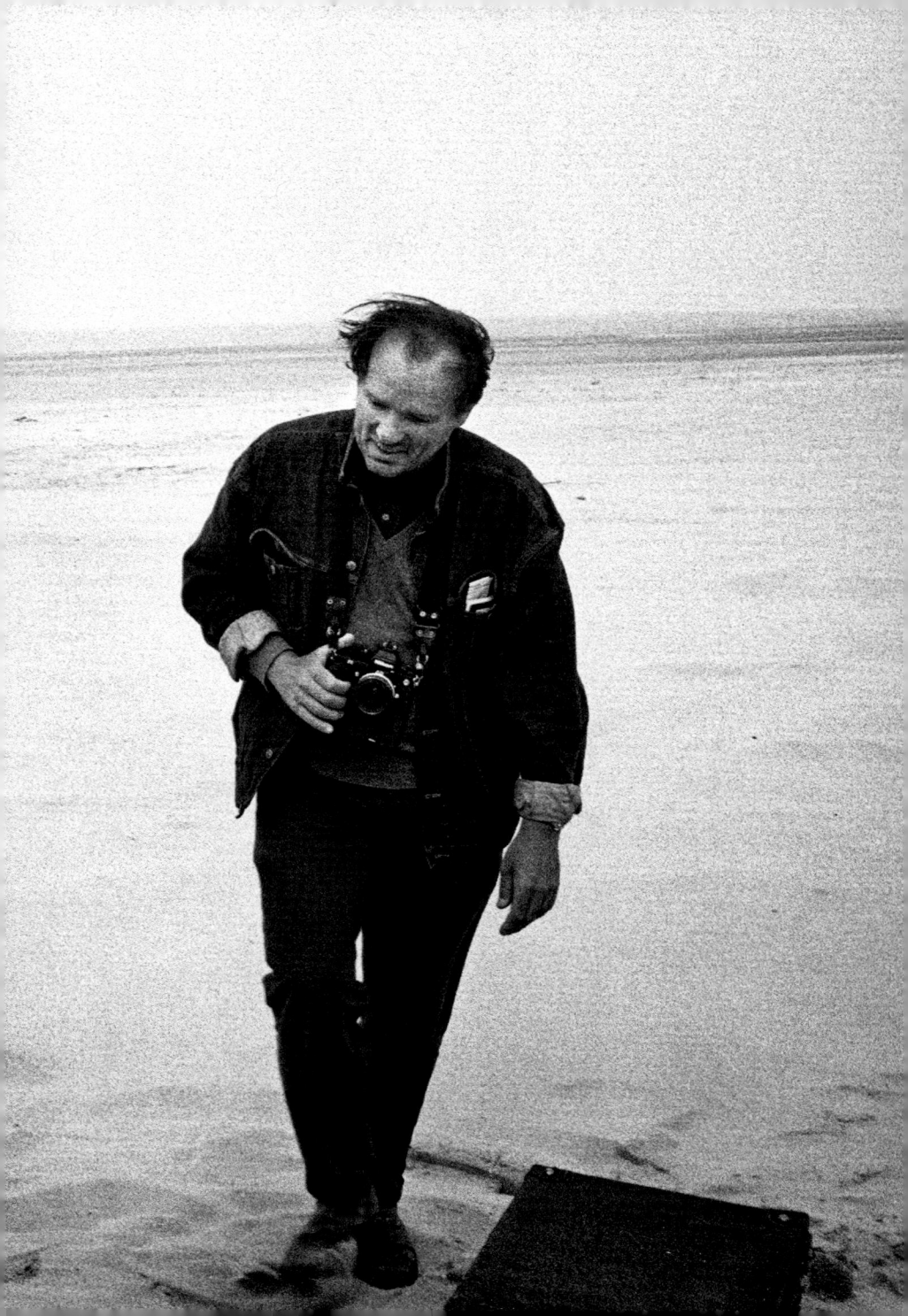

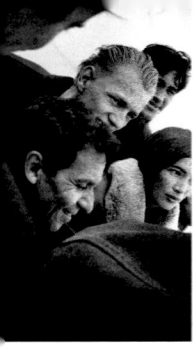
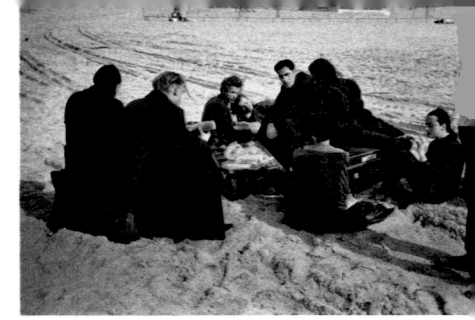
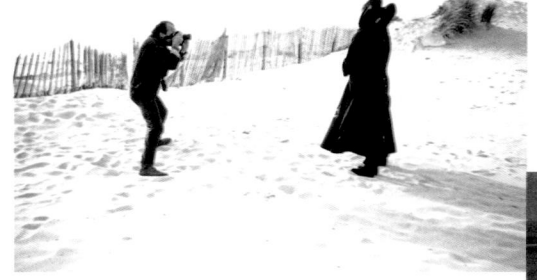
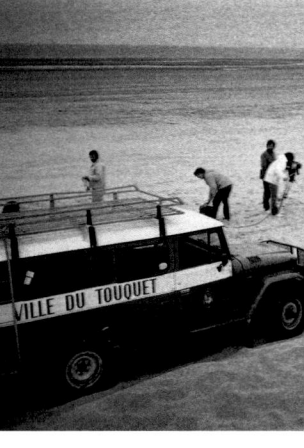
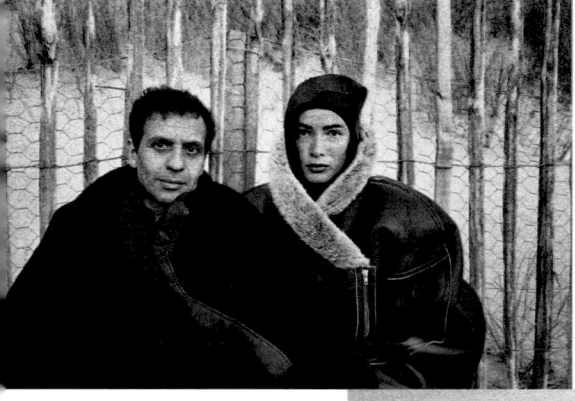
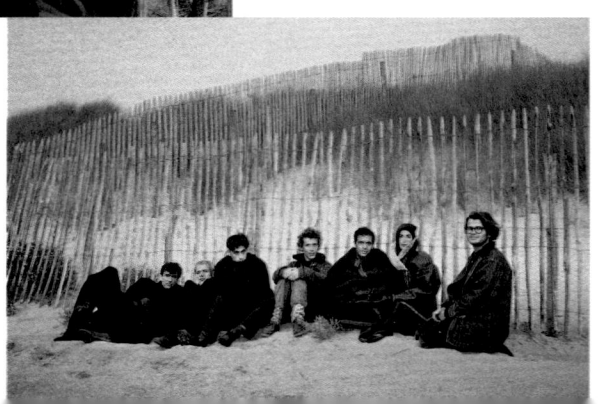

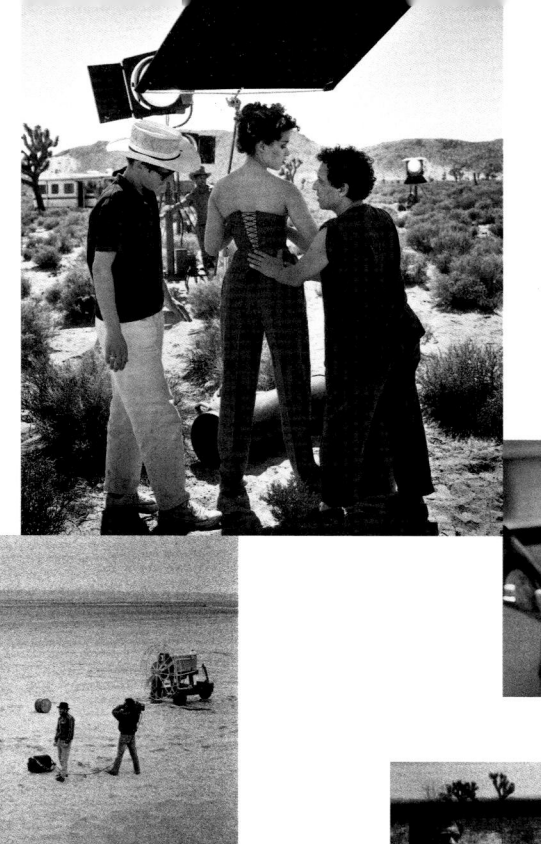
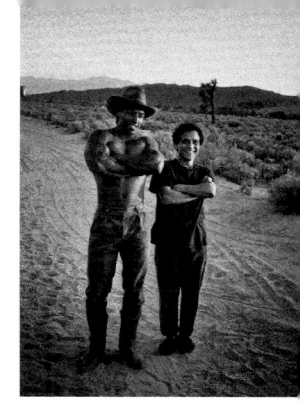
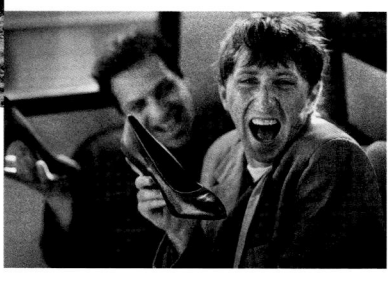
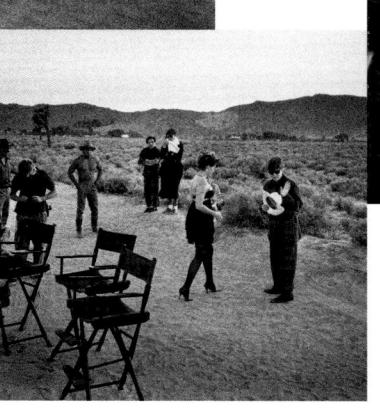
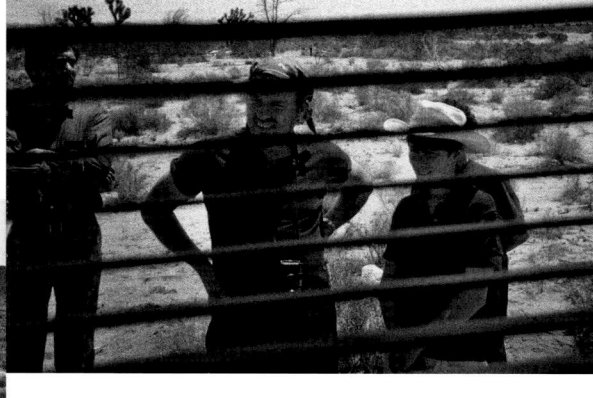
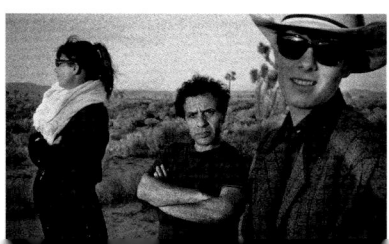

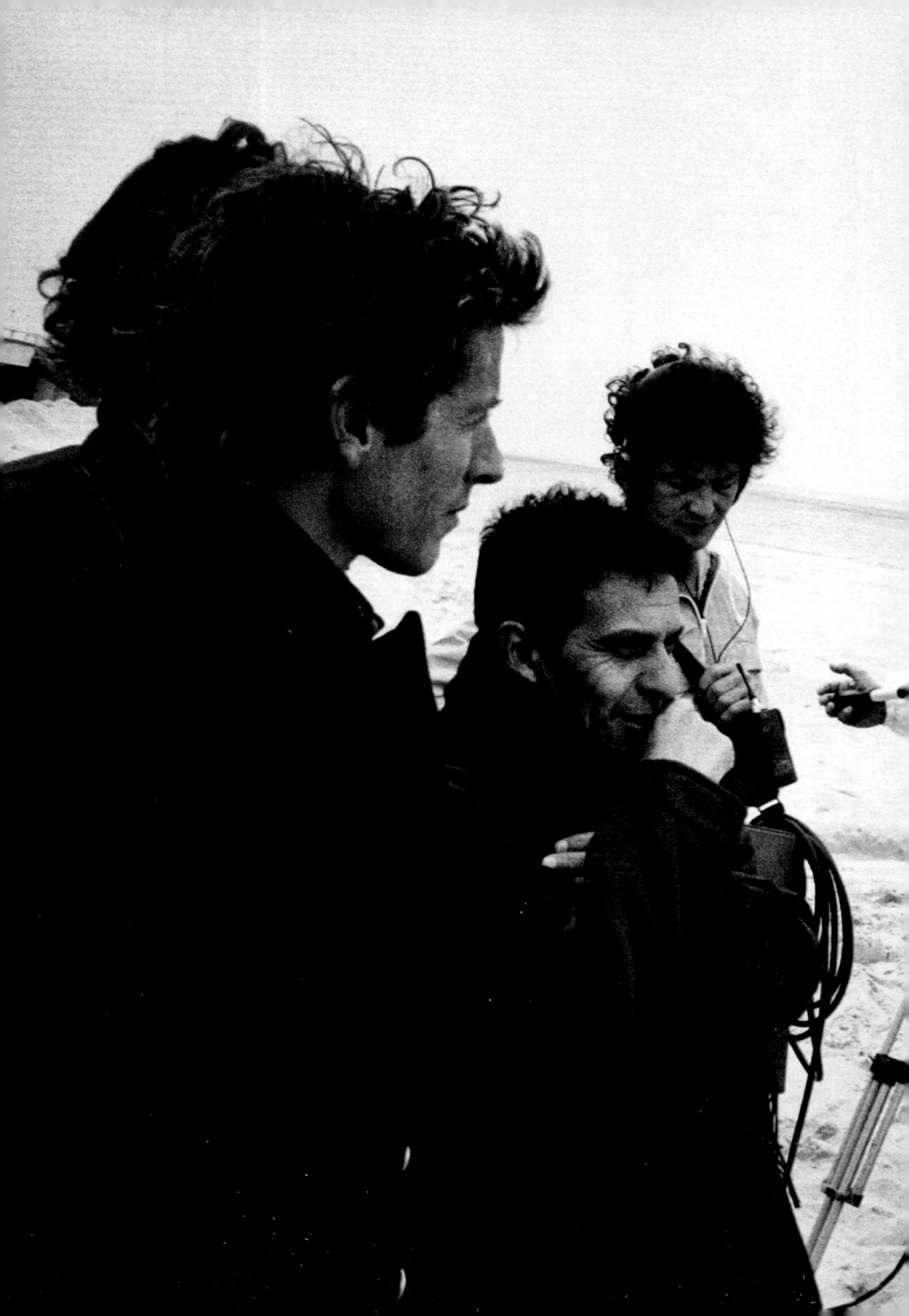

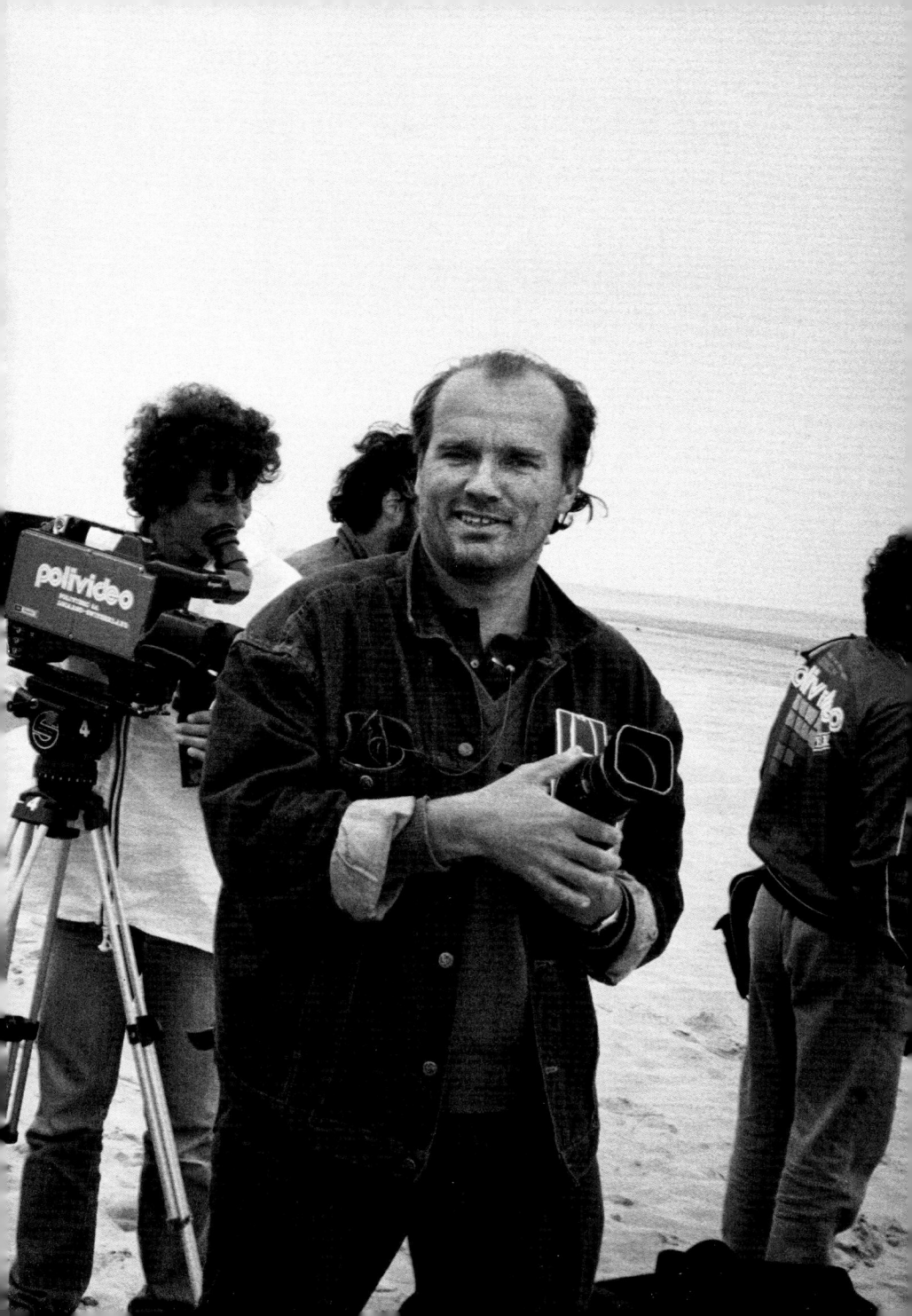

Want to see more? Visit taschen.com to view our current publications,
browse our latest magazine, and subscribe to our newsletter.

© 2025 TASCHEN GmbH
Hohenzollernring 53, D-50672 Köln, Germany
www.taschen.com

Photographs by Peter Lindbergh
© 2021 PETER LINDBERGH FOUNDATION

Texts
© 2021 Fabrice Hergott
© 2021 Paolo Roversi
© 2021 Olivier Saillard

Project Management
Simone Philippi

Translation
Charles Penwarden, Antonia Reiner

Printed in Italy
ISBN 978-3-7544-0422-5

Endpaper (front): *Le Touquet*, 1986
Endpaper (back): *Le Touquet*, 1987
Page 2: Peter Lindbergh, Kristen McMenamy and Azzedine Alaïa, *Paris*, 1995

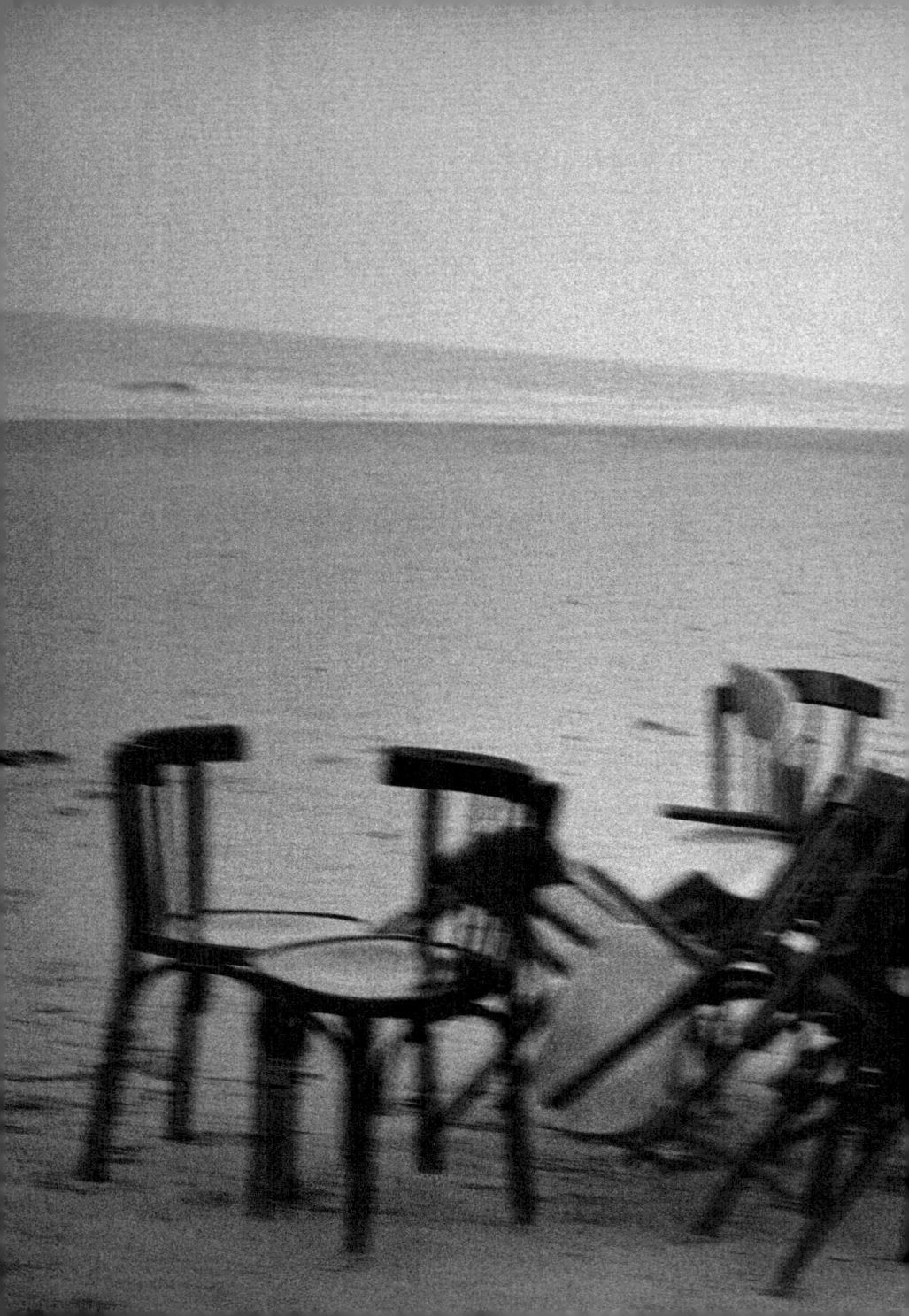